Gradle Effective Implementations Guide

Second Edition

A comprehensive guide to get up and running with build automation using Gradle

Hubert Klein Ikkink

BIRMINGHAM - MUMBAI

Gradle Effective Implementations Guide

Second Edition

First published: October 2012

Second edition: May 2016

Production reference: 1250516

Published by Packt Publishing Ltd.

Livery Place

35 Livery Street

Birmingham

B3 2PB, UK.

ISBN 978-1-78439-497-4

www.packtpub.com

Credits

Author

Hubert Klein Ikkink

Reviewer

Izzet Mustafaiev

Commissioning Editor

Amarabha Banerjee

Acquisition Editor

Manish Nainani

Content Development Editor

Shweta Pant

Technical Editor

Suwarna Patil

Copy Editor

Vibha Shukla

Project Coordinator

Shweta H Birwatkar

Proofreader

Safis Editing

Indexer

Mariammal Chettiyar

Graphics

Disha Haria

Production Coordinator

Nilesh Mohite

About the Author

Hubert Klein Ikkink was born in 1973 and currently lives in Tilburg, Netherlands, with his beautiful wife and gorgeous children. He is also known as mrhaki, which is simply the first letters of his name prepended with mr. He studied information systems and management at Tilburg University. After finishing his studies, he started working at a company specialized in knowledge-based software. There he started writing his first Java software (yes, an applet!) in 1996. During these years, his focus switched from applets to servlets to Java Enterprise Edition applications to Spring-based software.

In 2008, he wanted to have fun when writing software. The larger projects he was working on were more about writing configuration XML files and tuning performance and less about real development in his eyes, so he started to look around and noticed that Groovy was a very good language to learn. He could still use the existing Java code and libraries and use his Groovy classes in Java. The learning curve isn't steep and to support his learning phase, he wrote interesting Groovy facts on his blog with the title Groovy Goodness. He posts small articles with a lot of code samples to understand how to use Groovy. Since November 2011, he is also a DZone Most Valuable Blogger (MVB), where DZone post his blog items on their site. During these years, he also wrote about other subjects such as Grails, Gradle, Spock, Asciidoctor, and Ratpack.

Hubert was invited to speak at conferences such as Gr8Conf in Copenhagen, Minneapolis, and Greach, Madrid. Also, he gave presentations at Java conferences such as JFall in Netherlands and Javaland in Germany.

Hubert works for a company called JDriven in Netherlands. JDriven focuses on technologies that simplify and improve development of enterprise applications. Employees of JDriven have years of experience with Java and related technologies and are all eager to learn about new technologies. Hubert works on projects using Grails and Java combined with Groovy and Gradle.

It was a great honor to be asked by Packt Publishing to write this book. I knew it beforehand that it would be a lot of work and somehow needed to be combined with my daytime job. I couldn't have written the book without the help of a lot of people and I want to thank all these people.

First of all, I would like to thank my family for supporting me while writing the book. They gave me space and time to write the book. Thank you for your patience and a big kiss to Kim, Britt, Liam, and Chloë, I love you. Of course, I would also like to thank all the people at Gradle Inc. for making Gradle such a great build tool.

Finally, I would like to thank the great staff at Packt Publishing. Shweta Pant kept me on schedule and made sure everything was submitted on time. I would also like to thank all the editors for reviewing the book. They really helped me to keep focus and be concise with the text.

About the Reviewer

Izzet Mustafaiev is a family guy with a tendency of having BBQ parties and traveling.

Professionally, he's a software engineer, working with EPAM Systems with primary language—Java, hands on Groovy/Ruby, and exploring FP with Erlang/Elixir. Izzet has participated in different projects as a developer and architect. He advocates XP, clean code, and DevOps habits and practices, speaking at engineering conferences.

www.PacktPub.com

For support files and downloads related to your book, please visit www.PacktPub.com.

Did you know that Packt offers eBook versions of every book published, with PDF and ePub files available? You can upgrade to the eBook version at www.PacktPub.com and as a print book customer, you are entitled to a discount on the eBook copy. Get in touch with us at service@packtpub.com for more details.

At www.PacktPub.com, you can also read a collection of free technical articles, sign up for a range of free newsletters and receive exclusive discounts and offers on Packt books and eBooks.

https://www2.packtpub.com/books/subscription/packtlib

Do you need instant solutions to your IT questions? PacktLib is Packt's online digital book library. Here, you can search, access, and read Packt's entire library of books.

Why subscribe?

- Fully searchable across every book published by Packt
- Copy and paste, print, and bookmark content
- On demand and accessible via a web browser

Free access for Packt account holders

If you have an account with Packt at www.PacktPub.com, you can use this to access PacktLib today and view 9 entirely free books. Simply use your login credentials for immediate access.

Table of Contents

Preface

Gradle is the next generation in build automation. Gradle uses convention-over-configuration to provide good defaults, but it is also flexible to be used in every situation you encounter in daily development. Build logic is described with a powerful DSL and empowers developers to create reusable and maintainable build logic.

We will see more about Gradle in this book. We will discuss Gradle's features with code samples throughout the book. We will also discuss how to write tasks, work with files, and write build scripts using the Groovy DSL. Next, we will discuss how to use Gradle in projects to compile, package, test, check code quality, and deploy applications. Finally we will see how to integrate Gradle with continuous integration servers and development environments (IDEs).

After reading this book, you will know how to use Gradle in your daily development. We can write tasks, apply plugins, and write build logic using the Gradle build language.

What this book covers

Chapter 1, *Starting with Gradle*, introduces Gradle and how to install it. We will write our first Gradle script and discuss command-line and GUI features of Gradle.

Chapter 2, *Creating Gradle Build Scripts*, looks at tasks as part of the Gradle build scripts. We will see how to define tasks and how to use task dependencies to describe the build logic.

Chapter 3, *Working with Gradle Build Scripts*, covers more functionalities that we can apply in Gradle scripts. We will discuss how to work with files and directories, apply logging to our build scripts, and use properties to parameterize our build scripts.

Chapter 4, Using Gradle for Java Projects, discusses all about using the Java plugin for Gradle projects. Gradle offers several tasks and configuration convention that makes working with Java project very easy. We see how to customize the configuration for project that cannot follow the conventions.

Chapter 5, *Dependency Management*, covers the support for dependencies by Gradle. We will discuss how to use configurations to organize dependencies. We will also see how to use repositories with dependencies in our build scripts.

Chapter 6, *Testing, Building, and Publishing Artifacts*, introduces the support of Gradle to run tests from the build script. We will discuss how to build several artifacts for a project and how to publish the artifacts to a repository so that other developers can reuse our code.

Chapter 7, *Multi-project Builds*, covers Gradle's support for multi-project builds. With Gradle, we can configure multiple projects that can be related to each other easily. We will also see how Gradle can automatically build related or dependent projects if necessary.

Chapter 8, *Mixed Languages*, explains the Scala and Groovy plugin that is included with Gradle to work with projects that have Scala or Groovy code.

Chapter 9, *Maintaining Code Quality*, introduces the code quality plugins of Gradle. We will see how to use and configure the plugins to include code analysis in our build process.

Chapter 10, *Writing Custom Tasks and Plugins*, introduces what we need to do to write our own custom task and plugins. We will see how to decouple the definition and usage of a custom task and plugin in separate source files. We will also discuss how to reuse our custom task and plugin in other projects.

Chapter 11, *Gradle in the Enterprise*, introduces the support of several continuous integration tools for Gradle. We will discuss how to configure a continuous integration server to automatically invoke our Gradle build scripts.

Chapter 12, *IDE Support*, looks at how Gradle can generate project files for Eclipse and IntelliJ IDEA. We will also see how the IDEs support Gradle from within the IDE in order to run, for example, tasks and keep track of dependencies defined in Gradle scripts.

What you need for this book

In order to work with Gradle and the code samples in the book, we need at least a Java Development Toolkit (JDK, 1.6 or higher version), Gradle, and a good text editor. In the first chapter, we will see how to install Gradle on our computer.

Who this book is for

You are working on Java (Scala and Groovy) applications and want to use build automation to automatically compile, package, and deploy your application. You might have worked with other build automation tools, such as Maven or ANT, but this is not necessary to understand the topics in this book.

Conventions

In this book, you will find a number of text styles that distinguish between different kinds of information. Here are some examples of these styles and an explanation of their meaning.

Code words in text, database table names, folder names, filenames, file extensions, pathnames, dummy URLs, user input, and Twitter handles are shown as follows: "We can include other contexts through the use of the include directive."

A block of code is set as follows:

```
task helloWorld << {
    println 'Hello world.'
}
```

Any command-line input or output is written as follows:

```
$ gradle -v
------------------------------------------------------------
Gradle 2.12
------------------------------------------------------------
Build time: 2016-03-14 08:32:03 UTC
Chapter 1
[ 5 ]
 Build number: none
 Revision: b29fbb64ad6b068cb3f05f7e40dc670472129bc0
 Groovy: 2.4.4
 Ant: Apache Ant(TM) version 1.9.3 compiled on
December23 2013
 JVM: 1.8.0_66 (Oracle Corporation 25.66-b17)
 OS: Mac OS X 10.11.3 x86_64
```

New terms and important words are shown in bold. Words that you see on the screen, for example, in menus or dialog boxes, appear in the text like this: "With the **Gradle GUI**, we have a graphical overview of the tasks in a project and we can execute them by simply clicking on the mouse."

 Warnings or important notes appear in a box like this.

 Tips and tricks appear like this.

Reader feedback

Feedback from our readers is always welcome. Let us know what you think about this book—what you liked or disliked. Reader feedback is important for us as it helps us develop titles that you will really get the most out of.

To send us general feedback, simply e-mail feedback@packtpub.com, and mention the book's title in the subject of your message.

If there is a topic that you have expertise in and you are interested in either writing or contributing to a book, see our author guide at www.packtpub.com/authors.

Customer support

Now that you are the proud owner of a Packt book, we have a number of things to help you to get the most from your purchase.

Downloading the example code

You can download the example code files for this book from your account at http://www.packtpub.com. If you purchased this book elsewhere, you can visit http://www.packtpub.com/support and register to have the files e-mailed directly to you.

You can download the code files by following these steps:

1. Log in or register to our website using your e-mail address and password.
2. Hover the mouse pointer on the **SUPPORT** tab at the top.
3. Click on **Code Downloads & Errata**.
4. Enter the name of the book in the **Search** box.
5. Select the book for which you're looking to download the code files.
6. Choose from the drop-down menu where you purchased this book from.
7. Click on **Code Download**.

Once the file is downloaded, please make sure that you unzip or extract the folder using the latest version of:

- WinRAR / 7-Zip for Windows
- Zipeg / iZip / UnRarX for Mac
- 7-Zip / PeaZip for Linux

The code bundle for the book is also hosted on GitHub at `https://github.com/PacktPublishing/Gradle-Effective-Implementations-Guide-Second-Edition`. We also have other code bundles from our rich catalog of books and videos available at `https://github.com/PacktPublishing/`. Check them out!

Errata

Although we have taken every care to ensure the accuracy of our content, mistakes do happen. If you find a mistake in one of our books-maybe a mistake in the text or the code-we would be grateful if you could report this to us. By doing so, you can save other readers from frustration and help us improve subsequent versions of this book. If you find any errata, please report them by visiting `http://www.packtpub.com/submit-errata`, selecting your book, clicking on the **Errata Submission Form** link, and entering the details of your errata. Once your errata are verified, your submission will be accepted and the errata will be uploaded to our website or added to any list of existing errata under the **Errata** section of that title.

To view the previously submitted errata, go to `https://www.packtpub.com/books/content/support` and enter the name of the book in the search field. The required information will appear under the **Errata** section.

Piracy

Piracy of copyrighted material on the Internet is an ongoing problem across all media. At Packt, we take the protection of our copyright and licenses very seriously. If you come across any illegal copies of our works in any form on the Internet, please provide us with the location address or website name immediately so that we can pursue a remedy.

Please contact us at `copyright@packtpub.com` with a link to the suspected pirated material.

We appreciate your help in protecting our authors and our ability to bring you valuable content.

Questions

If you have a problem with any aspect of this book, you can contact us at `questions@packtpub.com`, and we will do our best to address the problem.

1
Starting with Gradle

When we develop a software, we write, compile, test, package, and finally, distribute the code. We can automate these steps by using a build system. The big advantage is that we have a repeatable sequence of steps. The build system will always follow the steps that we have defined, so we can concentrate on writing the actual code and don't have to worry about the other steps.

Gradle is one such build system.

In this chapter, we will cover the following topics:

- Getting started with Gradle
- Writing our first build script
- Looking at default tasks
- Learning about command-line options
- Discussing the Gradle graphical user interface

Gradle is a tool for build automation. With Gradle, we can automate compiling, testing, packaging, and deployment of our software or any other types of projects. Gradle is flexible, but has sensible defaults for most projects. This means that we can rely on the defaults if we don't want something special, but we can still can use the flexibility to adapt a build to certain custom needs.

Gradle is already used by large open source projects such as Spring, Hibernate, and Grails. Enterprise companies such as LinkedIn and Netflix also use Gradle.

In this chapter, we will explain what Gradle is and how to use it in our development projects.

Let's take a look at some of Gradle's features.

Declarative builds and convention over configuration

Gradle uses a **Domain Specific Language** (**DSL**) based on Groovy to declare builds. The DSL provides a flexible language that can be extended by us. As the DSL is based on Groovy, we can write Groovy code to describe a build and use the power and expressiveness of the Groovy language. Groovy is a language for the **Java Virtual Machine** (**JVM**), such as Java and Scala. Groovy makes it easy to work with collections, has closures, and a lot of useful features. The syntax is closely related to the Java syntax. In fact, we could write a Groovy class file with Java syntax and it will compile. However, using the Groovy syntax makes it easier to express the code intent and we need less boilerplate code than with Java. To get the most out of Gradle, it is best to also learn the basics of the Groovy language, but it is not necessary to start writing Gradle scripts.

Gradle is designed to be a build language and not a rigid framework. The Gradle core itself is written in Java and Groovy. To extend Gradle, we can use Java and Groovy to write our custom code. We can even write our custom code in Scala if we want to.

Gradle provides support for Java, Groovy, Scala, web, and OSGi projects out of the box. These projects have sensible convention-over-configuration settings that we probably already use ourselves. However, we have the flexibility to change these configuration settings if required for our projects.

Support for Ant Tasks and Maven repositories

Gradle supports **Ant Tasks** and projects. We can import an Ant build and reuse all the tasks. However, we can also write Gradle tasks dependent on Ant Tasks. The integration also applies for properties, paths, and so on.

Maven and Ivy repositories are supported to publish or fetch dependencies. So, we can continue to use any repository infrastructure that we already have.

Incremental builds

With Gradle, we have incremental builds. This means the tasks in a build are only executed if necessary. For example, a task to compile source code will first check whether the sources have changed since the last execution of the task. If the sources have changed, the task is executed; but if the sources haven't changed, the execution of the task is skipped and the task is marked as being up to date.

Gradle supports this mechanism for a lot of provided tasks. However, we can also use this for tasks that we write ourselves.

Multi-project builds

Gradle has great support for multi-project builds. A project can simply be dependent on other projects or be a dependency of other projects. We can define a graph of dependencies among projects, and Gradle can resolve these dependencies for us. We have the flexibility to define our project layout as we want.

Gradle has support for partial builds. This means that Gradle will figure out whether a project, which our project depends on, needs to be rebuild or not. If the project needs rebuilding, Gradle will do this before building our own project.

Gradle Wrapper

The **Gradle Wrapper** allows us to execute Gradle builds even if Gradle is not installed on a computer. This is a great way to distribute source code and provide the build system with it so that the source code can be built.

Also in an enterprise environment, we can have a zero-administration way for client computers to build the software. We can use the wrapper to enforce a certain Gradle version to be used so that the whole team is using the same version. We can also update the Gradle version for the wrapper, and the whole team will use the newer version as the wrapper code is checked in to version control.

Free and open source

Gradle is an open source project and it is licensed under the **Apache License (ASL)**.

Getting started

In this section, we will download and install Gradle before writing our first Gradle build script.

Before we install Gradle, we must make sure that we have a **Java Development SE Kit (JDK)** installed on our computer. Gradle requires JDK 6 or higher. Gradle will use the JDK found on the path of our computer. We can check this by running the following command on the command line:

```
$ java -version
```

Although Gradle uses Groovy, we don't have to install Groovy ourselves. Gradle bundles the Groovy libraries with the distribution and will ignore a Groovy installation that is already available on our computer.

Gradle is available on the Gradle website at `http://www.gradle.org/downloads`. From this page, we can download the latest release of Gradle. We can also download an older version if we want. We can choose among three different distributions to download. We can download the complete Gradle distribution with binaries, sources, and documentation; or we can only download the binaries; or we can only download the sources.

To get started with Gradle, we will download the standard distribution with the binaries, sources, and documentation. At the time of writing this book, the current release is 2.12.

Installing Gradle

Gradle is packaged as a ZIP file for one of the three distributions. So when we have downloaded the Gradle full-distribution ZIP file, we must unzip the file. After unpacking the ZIP file we have:

- Binaries in the `bin` directory
- Documentation with the user guide, Groovy DSL, and API documentation in the `doc` directory
- A lot of samples in the `samples` directory
- Source code of Gradle in the `src` directory
- Supporting libraries for Gradle in the `lib` directory
- A directory named `init.d`, where we can store Gradle scripts that need to be executed each time we run Gradle

Once we have unpacked the Gradle distribution to a directory, we can open a command prompt. We go to the directory where we have installed Gradle. To check our installation, we run `gradle -v` and get an output with the used JDK and library versions of Gradle, as follows:

```
$ gradle -v

------------------------------------------------------------
Gradle 2.12
------------------------------------------------------------

Build time:   2016-03-14 08:32:03 UTC
Build number: none
Revision:     b29fbb64ad6b068cb3f05f7e40dc670472129bc0
Groovy:       2.4.4
Ant:          Apache Ant(TM) version 1.9.3 compiled on
 December23 2013
JVM:          1.8.0_66 (Oracle Corporation 25.66-b17)
OS:           Mac OS X 10.11.3 x86_64
```

Here, we can check whether the displayed version is the same as the distribution version that we have downloaded from the Gradle website.

To run Gradle on our computer, we have to only add `$GRADLE_HOME/bin` to our `PATH` environment variable. Once we have done that, we can run the `gradle` command from every directory on our computer.

If we want to add **JVM** options to Gradle, we can use the `JAVA_OPTS` and `GRADLE_OPTS` environment variables. `JAVA_OPTS` is a commonly used environment variable name to pass extra parameters to a Java application. Gradle also uses the `GRADLE_OPTS` environment variable to pass extra arguments to Gradle. Both environment variables are used, so we can even set them both with different values. This is mostly used to set, for example, an HTTP proxy or extra memory options.

Installing with SKDMAN!

Software Development Kit Manager (SDKMAN!) is a tool to manage versions of software development kits such as Gradle. Once we have installed SKDMAN!, we can simply use the `install` command and SDKMAN! downloads Gradle and makes sure that it is added to our `$PATH` variable. SDKMAN! is available for Unix-like systems, such as Linux, Mac OSX, and Cygwin (on Windows).

First, we need to install SDKMAN! with the following command in our shell:

```
$ curl -s get.sdkman.io | bash
```

Next, we can install Gradle with the `install` command:

```
$ sdk install gradle
Downloading: gradle 2.12
% Total    % Received % Xferd  Average Speed   Time    Time     Time
Current
                                 Dload  Upload   Total   Spent    Left
Speed
      0       0    0    0    0     0       0        0 --:--:-- --:--:-- --:--:-
-      0
      0     354    0    0    0     0       0        0 --:--:-- --:--:-- --:--:-
-      0
    100 42.6M  100 42.6M    0     0    1982k        0  0:00:22  0:00:22 --:--:-
- 3872k
Installing: gradle 2.12
Done installing!
Do you want gradle 2.12 to be set as default? (Y/n): Y
Setting gradle 2.12 as default.
```

If we have multiple versions of Gradle, it is very easy to switch between versions with the `use` command:

```
$ sdk use gradle 2.12
Using gradle version 2.12 in this shell.
```

Writing our first build script

We now have a running Gradle installation. It is time to create our first Gradle build script. Gradle uses the concept of projects to define a related set of tasks. A Gradle build can have one or more projects. A project is a very broad concept in Gradle, but it is mostly a set of components that we want to build for our application.

A project has one or more tasks. Tasks are a unit of work that need to be executed by the build. Examples of tasks are compiling source code, packaging class files into a JAR file, running tests, and deploying the application.

We now know a task is a part of a project, so to create our first task, we also create our first Gradle project. We use the `gradle` command to run a build. Gradle will look for a file named `build.gradle` in the current directory. This file is the build script for our project. We define our tasks that need to be executed in this build script file.

We create a new `build.gradle` file and open this in a text editor. We type the following code to define our first Gradle task:

```
task helloWorld << {
    println 'Hello world.'
}
```

With this code, we will define a `helloWorld` task. The task will print the words `Hello world.` to the console. The `println` is a **Groovy** method to print text to the console and is basically a shorthand version of the `System.out.println` Java method.

The code between the brackets is a **closure**. A closure is a code block that can be assigned to a variable or passed to a method. Java doesn't support closures, but Groovy does. As Gradle uses Groovy to define the build scripts, we can use closures in our build scripts.

The `<<` syntax is, technically speaking, an operator shorthand for the `leftShift()` method, which actually means **add to**. Therefore, here we are defining that we want to add the closure (with the `println 'Hello world'` statement) to our task with the `helloWorld` name.

First, we save `build.gradle`, and with the `gradle helloWorld` command, we execute our build:

```
$ gradle helloWorld
:helloWorld
Hello world.
BUILD SUCCESSFUL
Total time: 2.384 secs
This build could be faster, please consider using the Gradle  Daemon:
https://docs.gradle.org/2.12/userguide/gradle_daemon.html
```

The first line of output shows our line `Hello world`. Gradle adds some more output such as the fact that the build was successful and the total time of the build. As Gradle runs in the JVM, every time we run a Gradle build, the JVM must be also started. The last line of the output shows a tip that we can use the Gradle daemon to run our builds. We will discuss more about the Gradle daemon later, but it essentially keeps Gradle running in memory so that we don't get the penalty of starting the JVM each time we run Gradle. This drastically speeds up the execution of tasks.

We can run the same build again, but only with the output of our task using the Gradle `--quiet` or `-q` command-line option. Gradle will suppress all messages except error messages. When we use the `--quiet` (or `-q`) option, we get the following output:

```
$ gradle --quiet helloWorld
Hello world.
```

Default Gradle tasks

We can create our simple build script with one task. We can ask Gradle to show us the available tasks for our project. Gradle has several built-in tasks that we can execute. We type `gradle -q tasks` to see the tasks for our project:

```
$ gradle -q tasks
------------------------------------------------------------
All tasks runnable from root project
------------------------------------------------------------
Build Setup tasks
-----------------
init - Initializes a new Gradle build. [incubating]
wrapper - Generates Gradle wrapper files. [incubating]
Help tasks
----------
components - Displays the components produced by root project
'hello-world'. [incubating]
dependencies - Displays all dependencies declared in root project  'hello-
world'.
dependencyInsight - Displays the insight into a specific n        dependency
in root project 'hello-world'.
help - Displays a help message.
model - Displays the configuration model of root project  'hello-world'.
[incubating]
projects - Displays the sub-projects of root project 'hello-world'.
properties - Displays the properties of root project 'hello-world'.
tasks - Displays the tasks runnable from root project 'hello-world'.
Other tasks
-----------
helloWorld
To see all tasks and more detail, run gradle tasks --all
To see more detail about a task, run gradle help --task <task>
```

Here, we see our `helloWorld` task in the `Other tasks` section. The Gradle built-in tasks are displayed in the `Help tasks` section. For example, to get some general help information, we execute the `help` task:

```
$ gradle -q help
Welcome to Gradle 2.12.
To run a build, run gradle <task> ...
To see a list of available tasks, run gradle tasks
To see a list of command-line options, run gradle --help
To see more detail about a task, run gradle help --task <task>
```

The `properties` task is very useful to see the properties available for our project. We haven't defined any property ourselves in the build script, but Gradle provides a lot of built-in properties. The following output shows some of the properties:

```
$ gradle -q properties
------------------------------------------------------------
Root project
------------------------------------------------------------
allprojects: [root project 'hello-world']
ant: org.gradle.api.internal.project.DefaultAntBuilder@3bd3d05e
antBuilderFactory:
org.gradle.api.internal.project.DefaultAntBuilderFactory@6aba5d30
artifacts:
org.gradle.api.internal.artifacts.dsl.DefaultArtifactHandler_Decorated@61d3
4b4
asDynamicObject: org.gradle.api.internal.ExtensibleDynamicObject@588307f7
baseClassLoaderScope:
org.gradle.api.internal.initialization.DefaultClassLoaderScope@7df76d99
buildDir: /Users/mrhaki/Projects/gradle-effective-implementation-
guide-2/gradle-impl-guide-2/src/docs/asciidoc/Chapter1/Code_Files/hello-
world/build
buildFile: /Users/mrhaki/Projects/gradle-effective-implementation-
guide-2/gradle-impl-guide-2/src/docs/asciidoc/Chapter1/Code_Files/hello-
world/build.gradle
buildScriptSource: org.gradle.groovy.scripts.UriScriptSource@459cfcca
buildscript:
org.gradle.api.internal.initialization.DefaultScriptHandler@2acbc859
childProjects: {}
class: class org.gradle.api.internal.project.DefaultProject_Decorated
classLoaderScope:
org.gradle.api.internal.initialization.DefaultClassLoaderScope@6ab7ce48
components: []
configurationActions:
org.gradle.configuration.project.DefaultProjectConfigurationActionContainer
@2c6aed22 ...
```

The `dependencies` task will show dependencies (if any) for our project. Our first project doesn't have any dependencies, as the output shows when we run the task:

```
$ gradle -q dependencies
------------------------------------------------------------
Root project
------------------------------------------------------------

No configurations
```

The `projects` tasks will display subprojects (if any) for a root project. Our project doesn't have any subprojects. Therefore, when we run the `projects` task, the output shows us our project has no subprojects:

```
$ gradle -q projects
------------------------------------------------------------
Root project
------------------------------------------------------------

Root project 'hello-world'
No sub-projects
To see a list of the tasks of a project, run gradle <project-path>:tasks
For example, try running gradle :tasks
```

The `model` tasks displays information about the model that Gradle builds internally from our project build file. This feature is incubating, which means that the functionality can change in future versions of Gradle:

```
$ gradle -q model
------------------------------------------------------------
Root project
------------------------------------------------------------
 + model
    + tasks
        | Type:        org.gradle.model.ModelMap<org.gradle.api.Task>
          | Creator:     Project.<init>.tasks()
        + components
          | Type:
org.gradle.api.reporting.components.ComponentReport
          | Value:       task ':components'
          | Creator:     tasks.addPlaceholderAction(components)
          | Rules:
            ▯ copyToTaskContainer
        + dependencies
          | Type:
org.gradle.api.tasks.diagnostics.DependencyReportTask
          | Value:       task ':dependencies'
          | Creator:     tasks.addPlaceholderAction(dependencies)
          | Rules:
   ...
```

We will discuss more about these and the other tasks in this book.

Task name abbreviation

Before we look at more Gradle command-line options, it is good to discuss a real-time save feature of Gradle: task name abbreviation. With task name abbreviation, we don't have to type the complete task name on the command line. We only have to type enough of the name to make it unique within the build.

In our first build, we only have one task, so the `gradle h` command should work just fine. However, we didn't take the built-in `help` task into account. So, to uniquely identify our `helloWorld` task, we use the `hello` abbreviation:

```
$ gradle -q hello
Hello world.
```

We can also abbreviate each word in a CamelCase task name. For example, our `helloWorld` task name can be abbreviated to `hW`:

```
$ gradle -q hW
Hello world.
```

This feature saves us the time spent in typing the complete task name and can speed up the execution of our tasks.

Executing multiple tasks

With just a simple build script, we already discussed that we have a couple of default tasks besides our own task that we can execute. To execute multiple tasks, we only have to add each task name to the command line. Let's execute our `helloWorld` custom task and built-in `tasks` task:

```
$ gradle helloWorld tasks
:helloWorld
Hello world.
:tasks

------------------------------------------------------------
All tasks runnable from root project
------------------------------------------------------------

Build Setup tasks
-----------------
init - Initializes a new Gradle build. [incubating]
wrapper - Generates Gradle wrapper files. [incubating]
Help tasks
----------
components - Displays the components produced by root project 'hello-
```

```
world'. [incubating]
 dependencies - Displays all dependencies declared in root project 'hello-
world'.
    dependencyInsight - Displays the insight into a specific  dependency in
root project 'hello-world'.
    help - Displays a help message.
    model - Displays the configuration model of root project 'hello-world'.
[incubating]
    projects - Displays the sub-projects of root project 'hello-world'.
    properties - Displays the properties of root project 'hello-world'.
    tasks - Displays the tasks runnable from root project 'hello-world'.
    Other tasks
    -----------
    helloWorld
    To see all tasks and more detail, run gradle tasks --all
    To see more detail about a task, run gradle help --task <task>
    BUILD SUCCESSFUL
    Total time: 2.028 secs
    This build could be faster, please consider using the Gradle Daemon:
https://docs.gradle.org/2.12/userguide/gradle_daemon.html
```

We see the output of both tasks. First, `helloWorld` is executed, followed by `tasks`. In the output, we see the task names prepended with a colon (`:`) and the output is in the next lines.

Gradle executes the tasks in the same order as they are defined in the command line. Gradle will only execute a task once during the build. So even if we define the same task multiple times, it will only be executed once. This rule also applies when tasks have dependencies on other tasks. Gradle will optimize the task execution for us and we don't have to worry about that.

Command-line options

The `gradle` command is used to execute a build. This command accepts several command-line options. We know the `--quiet` (or `-q`) option to reduce the output of a build. If we use the `--help` (or `-h` or `-?`) option, we see the complete list of options, as follows:

```
$ gradle --help
USAGE: gradle [option...] [task...]
-?, -h, --help          Shows this help message.
-a, --no-rebuild        Do not rebuild project dependencies.
-b, --build-file        Specifies the build file.
-c, --settings-file     Specifies the settings file.
--configure-on-demand   Only relevant projects are configured in this build
```

run. This means faster build for large multi-project builds. [incubating]

    --console   Specifies which type of console output to generate. Values are 'plain', 'auto' (default) or 'rich'.

    --continue   Continues task execution after a task failure.

    -D, --system-prop   Set system property of the JVM (e.g. -Dmyprop=myvalue).

    -d, --debug   Log in debug mode (includes normal stacktrace).

    --daemon   Uses the Gradle daemon to run the build. Starts the daemon if not running.

    --foreground   Starts the Gradle daemon in the foreground. [incubating]

    -g, --gradle-user-home Specifies the gradle user home directory.

    --gui   Launches the Gradle GUI.

    -I, --init-script   Specifies an initialization script.

    -i, --info   Set log level to info.

    -m, --dry-run   Runs the builds with all task actions disabled.

    --max-workers   Configure the number of concurrent workers Gradle is allowed to use. [incubating]

    --no-color   Do not use color in the console output. [deprecated - use --console=plain instead]

    --no-daemon   Do not use the Gradle daemon to run the build.

    --offline   The build should operate without accessing network resources.

    -P, --project-prop   Set project property for the build script (e.g. -Pmyprop=myvalue).

    -p, --project-dir   Specifies the start directory for Gradle. Defaults to current directory.

    --parallel   Build projects in parallel. Gradle will attempt to determine the optimal number of executor threads to use. [incubating]

    --parallel-threads   Build projects in parallel, using the specified number of executor threads. [deprecated - Please use --parallel, optionally in conjunction with --max-workers.] [incubating]

    --profile   Profiles build execution time and generates a report in the <build_dir>/reports/profile directory.

    --project-cache-dir   Specifies the project-specific cache directory. Defaults to .gradle in the root project directory.

    -q, --quiet   Log errors only.

    --recompile-scripts   Force build script recompiling.

    --refresh-dependencies Refresh the state of dependencies.

    --rerun-tasks   Ignore previously cached task results.

    -S, --full-stacktrace   Print out the full (very verbose) stacktrace for all exceptions.

    -s, --stacktrace   Print out the stacktrace for all exceptions.

    --stop   Stops the Gradle daemon if it is running.

    -t, --continuous   Enables continuous build. Gradle does not exit and will re-execute tasks when task file inputs change. [incubating]

    -u, --no-search-upward Don't search in parent folders for a settings.gradle file.

```
-v, --version              Print version info.
-x, --exclude-task         Specify a task to be excluded from execution.
```

Logging options

Let's look at some of the options in more detail. The --quiet (or -q), --debug (or -d), --info (or -i), --stacktrace (or-s), and --full-stacktrace (or-S) options control how much output we see when we execute tasks. To get the most detailed output, we use the --debug (or -d) option. This option provides a lot of output with information about the steps and classes used to run the build. The output is very verbose, therefore, we will not use it much.

To get a better insight on the steps that are executed for our task, we can use the --info (or -i) option. The output is not as verbose as with --debug, but it can provide a better understanding of the build steps:

```
$ gradle --info helloworld
Starting Build
Settings evaluated using settings file '/master/settings.gradle'.
    Projects loaded. Root project using build file
'/Users/mrhaki/Projects/gradle-effective-implementation-guide-2/gradle-
impl-guide-2/src/docs/asciidoc/Chapter1/Code_Files/hello-
world/build.gradle'.
    Included projects: [root project 'hello-world']
    Evaluating root project 'hello-world' using build file
'/Users/mrhaki/Projects/gradle-effective-implementation-guide-2/gradle-
impl-guide-2/src/docs/asciidoc/Chapter1/Code_Files/hello-
world/build.gradle'.
    All projects evaluated.
    Selected primary task 'helloWorld' from project :
    Tasks to be executed: [task ':helloWorld']
    :helloWorld (Thread[main,5,main]) started.
    :helloWorld
    Executing task ':helloWorld' (up-to-date check took 0.001 secs) due to:
      Task has not declared any outputs.
    Hello world.
    :helloWorld (Thread[main,5,main]) completed. Took 0.021 secs.
    BUILD SUCCESSFUL
    Total time: 1.325 secs
    This build could be faster, please consider using the Gradle Daemon:
https://docs.gradle.org/2.12/userguide/gradle_daemon.html
```

If our build throws exceptions, we can see the stack trace information with the `--stacktrace` (or `-s`) and `--full-stacktrace` (or `-S`) options. The latter option will output the most information and is the most verbose. The `--stacktrace` and `--full-stacktrace` options can be combined with the other logging options.

Changing the build file and directory

We created our build file with the `build.gradle` name. This is the default name for a build file. Gradle will look for a file with this name in the current directory to execute the build. However, we can change this with the `--build-file` (or `-b`) and `--project-dir` (or `-p`) command-line options.

Let's run the `gradle` command from the parent directory of our current directory:

```
$ cd ..
$ gradle --project-dir hello-world -q helloWorld
Hello world.
```

We can also rename our `build.gradle` to, for example, `hello.build` and still execute our build:

```
$ mv build.gradle hello.build
$ gradle --build-file hello.build -q helloWorld
Hello world.
```

Running tasks without execution

With the `--dry-run` (or `-m`) option, we can run all tasks without really executing them. When we use the `dry-run` option, we can see the tasks that are executed, so we get an insight on the tasks that are involved in a certain build scenario. We don't even have to worry whether the tasks are actually executed. Gradle builds up a **Directed Acyclic Graph (DAG)** with all tasks before any task is executed. The DAG is build so that the tasks will be executed in order of dependencies, and a task is only executed once:

```
$ gradle --dry-run helloWorld
:helloWorld SKIPPED
BUILD SUCCESSFUL
Total time: 1.307 secs
This build could be faster, please consider using the Gradle Daemon:
https://docs.gradle.org/2.12/userguide/gradle_daemon.html
```

Gradle daemon

We already discussed that Gradle executes in a JVM, and each time we invoke the `gradle` command, a new JVM is started, the Gradle classes and libraries are loaded, and the build is executed. We can reduce the build execution time if we don't have to load JVM and Gradle classes and libraries each time we execute a build. The `--daemon` command-line option starts a new Java process that will have all Gradle classes and libraries already loaded and then execute the build. Next time when we run Gradle with the `--daemon` option, only the build is executed as the JVM with the required Gradle classes and libraries is already running.

The first time we execute Gradle with the `--daemon` option, the execution speed will not have improved as the Java background process was not started yet. However, the next time, we can see a major improvement:

```
$ gradle --daemon helloWorld
Starting a new Gradle Daemon for this build (subsequent builds will be
faster).
:helloWorld
Hello world.
BUILD SUCCESSFUL
Total time: 2.136 secs
$ gradle helloWorld
:helloWorld
 Hello world.
BUILD SUCCESSFUL
Total time: 0.594 secs
```

Even though the daemon process is started, we can still run Gradle tasks without using the daemon. We use the `--no-daemon` command-line option to run a Gradle build, and then the daemon is not used:

```
$ gradle --no-daemon helloWorld
:helloWorld
Hello world.
BUILD SUCCESSFUL
Total time: 1.325 secs
```

To stop the daemon process, we use the `--stop` command-line option:

```
$ gradle --stop
Stopping daemon(s).
Gradle daemon stopped.
```

This will stop the Java background process completely.

To always use the --daemon command-line option, but we don't want to type it every time we run the gradle command, we can create an alias if our operating system supports aliases. For example, on a Unix-based system, we can create an alias and then use the alias to run the Gradle build:

```
$ alias gradled='gradle --daemon'
$ gradled helloWorld
:helloWorld
Hello world.
BUILD SUCCESSFUL
Total time: 0.572 secs
```

Instead of using the --daemon command-line option, we can use the org.gradle.daemon Java system property to enable the daemon. We can add this property to the GRADLE_OPTS environment variable so that it is always used when we run a Gradle build:

```
$ export GRADLE_OPTS="-Dorg.gradle.daemon=true"
$ gradle helloWorld
:helloWorld
Hello world.
BUILD SUCCESSFUL
Total time: 0.575 secs
```

Finally, we can add a gradle.properties file to the root of our project directory. In the file, we can define a org.gradle.daemon property and assign the true value to enable the Gradle daemon for all builds that are executed from this directory.

Let's create a gradle.properties file with the following contents:

```
org.gradle.daemon=true
```

We can run our example task, helloWorld, and the build will use the Gradle daemon:

```
$ gradle helloWorld
:helloWorld
Hello world.
BUILD SUCCESSFUL
Total time: 0.58 secs
```

Profiling

Gradle also provides the `--profile` command-line option. This option records the time that certain tasks take to complete. The data is saved in an HTML file in the `build/reports/profile` directory. We can open this file in a web browser and check the time taken for several phases in the build process. The following image shows the HTML contents of the profile report:

Profile report

Profiled build: helloWorld

Started on: 2015/08/30 - 07:13:48

Summary	Configuration	Dependency Resolution	Task Execution

Description	Duration
Total Build Time	0.577s
Startup	0.561s
Settings and BuildSrc	0.002s
Loading Projects	0.001s
Configuring Projects	0.004s
Task Execution	0.001s

Generated by Gradle 2.6 at Aug 30, 2015 7:13:48 AM

HTML page with profiling information

Offline usage

If we don't have access to a network at some location, we might get errors from our Gradle build, when a task needs to download something from the Internet, for example. We can use the `--offline` command-line option to instruct Gradle to not access any network during the build. This way we can still execute the build if all necessary files are already available offline and we don't get an error.

Understanding the Gradle graphical user interface

Finally, we take a look at the `--gui` command-line option. With this option, we start a graphical shell for our Gradle builds. Until now, we used the command line to start a task. With the **Gradle GUI**, we have a graphical overview of the tasks in a project and we can execute them by simply clicking on the mouse.

To start the GUI, we invoke the following command:

```
$ gradle --gui
```

A window is opened with a graphical overview of our task tree. We only have one task that one is shown in the task tree, as we can seen in the following screenshot:

Overview of tasks in the Gradle GUI

The output of running a task is shown at the bottom of the window. When we start the GUI for the first time, the tasks task is executed and we see the output in the window.

Task tree

The Task Tree tab shows projects and tasks found in our build project. We can execute a task by double-clicking on the task name.

By default, all the tasks are shown, but we can apply a filter to show or hide certain projects and tasks. The **Edit filter** button opens a new dialog window where we can define the tasks and properties that are a part of the filter. The **Toggle filter** button makes the filter active or inactive.

We can also right-click on the project and task names. This opens a context menu where we can choose to execute the task, add it to the favorites, hide it (adds it to the filter), or edit the build file. If we have associated the .gradle extension to a text editor in our operating system, then the editor is opened with the content of the build script. These options can be seen in the following screenshot:

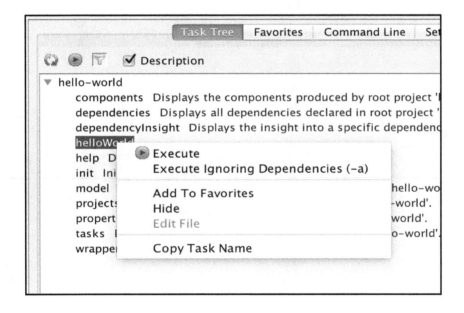

Available actions for a task in the Gradle GUI

Favorites

The Favorites tab stores tasks we want to execute regularly. We can add a task by right-clicking on the task in the **Task Tree** tab and selecting the **Add To Favorites** menu option, or if we have opened the **Favorites** tab, we can select the **Add** button and manually enter the project and task name that we want to add to our favorites list. We can see the **Add Favorite** dialog window in the following screenshot:

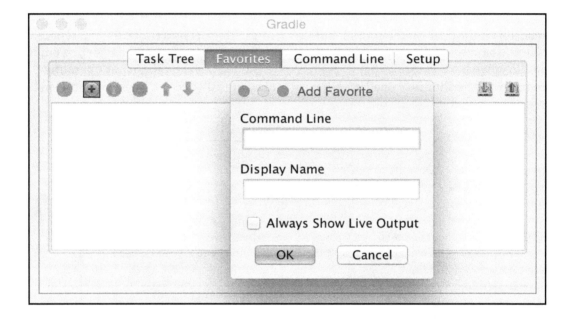

Add favorites in the Gradle GUI

Command line

On the Command Line tab, we can enter any Gradle command that we normally would enter on the command prompt. The command can be added to **Favorites** as well. We see the **Command Line** tab contents in the following image:

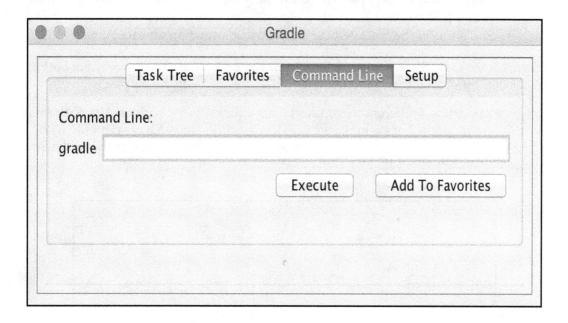

Execute task with command-line optins

Setup

The last tab is the Setup tab. Here, we can change the project directory, which is set to the current directory by default.

We discussed about the different logging levels as command-line options previously in this chapter. With the GUI, we can select the logging level from the **Log Level** select box with the different log levels. We can choose **debug**, **info**, **Lifecycle**, and **error** as log levels. The error log level only shows errors and is the least verbose, while debug is the most verbose log level. The lifecycle log level is the default log level.

Here, we also can set how detailed the exeption stack trace information should be. In the **Stack Trace Output** section, we can choose from the following three options:

- **Exceptions Only**: This is for only showing the exceptions when they occur, which is the default value
- **Standard Stack Trace (-s)**: This is for showing more stack trace information for the exceptions
- **-S)**: This is for the most verbose stack trace information for exceptions

If we enable the **Only Show Output When Error Occurs** option, then we only get output from the build process if the build fails. Otherwise, we don't get any output.

Finally, we can define a different way to start Gradle for the build with the **Use Custom Gradle Executor** option. For example, we can define a different batch or script file with extra setup information to run the build process. The following screenshot shows the **Setup** tab page and all the options that we can set:

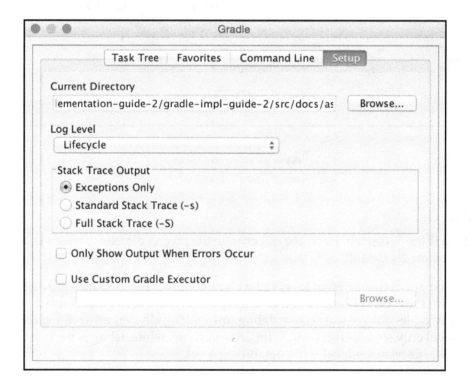

Setup Gradle options in the Gradle GUI

Summary

So, now we have discussed how to install Gradle on our computers. We have written our first Gradle build script with a simple task.

We have also seen how we use the built-in tasks of Gradle to get more information about a project. We discussed how to use the command-line options to help us run the build scripts. We have looked at the Gradle GUI and how we can use it to run Gradle build scripts.

In the next chapter, we will take a further look at tasks. We will discuss how to add actions to a task. We write more complex tasks, where the tasks will depend on other tasks. We will also discuss how Gradle builds up a task graph internally and how to use this in our projects.

2
Creating Gradle Build Scripts

In Gradle, projects and tasks are two important concepts. A Gradle build always consists of one or more projects. A project defines some sort of component that we want to build. There are no defining rules about what the component is. It can be a JAR file with utility classes to be used in other projects, or a web application to be deployed to the corporate intranet. A project doesn't have to be about building and packaging code, it can also be about doing things such as copying files on a remote server or deployment of applications to servers.

A project has one or more tasks. A task is a small piece of work that is executed when we run a build, for example, compiling source code, packaging code in an archive file, generating documentation, and so on.

In this chapter, we will discuss how to define a project with tasks and use it as a Gradle build. We will cover the following topics:

- Defining tasks
- Defining dependencies between tasks
- Organizing tasks and ways to handle it

Writing a build script

In the first chapter, we have already written our first build script. Let's create a similar build script with a simple task. Gradle will look for a file with the name `build.gradle` in the current directory. The `build.gradle` file contains the tasks that make up our project. In this example, we define a simple task that prints out a simple message to the console:

```
// Assign value to description property.
project.description = 'Simple project'

// DSL to create a new task using
```

```
// Groovy << operator.
task simple << {
    println 'Running simple task for project ' +
        project.description
}
```

If we run the build, we see the following output in the console:

```
:simple
Running simple task for project Simple project
BUILD SUCCESSFUL
Total time: 0.57 secs
```

A couple of interesting things happen with this small build script. Gradle reads the script file and creates a `Project` object. The build script configures the `Project` object, and finally, the set of tasks to be executed is determined and executed.

So, it is important to note that Gradle creates a `Project` object for us. The `Project` object has several properties and methods and it is available in our build scripts. We can use the `project` variable name to reference the `Project` object, but we can also leave out this variable name to reference properties and methods of the `Project` object. Gradle will automatically try to map properties and methods in the build script to the `Project` object.

In our simple build script, we assign the `Simple project` value to the `description` project property. We used the explicit project variable name and Groovy property assignment syntax. The following build script uses a different syntax, which is a bit more like Java, to get the same result:

```
// Use setDescription method
// to assign value instead of
// Groovy assignment.
project.setDescription('Simple project')

// Use create method to add new
// task instead of Groovy << operator.
project.getTasks().create('simple') {
    println 'Running simple task for project ' +
        project.description
}
```

Here, we use the Java syntax to set and get the value of the description property of the `Project` object. We are very flexible in our syntax, but we will stick to the Groovy syntax for the rest of the book as it results in more readable build scripts.

Defining tasks

A project has one or more tasks to execute some actions, so a task is made up of actions. These actions are executed when the task is executed. Gradle supports several ways to add actions to our tasks. In this section, we discuss about the different ways to add actions to a task.

We can use the doFirst and doLast methods to add actions to our task, and we can use the left-shift operator (<<) as a synonym for the doLast method. With the doLast method or the left-shift operator (<<), we add actions at the end of the list of actions for the task. With the doFirst method, we can add actions to the beginning of the list of actions. The following script shows how we can use the several methods:

```
task first {
    doFirst {
        println 'Running first'
    }
}

task second {
    doLast { Task task ->
        println "Running ${task.name}"
    }
}

// Here we use the << operator
// as synonym for the doLast method.
task third << { taskObject ->
    println 'Running ' + taskObject.name
}
```

When we run the script, we get the following output:

```
$ gradle first second third
:first
Running first
:second
Running second
:third
Running third
BUILD SUCCESSFUL
Total time: 0.592 secs
```

For the `second` task, we add the action to print text with the `doLast` method. The method accepts a closure as an argument. The `task` object is passed to the closure as a parameter. This means that we can use the `task` object in our actions. In the sample build file, we get the value for the `name` property of `task` and print it to the console.

Maybe it is a good time to look more closely at closures as they are an important part of Groovy and are used throughout Gradle build scripts. Closures are basically reusable pieces of code that can be assigned to a variable or passed to a method. A closure is defined by enclosing the piece of code with curly brackets (`{ ... }`). We can pass one or more parameters to the closures. If the closure has only one argument, an implicit parameter, `it`, can be used to reference the parameter value. We could have written the `second` task as follows, and the result would still be the same:

```
task second {
    doLast {
        // Using implicit 'it' closure parameter.
        // The type of 'it' is a Gradle task.
        println "Running ${it.name}"
    }
}
```

We can also define a name for the parameter and use this name in the code. This is what we did for the `second` and `third` tasks; wherein, we named the closure parameter `task` and `taskObject`, respectively. The resulting code is more readable if we define the parameter `name` explicitly in our closure, as follows:

```
task second {
    doLast { Task task ->
        // Using explicit name 'task' as closure parameter.
        // We also defined the type of the parameter.
        // This can help the IDE to add code completion.
        println "Running ${task.name}"
    }
}
```

Defining actions with the Action interface

Gradle often has more than one way of defining something, as we will see throughout the book. Besides using closures to add actions to a task, we can also follows a more verbose way of passing an implementation class of the `org.gradle.api.Action` interface. The `Action` interface has one method: `execute`. This method is invoked when the task is executed. The following piece of code shows a reimplementation of the first task in our build script:

```
task first {
    doFirst(
        new Action() {
          void execute(O task) {
            println "Running ${task.name}"
          }
        }
    )
}
```

It is good to know that we have choices when we define actions for a task, but the closure syntax is denser and more readable. We will use closure to configure objects further in this book.

Build scripts are Groovy code

We must keep in mind that Gradle scripts use Groovy. This means that we can use all the Groovy's good stuff in our scripts. We already saw the use of so-called Groovy `GString` in our sample script. The `GString` object is defined as a `String` with double quotes and can contain references to variables defined in a `${...}` section. The variable reference is resolved when we get the value of the `GString`.

However, other great Groovy constructs can also be used in Gradle scripts. The following sample script shows some of these constructs:

```
task numbers << {
    // To define a range of numbers
    // we can use the following syntax:
    // start..end.
    // The each method executes the code
    // in the closure for each element
    // in a collection, like a range.
    (1..4).each { number ->
        // def is short for define.
```

```
        // Used to define a variable without
        // an explicit type of the variable.
        def squared = number * number

        // Use GString with ${} expression
        // to get a new string value where
        // the value references are replaced
        // with the actual values.
        println "Square of ${number} = ${squared}"
    }
}

task list {
    doFirst {
        // Simple notation to define a list of values
        // in Groovy using square brackets.
        def list = ['Groovy', 'Gradle']

        // Groovy makes working with collections
        // easy and adds utility methods to work
        // with elements in the collection.
        // The collect method transform each element
        // in the original collection with the return
        // value of the closure. Here all string elements
        // are turned into lower case values.
        // The join method joins all elements separated by
        // the given character. The end result is
        // groovy&gradle
        println list.collect { it.toLowerCase() }.join('&')
    }
}
```

When we run the script, we get the following output:

```
$ gradle -q numbers list
Square of 1 = 1
Square of 2 = 4
Square of 3 = 9
Square of 4 = 16
groovy&gradle
```

Defining dependencies between tasks

Until now, we have defined tasks independent of each other. However, in our projects, we need dependencies between tasks. For example, a task to package compiled class files is dependent on the task to compile the class files. The build system should then run the compile task first, and when the task is finished, the package task must be executed.

In Gradle, we can add task dependencies with the dependsOn method for a task. We can specify a task name as the String value or task object as the argument. We can even specify more than one task name or object to specify multiple task dependencies. First, let's look at a simple task dependency:

```
task first << { task ->
    println "Run ${task.name}"
}

task second << { task ->
    println "Run ${task.name}"
}

// Define dependency of task second on task first
second.dependsOn 'first'
```

Note that we define the dependency of the second task on the first task, in the last line. When we run the script, we see that the first task is executed before the second task:

```
$ gradle second
:first
Run first
:second
Run second
BUILD SUCCESSFUL
Total time: 0.583 secs
```

Another way of defining the dependency between tasks is to set the dependsOn property instead of using the dependsOn method. There is a subtle difference, Gradle just offers several ways to achieve the same result. In the following piece of code, we use the property to define the dependency of the second task. For the third task, we immediately define the property when we define the task:

```
task first << { task ->
    println "Run ${task.name}"
}

task second << { task ->
    println "Run ${task.name}"
```

```
}

// Use property syntax to define dependency.
// dependsOn expects a collection object.
second.dependsOn = ['first']

// Define dependsOn when we create the task.
task third(dependsOn: 'second') << { task ->
    println "Run ${task.name}"
}
```

When we run the `third` task on the command line, we see that all three tasks are executed, as follows:

```
$ gradle -q third
Run first
Run second
Run third
```

The dependency between tasks is lazy. We can define a dependency on a task that is defined later in the build script. Gradle will set up all task dependencies during the configuration phase and not during the execution phase. The following script shows that the order of the tasks doesn't matter in the build script:

```
task third(dependsOn: 'second') << { task ->
    println "Run ${task.name}"
}

task second(dependsOn: 'first') << { task ->
    println "Run ${task.name}"
}

task first << { task ->
    println "Run ${task.name}"
}
```

We now have our build script with three tasks, but each task does the same thing: it prints a string with the name of the task. It is better to keep in mind that our build script is just code, and code can be organized and refactored to create cleaner code. This applies to Gradle build scripts as well. It is important to take a good look at your build scripts and see if things can be organized better and if the code can be reused instead of repeated. Even our simple build script can be rewritten as follows:

```
// We assign the task closure
// to a variable. We can reuse
// the variable name in our task definitions.
def printTaskName = { task ->
```

```
        println "Run ${task.name}"
}

// We use the variable with the closure.
task third(dependsOn: 'second') << printTaskName

task second(dependsOn: 'first') << printTaskName

task first << printTaskName
```

This might seem trivial, but it is important to understand that we can apply the same coding techniques that we use in our application code to our build code.

Defining dependencies via tasks

In our build scripts, we defined the task dependencies using the task name. However, there are more ways to define a task dependency. We can use the `task` object instead of the task name to define a task dependency:

```
def printTaskName = { task ->
    println "Run ${task.name}"
}

task first << printTaskName

// Here we use first (not the string value 'first')
// as a value for dependsOn.
task second(dependsOn: first) << printTaskName
```

Defining dependencies via closures

We can also use a closure to define the task dependencies. The closure must return a single task name or object, or a collection of task names or `task` objects. Using this technique, we can really fine-tune the dependencies for our task. For example, in the following build script, we define a dependency for the `second` task on all tasks in the project with task names that have the letter `f` in the task name:

```
def printTaskName = { task ->
    println "Run ${task.name}"
}

task second << printTaskName

// We use the dependsOn method
```

```
// with a closure.
second.dependsOn {
    // We use the Groovy method findAll
    // that returns all tasks that
    // apply to the condition we define
    // in the closure: the task name
    // starts with the letter 'f'.
    project.tasks.findAll { task ->
        task.name.contains 'f'
    }
}

task first << printTaskName

task beforeSecond << printTaskName
```

When we run the build project, we get the following output:

```
$ gradle second
:beforeSecond
Run beforeSecond
:first
Run first
:second
Run second
BUILD SUCCESSFUL
Total time: 0.602 secs
```

Setting default tasks

To execute a task, we use the task name on the command line when we run `gradle`. So, if our build script contains a task with the `first` name, we can run the task with the following command:

```
$ gradle first
```

However, we can also define a default task or multiple default tasks that need to be executed, even if we don't explicitly set the task name. So, if we run the `gradle` command without arguments, the default task of our build script will be executed.

To set the default task or tasks, we use the `defaultTasks` method. We pass the names of the tasks that need to be executed to the method. In the following build script, we make the `first` and `second` tasks the default tasks:

```
defaultTasks 'first', 'second'
```

```
task first {
    doLast {
        println "I am first"
    }
}

task second {
    doFirst {
        println "I am second"
    }
}
```

We can run our build script and get the following output:

```
$ gradle
:first
I am first
:second
I am second
BUILD SUCCESSFUL
Total time: 0.558 secs
```

Organizing tasks

In Chapter 1, *Starting with Gradle*, we already discussed that we could use the tasks task of Gradle to see the tasks that are available for a build. Let's suppose we have the following simple build script:

```
defaultTasks 'second'

task first << {
    println "I am first"
}

task second(dependsOn: first) << {
    println "I am second"
}
```

Nothing fancy here. The second task is the default task and depends on the first task. When we run the tasks task on the command line, we get the following output:

```
$ gradle -q tasks
-----------------------------------------------------------
   All tasks runnable from root project
-----------------------------------------------------------
Default tasks: second
```

```
Build Setup tasks
-----------------
init - Initializes a new Gradle build. [incubating]
wrapper - Generates Gradle wrapper files. [incubating]
Help tasks
----------
components - Displays the components produced by root project 'organize'.
[incubating]
    dependencies - Displays all dependencies declared in root project
'organize'.
    dependencyInsight - Displays the insight into a specific dependency in
root project 'organize'.
    help - Displays a help message.
    model - Displays the configuration model of root project 'organize'.
[incubating]
    projects - Displays the sub-projects of root project 'organize'.
    properties - Displays the properties of root project 'organize'.
    tasks - Displays the tasks runnable from root project 'organize'.
    Other tasks
    -----------
    second
To see all tasks and more detail, run gradle tasks --all
To see more detail about a task, run gradle help --task <task>
```

We see our task with the name `second` in the section `Other tasks`, but not the task with the name `first`. To see all tasks, including the tasks other tasks depend on, we must add the option `--all` to the tasks command:

```
$ gradle tasks --all
 . . .
Other tasks
-----------
   second
      first
```

Now we see our task with the name `first`. Gradle even indents the dependent tasks so that we can see that the `second` task depends on the `first` task.

At the beginning of the output, we see the following line:

```
Default tasks: second
```

Gradle shows us the default task in our build.

Adding a description to tasks

To describe our task, we can set the description property of a task. The value of the description property is used by the task of Gradle. Let's add a description to our two tasks, as follows:

```
defaultTasks 'second'

// Use description property to set description.
task first(description: 'Base task') << {
    println "I am first"
}

task second(
    dependsOn: first,
    description: 'Secondary task') << {

    println "I am second"
}
```

Now when we run the tasks task, we get a more descriptive output:

```
$ gradle tasks --all
. . .
Other tasks
-----------
second - Secondary task
       first - Base task
```

Grouping tasks together

With Gradle, we can also group tasks together in so-called **task groups**. A task group is a set of tasks that belong together, logically. The task group is used, for example, in the output of the tasks task that we used earlier. Let's expand our sample build script by grouping the two tasks together in a sample task group. We must assign a value to the group property of a task:

```
defaultTasks 'second'

// Define name of the
// task group we want to use.
def taskGroup = 'base'

task first(
    description: 'Base task',
```

```
        group: taskGroup) << {

        println "I am first"
    }

task second(
    dependsOn: first,
    description: 'Secondary task',
    group: taskGroup) << {

        println "I am second"
    }
```

Next time when we run the `tasks` task, we can see our tasks grouped together in a `Base tasks` section:

```
$ gradle -q tasks --all
...
 Base tasks
 ----------
 first - Base task
 second - Secondary task [first]
 ...
```

Note that the task dependency is appended to the `description` property of the `second` task.

Getting more information about a task

We can get some more information about a task with the Gradle `help` task. We need to specify an extra argument for the `help` task: `--task`, with the name of the task that we want more information about. Gradle will print some details about our task in the console. For example, the description and type of the task. This can be very useful to learn more about a task.

We will invoke the `help` task to get more information about our `second` task:

```
$ gradle help --task second
:help
Detailed task information for second
 Path :second
 Type  Task (org.gradle.api.Task)
 Description  Secondary task
```

```
Group  base
BUILD SUCCESSFUL
Total time: 0.58 secs
```

Adding tasks in other ways

Until now, we have added tasks to our build project using the `task` keyword, followed by the name of the task. However, there are more ways to add tasks to our project. We can use a `String` value with the task name to define a new task, as follows:

```
task 'simple' << { task ->
    println "Running ${task.name}"
}
```

We can also use variable expressions to define a new task. If doing so, we must use parenthesis, otherwise the expression cannot be resolved. The following sample script defines a `simpleTask` variable with the `simple` string value. This expression is used to define the task. The result is that our project now contains a task with the name `simple`:

```
// Define name of task
// as a variable.
def simpleTask = 'simple'

// Variable is used for the task name.
task(simpleTask) << { task ->
    println "Running ${task.name}"
}
```

We can run the `tasks` task to see our newly created task:

```
$ gradle -q tasks
 . . .

Other tasks
-----------
  simple
 . . .
```

We can also use the power of Groovy to add new tasks. We can use Groovy's GString notation to dynamically create a task name. It is just like using expressions in the previous sample, but expressed in a Groovy GString:

```
// Name of task as variable.
def simpleTask = 'simple'

// Using Groovy GString with
// ${} expression to use variable
// as task name.
task "${simpleTask}" << { task ->
    println "Running ${task.name}"
}

// Or use loops to create multiple tasks.
['Dev', 'Acc', 'Prod'].each { environment ->
    // A new task is created for each element
    // in the list ['Dev', 'Acc', 'Prod'].
    task "deployTo${environment}" << { task ->
        println "Deploying to ${environment}"
    }
}
```

If we run the tasks task, we can see that we have four new tasks, as follows:

```
$ gradle -q tasks
. . .
Other tasks
-----------
deployToAcc
deployToDev
deployToProd
  simple
  . . .
```

Another way to add a new task is through the tasks property of a project. Remember that in our build script, we have access to the Project object; either we use the project variable explicitly or we use methods and properties of the Project object implicitly, without using the project variable. The tasks property of a project is basically a container for all tasks in our project. In the following build script, we use the create method to add a new task:

```
def printTaskName = { task ->
    println "Running ${task.name}"
}

// Use tasks project variable to get access
```

```
// to the TaskContainer object.
// Then we use the create method of
// TaskContainer to create a new task.
project.tasks.create(name: 'first') << printTaskName

// Let Gradle resolve tasks to project variable.
tasks.create(name: 'second', dependsOn: 'first') << printTaskName
```

Using task rules

We have seen how to add tasks dynamically to our build project. However, we can also define so-called **task rules**. These rules are very flexible and allow us to add tasks to our project based on several parameters and project properties.

Suppose, we want to add an extra task that shows the description of every task in our project. If we have a task first in our project, we want to add a descFirst task to show the description property of the first task. With task rules, we define a pattern for new tasks. In our sample, this is desc<TaskName>; it is the desc prefix, followed by the name of the existing task. The following build script shows the implementation of the task rule:

```
task first(description: 'First task')

task second(description: 'Second task')

tasks.addRule(
    "Pattern: desc<TaskName>: " +
    "show description of a task.") { taskName ->

    if (taskName.startsWith('desc')) {
        // Remove 'desc' from the task name.
        def targetTaskName = taskName - 'desc'

      // Uncapitalize the task name.
      def targetTaskNameUncapitalize =
        targetTaskName[0].toLowerCase() +
          targetTaskName[1..-1]

      // Find the task in the project we search
      // the description for.
      def targetTask =
        project.tasks.findByName(
          targetTaskNameUncapitalize)

      if (targetTask) {
          task(taskName) << {
```

```
            println "Description of task ${targetTask.name} " +
                " -> ${targetTask.description}"
        }
      }
    }
  }
```

If we run the `tasks` task, we see an extra `Rules` section in the output:

```
$ gradle tasks
...
Rules
-----
Pattern: desc<TaskName>: show description of a task.
...
```

So, we know we can invoke `descFirst` and `descSecond` for our project. Note that these two extra tasks are not shown in the `Other tasks` section, but the `Rules` section shows the pattern we can use.

If we execute the `descFirst` and `descSecond` tasks, we get the following output:

```
$ gradle descFirst descSecond
:descFirst
Description of task first  -> First task
:descSecond
Description of task second  -> Second task
BUILD SUCCESSFUL
Total time: 0.56 secs
```

Accessing tasks as project properties

Each task that we add is also available as a `project` property, and we can reference this property like we can reference any other property in our build script. We can, for example, invoke methods or get and set the property values of our task through the property reference. This means that we are very flexible in how we create our tasks and add behavior to the tasks. In the following script, we use the `project` property reference to a task to change the `description` property:

```
// Create a simple task.
task simple << { task ->
    println "Running ${task.name}"
}

// The simple task is available as
```

```
// project property.
simple.description = 'Print task name'

// We can invoke methods from the
// Task object.
simple.doLast {
    println "Done"
}

// We can also reference the task
// via the project property
// explicitly.
project.simple.doFirst {
    println "Start"
}
```

When we run our task from the command line, we get the following output:

```
$ gradle -q simple
Start
Running simple
Done
```

Adding additional properties to tasks

A task object already has several properties and methods. However, we can add any arbitrary new property to a task and use it. Gradle provides an ext namespace for the task object. We can set new properties and use them again once they are set. We can either set a property directly or use a closure to set a property with a value. In the following sample, we print the value of the message task property. The value of the property is assigned with the simple.ext.message = 'world' statement:

```
// Create simple task.
task simple << {
    println "Hello ${message}"
}

// We set the value for
// the non-existing message
// property with the task extension
// support.
simple.ext.message = 'world'
```

When we run the task, we get the following output:

```
: simple
Hello world
BUILD SUCCESSFUL
Total time: 0.584 secs
```

Avoiding common pitfalls

A common mistake when creating a task and adding actions for this task is that we forget the left-shift operator (<<). Then we are left with a valid syntax in our build script, so we don't get an error when we execute the task. However, instead of adding actions, we have configured our task. The closure we use is then interpreted as a configuration closure. All methods and properties in the closure are applied to the task. We can add actions for our tasks in the configuration closure, but we must use the doFirst and doLast methods. We cannot use the left-shift operator (<<).

The following tasks do the same thing, but note the subtle differences when we define the tasks:

```
def printTaskName = { task ->
    println "Running ${task.name}"
}

task 'one' {
    // Invoke doFirst method to add action.
    doFirst printTaskName
}

// Assign action through left-shift operator (<<).
task 'two' << printTaskName

task 'three' {
    // This line will be displayed during configuration
    // and not when we execute the task,
    // because we use the configuration closure
    // and forgot the << operator.
    println "Running three"
}

defaultTasks 'one', 'two'
```

Skipping tasks

Sometimes, we want tasks to be excluded from a build. In certain circumstances, we just want to skip a task and continue executing other tasks. We can use several methods to skip tasks in Gradle.

Using onlyIf predicates

Every task has an `onlyIf` method that accepts a closure as an argument. The result of the closure must be `true` or `false`. If the task must be skipped, the result of the closure must be `false`, otherwise the task is executed. The `task` object is passed as a parameter to the closure. Gradle evaluates the closure just before the task is executed.

The following build file will skip the `longrunning` task, if the file is executed during weekdays, but will execute it during the weekend:

```
import static java.util.Calendar.*

task longrunning {
    // Only run this task if the
    // closure returns true.
    onlyIf { task ->
        def now = Calendar.instance
        def weekDay = now[DAY_OF_WEEK]
        def weekDayInWeekend = weekDay in [SATURDAY, SUNDAY]
        return weekDayInWeekend
    }

    // Add an action.
    doLast {
        println "Do long running stuff"
    }
}
```

If we run our build during weekdays, we get the following output:

```
$ gradle longrunning
:longrunning SKIPPED
BUILD SUCCESSFUL
Total time: 0.581 secs
```

If we run the build during the weekend, we see that the task is executed:

```
$ gradle longrunning
:longrunning
```

```
Do long running stuff
BUILD SUCCESSFUL
Total time: 0.561 secs
```

We can invoke the `onlyIf` method multiple times for a task. If one of the predicates returns `false`, the task is skipped. Besides using a closure to define the condition that determines whether the task needs to be executed or not, we can use an implementation of the `org.gradle.api.specs.Spec` interface. The `Spec` interface has one method: `isSatisfiedBy`. We must write an implementation and return `true` if the task must be executed and `false` if we want the task to be skipped. The current `task` object is passed as a parameter to the `isSatisfiedBy` method.

In the following sample, we check whether a file exists. If the file exists, we can execute the task, otherwise the task is skipped:

```
// Create a new File object.
def file = new File('data.sample')

task handleFile {
    // Use Spec implementation to write
    // a conditon for the onlyIf method.
    onlyIf(new Spec() {
        boolean isSatisfiedBy(task) {
            file.exists()
        }
    })

    doLast {
        println "Work with file ${file.name}"
    }
}
```

Skipping tasks by throwing StopExecutionException

Another way to the skip execution of a task is to throw a `StopExecutionException` exception. If such an exception is thrown, the build will stop the current task and continue with the next task. We can use the `doFirst` method to add a precondition check for a task. In the closure, when we pass to the `doFirst` method, we can check for a condition and throw a `StopExecutionException` exception if necessary.

In the following build script, we check whether the script is executed during working hours. If so, the exception is thrown and the `first` task is skipped:

```
// Define closure with the task actions.
def printTaskName = { task ->
    println "Running ${task.name}"
}

// Create first task.
task first << printTaskName

// Use doFirst method with closure
// that throws exception when task
// is executed during work hours.
first.doFirst {
    def today = Calendar.instance
    def workingHours = today[Calendar.HOUR_OF_DAY] in 8..17

    if (workingHours) {
        throw new StopExecutionException()
    }
}

// Create second task that depends on first task.
task second(dependsOn: 'first') << printTaskName
```

If we run our script during working hours and check the output of our build script, we will notice that we cannot see that the task has been skipped. If we use the `onlyIf` method, Gradle will add `SKIPPED` to a task that is not executed:

```
:first
:second
Running second
BUILD SUCCESSFUL
Total time: 0.637 secs
```

Enabling and disabling tasks

We have seen how we can skip tasks with the `onlyIf` method or by throwing `StopExecutionException`. However, we can also use another method to skip a task. Every task has an `enabled` property. By default, the value of the property is `true`, which means that the task is enabled and executed. We can change the value and set it to `false` in order to disable the task and skip its execution.

In the following sample, we check the existence of a directory, and if it exists, the `enabled` property is set to `true`; if not, it is set to `false`:

```
task listDirectory {
    def dir = new File('assemble')

    // Set value for enabled task property.
    enabled = dir.exists()

    // This is only executed if enabled is true.
    doLast {
        println "List directory contents: " +
                dir.listFiles().join(',')
    }
}
```

If we run the task and the directory doesn't exist, we get the following output:

```
$ gradle listDirectory
 :listDirectory SKIPPED
BUILD SUCCESSFUL
 Total time: 0.563 secs
```

If we run the task, and this time the directory exists, containing a single file with the name `sample.txt`, we get the following output:

```
$ gradle listDirectory
 :listDirectory
List directory contents: assemble/sample.txt
BUILD SUCCESSFUL
Total time: 0.566 secs
```

Skipping from the command line

Until now, we have defined the rules to skip a task in the build file. However, we can use the `--exclude-tasks` (`-x`) command-line option if we run the build. We must define, as an argument, the task that we want to exclude from the tasks to be executed.

The following script has three tasks with some task dependencies:

```
// Define closure with task action.
def printTaskName = { task ->
    println "Run ${task.name}"
}

task first << printTaskName
```

```
task second(dependsOn: first) << printTaskName

task third(dependsOn: [second, first]) << printTaskName
```

If we run the `gradle` command and exclude the `second` task, we get the following output:

```
$ gradle third -x second
:first
Run first
:third
Run third
BUILD SUCCESSFUL
Total time: 0.573 secs
```

If our `third` task didn't depend on the first task, only the `third` task would be executed.

Skipping tasks that are up to date

Until now, we have defined conditions that are evaluated to determine whether a task needs to be skipped or not. However, with Gradle, we can be even more flexible. Suppose, we have a task that works on a file and generates some output based on the file. For example, a compile task fits this pattern. In the following sample build file, we have the `convert` task that will take an XML file, parse the contents, and write data to a text file, as shown in the following code:

```
task convert {
    def source = new File('source.xml')
    def output = new File('output.txt')

    doLast {
      def xml = new XmlSlurper().parse(source)

      output.withPrintWriter { writer ->
          xml.person.each { person ->
            writer.println "${person.name},${person.email}"
        }
      }

      println "Converted ${source.name} to ${output.name}"
    }
}
```

We can run this task a couple of times. Each time, the data is read from the XML file and written to the text file:

```
$ gradle convert
:convert
Converted source.xml to output.txt
BUILD SUCCESSFUL
Total time: 0.592 secs
$ gradle convert
:convert
Converted source.xml to output.txt
BUILD SUCCESSFUL
Total time: 0.592 secs
```

However, our input file hasn't changed between the task invocations, so the task doesn't have to be executed. We want the task to be executed only if the source file has changed, or the output file is missing, or has changed since the last run of the task.

Gradle supports this pattern, this support is known as **incremental build support**. A task only needs to be executed if necessary. This is a very powerful feature of Gradle. It will really speed up a build process as only the tasks that need to be executed are executed.

We need to change the definition of our task so that Gradle can determine whether the task needs to be executed based on changes in the input file or output file of the task. A task has the properties inputs and outputs that are used for this purpose. To define an input file, we invoke the file method of the inputs property with the value of our input file. We set the output file by invoking the file method of the outputs property.

Let's rewrite our task to make it support Gradle's incremental build feature:

```
task convert {
    def source = new File('source.xml')
    def output = new File('output.txt')

    // Define input file
    inputs.file source

    // Define output file
    outputs.file output

    doLast {
      def xml = new XmlSlurper().parse(source)

      output.withPrintWriter { writer ->
        xml.person.each { person ->
          writer.println "${person.name},${person.email}"
        }
```

```
        }

        println "Converted ${source.name} to ${output.name}"
      }
    }
```

When we run the build file a couple of times, we see that our task is skipped the second time we run it as the input and output file haven't changed:

```
$ gradle convert
:convert
Converted source.xml to output.txt
BUILD SUCCESSFUL
Total time: 0.592 secs
$ gradle convert
:convert UP-TO-DATE
BUILD SUCCESSFUL
Total time: 0.581 secs
```

We can use the `--rerun-tasks` command-line option to ignore the incremental build feature. Gradle will not check for any conditions when we use this command-line option and will execute the task regardless of the conditions for the `inputs` or `outputs` properties.

Let's use this option and run our `convert` task again. This time, the task is executed even though the source file and output files have not changed:

```
$ gradle --rerun-tasks convert
:convert
Converted source.xml to output.txt
BUILD SUCCESSFUL
Total time: 0.592 secs
```

We have defined a single file for the `inputs` and `outputs` properties. However, Gradle supports more ways to define values for these properties. The `inputs` property has methods to add a directory, multiple files, or even properties to be watched for changes. The `outputs` property has methods to add a directory or multiple files to be monitored for changes. If these methods are not appropriate for our build, we can even use the `upToDateWhen` method for the `outputs` property. We pass a closure or implementation of the `org.gradle.api.specs.Spec` interface to define a predicate that determines whether the output of the task is up to date.

The following build script uses some of these methods:

```
project.version = '1.0'

task createVersionDir {
```

```
    def outputDir = new File('output')

    // If project.version changes then the
    // task is no longer up-to-date
    inputs.property 'version', project.version

    outputs.dir outputDir

    doLast {
        println "Making directory ${outputDir.name}"
        mkdir outputDir
    }
}

task convertFiles {
    // Define multiple files to be checked as inputs.
    // Or use inputs.dir 'input' to check a complete directory.
    inputs.files 'input/input1.xml', 'input/input2.xml'

    // Use upToDateWhen method to define predicate.
    outputs.upToDateWhen {

        // If output directory contains any file which name
        // starts with output and has the xml extension,
        // then the task is up-to-date.
        // We use the Groovy method any to check
        // if at least one file applies to the condition.
        // The ==~ syntax is a Groovy shortcut to
        // check if a regular expression is true.
        new File('output')
            .listFiles()
            any { it.name ==~ /output.*\.xml$/ }
    }

    doLast {
        println "Running convertFiles"
    }
}
```

Summary

In this chapter, we discussed how to create tasks in a build project. We created tasks with actions in several ways and discussed how to configure tasks.

We skipped tasks by using predicates, throwing `StopExecutionException`, and enabling or disabling a task. We also discussed how to skip tasks from the command line.

A very powerful feature of Gradle is the incremental build support. If a task is up to date, it isn't executed. We can define the rules to determine the up-to-date state in the tasks definition.

In the next chapter, we will take a more in-depth look at the Gradle `Project` object. We will see how to work with files and project properties and how to use the Gradle Wrapper.

3
Working with Gradle Build Scripts

A Gradle script is a program. We use a Groovy DSL to express our build logic. Gradle has several useful built-in methods to handle files and directories as we often deal with files and directories in our build logic.

In this chapter, we will discuss how to use Gradle's features to work with files and directories. We will also take a look at how to set properties in a Gradle build and use Gradle's logging framework. Finally, we see will how to use the Gradle Wrapper task to distribute a configurable Gradle with our build scripts.

Working with files

It is very common in a build script that we have to work with files and directories. For example, when we need to copy a file from one directory to another or create a directory to store the output of a task or program.

Locating files

To locate a file or directory relative to the current project, we can use the `file()` method. This method is actually a method of the `Project` object that is connected to our build script. In the previous chapter, we discussed how to use an explicit reference to the `project` variable or simply invoke methods and properties of the `Project` object implicitly.

The `file()` method will resolve the location of a file or directory relative to the current project and not the current working directory. This is very useful as we can run a build script from a different directory than the location of the actual build script. File or directory references that are returned by the `file()` method are then resolved, relative to the project directory.

We can pass any object as an argument for the `file()` method. Usually, we will pass a `String` or `java.io.File` object.

In the next example, we will demonstrate how to use the `file()` method to get a reference to a `File` object:

```
// Use String for file reference.
File wsdl = file('src/wsdl/sample.wsdl')

// Use File object for file reference.
File xmlFile = new File('xml/input/sample.xml')
def inputXml = project.file(xmlFile)
```

There are many ways in which we can use the `file()` method. We can pass a `url` or `uri` instance as an argument. Only file based URLs are now supported by Gradle. We can also use closure to define the file or directory. Finally, we could also pass an instance of the `java.util.concurrent.Callable` interface, where the return value of the `call()` method is a valid reference to a file or directory:

```
import java.util.concurrent.Callable

// Use URL instance to locate file.
def url = new URL('file:/README')
File readme = file(url)

// Or a URI instance.
def uri = new URI('file:/README')
def readmeFile = file(uri)

// Use a closure to determine the
// file or directory name.
def fileNames = ['src', 'web', 'config']
def configDir = file {
    fileNames.find { fileName ->
        fileName.startsWith('config')
    }
}

// Use Callable interface.
def source = file(new Callable<String>() {
```

```
    String call() {
        'src'
    }
})
```

With the `file()` method, we create a new `File` object; this object can reference a file or directory. We can use the `isFile()` or `isDirectory()` method of the `File` object to see if we are dealing with a file or directory. In case we want to check whether the file or directory really exists, we use the `exists()` method. As our Gradle build script is written in Groovy, we can also use the extra properties and methods added by Groovy for the `File` class. For example, we can use the `text` property to read the contents of a file. However, we can only test the `File` object after we have used the `file()` method to create it. What if we want to stop the build in case a directory doesn't exist or we are dealing with a file and we expected to be dealing with a directory? In Gradle, we can pass an extra argument to the `file()` method, of the `org.gradle.api.PathValidation` type. Gradle then validates whether the created `File` object is valid for the `PathValidation` instance; if it isn't, the build is stopped and we get a nice error message telling us what went wrong.

Suppose, we want to work with a directory named `config` in our build script. The directory must be present, otherwise the build will stop:

```
def dir = project.file(new File('config'),    PathValidation.DIRECTORY)
```

Now we can run the build and see from the output that the directory doesn't exist:

```
$ gradle -q
FAILURE: Build failed with an exception.
* Where:
Build file '/Users/mrhaki/Projects/gradle-effective-implementation-
guide-2/Code_Files/build.gradle' line: 1
* What went wrong:
A problem occurred evaluating root project 'files'.
> Directory '/Users/mrhaki/Projects/gradle-effective-implementation-
guide-2/Code_Files/files/config' does not exist.
* Try:
Run with --stacktrace option to get the stack trace. Run with --info or --
debug option to get more log output.
```

We can also use the `PathValidation` argument to test whether a `File` object is really a file and not a directory. Finally, we can check whether the `File` object references an existing file or directory. If the file or directory doesn't exist, an exception is thrown and the build stops:

```
// Check file or directory exists.
def readme = project.file('README', PathValidation.EXISTS)

// Check File object is really a file.
def license = project.file('License.txt', PathValidation.FILE)
```

Using file collections

We can also work with a set of files or directories instead of just a single file or directory. In Gradle, a set of files is represented by the `ConfigurableFileCollection` interface. The nice thing is that a lot of classes in the Gradle API implement this interface.

We can use the `files()` method to define a file collection in our build script. This method is defined in the `Project` object that we can access in our build script. The `files()` method accepts many different types of arguments, which makes it very flexible to use. For example, we can use `String` and `File` objects to define a file collection.

As with the `file()` method, paths are resolved, relative to the project directory:

```
// Use String instances.
def multiple =
    files('README', 'licence.txt')

// Use File objects.
def userFiles =
    files(new File('README'), new File('INSTALL'))

// We can combine different argument types.
def combined = files('README', new File('INSTALL'))
```

However, these are not the only arguments we can use. We can pass a `URI` or `URL` object, just as we could with the `file()` method:

```
def urlFiles =
    files(new URI('file:/README'),
        new URL('file:/INSTALL'))
```

We can also use an array, `Collection`, or `Iterable` object with file names or another `ConfigurableFileCollection` instance as an argument:

```
// Use a Collection with file or directory names.
def listOfFileNames = ['src', 'test']
def mainDirectories = files(listOfFileNames)

// Use an array.
// We use the Groovy as keyword to
// force an object to a certain type.
mainDirectories = files(listOfFileNames as String[])

// Or an implementation of the Iterable interface.
mainDirectories = files(listOfFileNames as Iterable)

// Combine arguments and pass another file collection.
def allDirectories = files(['config'], mainDirectories)
```

We can also use a closure or instance of the `Callable` interface to define a list of files, as follows:

```
import java.util.concurrent.Callable

def dirs = files {
    [new File('src'), file('README')]
    .findAll { file ->
        file.directory
    }
}

def rootFiles = files(new Callable<List<File>>() {

    def files = [new File('src'),
            file('README'),
            file('INSTALL')]

    List<File> call() {
        files.findAll { fileObject ->
            fileObject.file
        }
    }

})
```

Finally, we can pass a `Task` object as an argument to the `files()` method. The `outputs` property of the task is used to determine the file collection or we can directly use the `TaskOutputs` object instead of letting Gradle resolve it via the `outputs` property of the `Task` object. Let's look at the `convert` task that we created in the previous chapter. This task has an `outputs` property with a single file, but this could also be multiple files or a directory. To get the file collection object in our build script, we simply pass the `Task` instance as an argument to the `files()` method:

```
task convert {
    def source = new File('source.xml')
    def output = new File('output.txt')

    // Define input file
    inputs.file source

    // Define output file
    outputs.file output

    doLast {
        def xml = new XmlSlurper().parse(source)
        output.withPrintWriter { writer ->
            xml.person.each { person ->
                writer.println "${person.name},${person.email}"
            }
        }
        println "Converted ${source.name} to ${output.name}"
    }
}

// Get the file collection from
// the task outputs property.
def taskOutputFiles = files(convert)

// Alternatively we could use
// the outputs property directly.
taskOutputFiles = files(convert.outputs)
```

It is also important to note that the file collection is lazy. This means the paths in the collection are not resolved when we define the collection. The paths in the collection are only resolved when the files are actually queried and used in the build script.

The `ConfigurableFileCollection` interface has useful methods to manipulate the collection, for example, we can use + and – operators to add or remove elements from the collection, respectively:

```
// Define collection.
def fileCollection = files('README', 'INSTALL')

// Remove INSTALL file from collection.
def readme = fileCollection - files('INSTALL')

// Add new collection to existing collection.
def moreFiles =
    fileCollection +
    files(file('config',
            PathValidation.DIRECTORY))
```

To get the absolute path names for the elements in `ConfigurableFileCollection`, we can use the `asPath` property. The path names are separated by the operating system's path separator. In a Microsoft Windows operating system, the semi-colon (`;`) is used as a path separator; and in Linux or Mac OS X operating systems, the colon (`:`) is used. This means that we can simply use the `asPath` property on any operating system and Gradle will automatically use the correct path separator:

```
task collectionPath << {
    def fileCollection = files('README', 'INSTALL')
    println fileCollection.asPath
}
```

When we run the build script on Mac OS X, we get the following output:

```
$ gradle -q collectionPath
/Users/mrhaki/gradle-book/Code_Files/files/README:/Users/mrhaki/gradle-
book/Code_Files/files/INSTALL
```

To get the `File` objects that make up the file collection, we can use the `files` property. We can also cast the collection to a list of `File` objects using the `as` keyword; if we know our collection is made up of just a single file or directory, then we can use the `singleFile` property to get the `File` object, as follows:

```
def fileCollection = files('README', [new File('INSTALL')])

// Get all elements as File objects.
def allFiles = fileCollection.files

// Or use casting with as keyword.
def fileObjects = fileCollection as File[]
```

```
    def singleFileCollection = files('INSTALL')

    // Get single file as File object.
    def installFile = singleFileCollection.singleFile
```

Finally, we can apply a filter to our file collection with the `filter()` method. We pass a closure that defines the elements that are to be in the filtered collection. The filtered collection is a live collection. This means that if we add new elements to the original collection, the filter closure is applied again for our filtered collection. In the following example, we have the `filterFiles` task, where we define a file collection of two files with the names `INSTALL.txt` and `README`. Next, we define a new file collection with a filter that contains all files that have the `.txt` filename extension. This collection is a live, filtered collection, as when we add a new file to the original collection, the filtered collection is also updated:

```
task filterFiles << {
    def rootFiles = files('INSTALL', 'README')

    // Filter for files with a txt extension.
    def smallFiles = rootFiles.filter { file ->
        file.name.endsWith 'txt'
    }

    rootFiles = rootFiles + files('LICENSE.txt')
    // smallFiles now contains 2 files:
    // INSTALL and LICENSE
}
```

Working with file trees

In Gradle, we can also work with file collections organized as a tree, for example, a directory tree on a disk or hierarchical content in a ZIP file. A hierarchical file collection is represented by a `ConfigurableFileTree` interface. This interface extends the `ConfigurableFileCollection` interface that we saw earlier.

To create a new file tree, we use the `fileTree()` method in our project. We can use several ways to define the file tree.

> If we don't provide a base directory, the current project directory is used as the base directory of the file tree.

We can use the `include` method and `includes` property to define a matching pattern to include a file (or files) in the file tree. With the `exclude` method and `excludes` property, we can use the same syntax to exclude a file or multiple files from the file tree. The matching pattern style is described as an Ant-style matching pattern as the Ant build tool uses this style to define a syntax to match filenames in file trees. The following patterns can be used:

- `*` to match any number of characters
- `?` to match any single character
- `**` to match any number of directories or files

The following example demonstrates how to create a file tree:

```
// Create file tree with base directory 'src/main'
// and only include files with extension .java
def srcDir = fileTree('src/main').include('**/*.java')

// Use map with arguments to create a file tree.
def resources =
    fileTree(dir: 'src/main',
        excludes: ['**/*.java', '**/*.groovy'])

// Create file tree with project directory as base
// directory and use method include() on tree
// object to include 2 files.
def base = fileTree('.')
base.include 'README', 'INSTALL'

// Use closure to create file tree.
def javaFiles = fileTree {
    from 'src/main/java'
    exclude '*.properties'
}
```

To filter a file tree, we can use the `filter()` method as we do with file collections, but we can also use the `matching()` method. We pass a closure to the `matching()` method or an instance of the `org.gradle.api.tasks.util.PatternFilterable` interface. We can use `include`, `includes`, `exclude`, and `excludes` methods to either include or exclude files from the file tree, as follows:

```
def sources = fileTree {
    from 'src'
}

def javaFiles = sources.matching {
```

```
        include '**/*.java'
    }

    def nonJavaFiles = sources.matching {
        exclude '**/*.java'
    }

    def nonLanguageFiles = sources.matching {
        exclude '**/*.scala', '**/*.groovy', '**/*.java'
    }

    def modifiedLastWeek = sources.matching {
        lastWeek = new Date() - 7
        include { file ->
            file.lastModified > lastWeek.time
        }
    }
```

We can use the `visit()` method to visit each tree node. We can check whether the node is a directory or file. The tree is then visited in breadth-wise order, as shown in the following code:

```
    def testFiles = fileTree(dir: 'src/test')

    testFiles.visit { fileDetails ->
        if (fileDetails.directory) {
            println "Entering directory ${fileDetails.relativePath}"
        } else {
            println "File name: ${fileDetails.name}"
        }
    }


    def projectFiles = fileTree(dir: 'src/test')

    projectFiles.visit(new FileVisitor() {
        void visitDir(FileVisitDetails details) {
            println "Directory: ${details.path}"
        }

        void visitFile(FileVisitDetails details) {
            println "File: ${details.path}, size: ${details.size}"
        }
    })
```

Copying files

To copy files in Gradle, we can use the `Copy` task. We must assign a set of source files to be copied and the destination of these files. This is defined with a copy spec. A copy spec is defined by the `org.gradle.api.file.CopySpec` interface. The interface has a `from()` method we can use to set the files or directories we want to copy. With the `into()` method that we specify in the destination directory or file.

The following example shows a simple `Copy` task called `simpleCopy` with a single source `src/xml` directory and a destination `definitions` directory:

```
task simpleCopy(type: Copy) {
    from 'src/xml'
    into 'definitions'
}
```

The `from()` method accepts the same arguments as the `files()` method. When the argument is a directory, all files in that directory—but not the directory itself—are copied to the destination directory. If the argument is a file, then only that file is copied.

The `into()` method accepts the same arguments as the `file()` method. To include or exclude files, we use the `include()` and `exclude()` methods of the `CopySpec` interface. We can apply the Ant-style matching patterns just like we do with the `fileTree()` method.

The following example defines a task with the name `copyTask` and uses the `include()` and `exclude()` methods to select the set of files to be copied:

```
// Define a closure with ANT-style
// pattern for files.
def getTextFiles = {
    '**/*.txt'
}

task copyTask(type: Copy) {
    // Copy from directory.
    from 'src/webapp'

    // Copy single file.
    from 'README.txt'

    // Include files with html extension.
    include '**/*.html', '**/*.htm'

    // Use closure to resolve files.
```

```
        include getTextFiles

        // Exclude file INSTALL.txt.
        exclude 'INSTALL.txt'

        // Copy into directory dist
        // resolved via closure.
        into { file('dist') }
}
```

Another way to copy files is with the `Project.copy()` method. The `copy()` method accepts a `CopySpec` interface implementation, just like the `Copy` task. Our `simpleCopy` task could also have been written as follows:

```
task simpleCopy << {
    // We use the project.copy()
    // method in our task. We can
    // leave out the project reference,
    // because Gradle knows how to
    // resolve it automatically.
    copy {
        from 'src/xml'
        into 'definitions'
    }
}
```

Archiving files

To create an archive file, we can use `Zip`, `Tar`, `Jar`, `War`, and `Ear` tasks. To define the source files for the archive and the destination inside the archive files, we use a `CopySpec` interface, just like with copying files. We can use `rename()`, `filter()`, `expand()`, `include()`, and `exclude()` methods in the same way so that you don't have to learn anything new, you can use what you have already learned.

To set the filename of the archive, we use any of these properties: `baseName`, `appendix`, `version`, `classifier`, or `extension`. Gradle will use the following pattern to create a filename: `[baseName]-[appendix]-[version]-[classifier].[extension]`. If a property is not set, then it is not included in the resulting filename. To override the default filename pattern, we can set the `archiveName` property and assign our own complete filename, which is used for the resulting archive file.

In the following example, we will create a ZIP archive with the `archiveZip` task. We will include all the files from the `dist` directory and put them in the root of the archive. The name of the file is set by the individual properties that follow Gradle's pattern:

```
task archiveDist(type: Zip) {
    from 'dist'

    // Create output filename.
    // Final filename is:
    // dist-files-archive-1.0-sample.zip
    baseName = 'dist-files'
    appendix = 'archive'
    extension = 'zip'
    version = '1.0'
    classifier = 'sample'
}
```

When we run the `archiveDist` task, a new `dist-files-archive-1.0-sample.zip` file is created in the root of our project. To change the destination directory of the archive file, we must set the `destinationDir` property. In the following example, we will set the destination directory to `build/zips`. We will also put the files in a `files` directory, inside the archive file with the `into()` method. The name of the file is now set by the `archiveName` property:

```
// By using task type Zip we instruct
// Gradle to create an archive
// in ZIP format.
task archiveFiles(type: Zip) {
    from 'dist'

    // Copy files to a directory inside the archive.
    into 'files'

    // Set destination directory for ZIP file.
    // $buildDir refers to default Gradle
    // build directory 'build/'.
    destinationDir = file("$buildDir/zips")

    // Set complete filename at once.
    archiveName = 'dist-files.zip'
}
```

To create a TAR archive with the optional `gzip` or `bzip2` compression, we must use the `tarFiles` task. The syntax is the same as the task for the `Zip` type, but we have an extra `compression` property that we can use to set the type of compression (`gzip`, `bzip2`) that we want to use. If we don't specify the `compression` property, no compression is used to create the archive file.

In the following example, we create a `tarFiles` task of the `Tar` type. We set the `compression` property to `gzip`. After running this task, we get a new `dist/tarballs/dist-files.tar.gz` file:

```
task tarFiles(type: Tar) {
    from 'dist'

    // Set destination directory.
    destinationDir = file("$buildDir/tarballs")

    // Set filename properties.
    baseName = 'dist-files'

    // Default extension for tar files
    // with gzip compression is tgz.
    extension = 'tar.gz'

    // Use gzip compression.
    compression = Compression.GZIP // or Compression.BZIP2
}
```

The `Jar`, `War`, and `Ear` task types follow the same pattern as the `Zip` and `Tar` task types. Each type has some extra properties and methods to include files specific for that type of archive. We will see examples of these tasks when we look at how we can use Gradle in Java projects.

Project properties

In a Gradle build file, we can access several properties that are defined by Gradle, but we can also create our own properties. We can set the value of our custom properties directly in the build script and we can also do this by passing values via the command line.

The default properties that we can access in a Gradle build are displayed in the following table:

Name	Type	Default value
project	Project	The project instance.
name	String	The name of the project directory. The name is read-only.
path	String	The absolute path of the project.
description	String	The description of the project.
projectDir	File	The directory containing the build script. The value is read-only.
buildDir	File	The directory with the build name in the directory, containing the build script.
rootDir	File	The directory of the project at the root of a project structure.
group	Object	Not specified.
version	Object	Not specified.
ant	AntBuilder	An AntBuilder instance.

The following build file has a task of showing the value of the properties:

```
version = '1.0'
group = 'Sample'
description = 'Sample build file to show project properties'

task defaultProperties << {
    println "Project: $project"
    println "Name: $name"
    println "Path: $path"
    println "Project directory: $projectDir"
    println "Build directory: $buildDir"
    println "Version: $version"
    println "Group: $project.group"
    println "Description: $project.description"
    println "AntBuilder: $ant"
}
```

When we run the build, we get the following output:

```
$ gradle defaultProperties
:defaultProperties
Project: root project 'props'
Name: defaultProperties
Path: :defaultProperties
Project directory: /Users/mrhaki/gradle-book/Code_Files/props
Build directory: /Users/mrhaki/gradle-book/Code_Files/props/build
Version: 1.0
Group: Sample
Description: Sample build file to show project properties
AntBuilder: org.gradle.api.internal.project.DefaultAntBuilder@3c95cbbd
BUILD SUCCESSFUL
Total time: 1.458 secs
```

Defining custom properties in script

To add our own properties, we have to define them in an `ext{}` script block in a build file. Prefixing the property name with `ext.` is another way to set the value. To read the value of the property, we don't have to use the `ext.` prefix, we can simply refer to the name of the property. The property is automatically added to the internal `project` property as well.

In the following script, we add a `customProperty` property with a `String` value custom. In the `showProperties` task, we show the value of the property:

```
// Define new property.
ext.customProperty = 'custom'

// Or we can use ext{} script block.
ext {
  anotherCustomProperty = 'custom'
}

task showProperties {
    ext {
        customProperty = 'override'
    }
    doLast {
        // We can refer to the property
        // in different ways:
        println customProperty
        println project.ext.customProperty
```

```
        println project.customProperty
    }
}
```

After running the script, we get the following output:

```
$ gradle showProperties
:showProperties
override
custom
custom
BUILD SUCCESSFUL
Total time: 1.469 secs
```

Defining properties using an external file

We can also set the properties for our project in an external file. The file needs to be named `gradle.properties`, and it should be a plain text file with the name of the property and its value on separate lines. We can place the file in the project directory or Gradle user home directory. The default Gradle user home directory is `$USER_HOME/.gradle`. A property defined in the `properties` file, in the Gradle user home directory, overrides the property values defined in a properties file in the project directory.

We will now create a `gradle.properties` file in our project directory, with the following contents.

We use our build file to show the property values:

```
task showProperties {
    doLast {
        println "Version: $version"
        println "Custom property: $customProperty"
    }
}
```

If we run the build file, we don't have to pass any command-line options, Gradle will use `gradle.properties` to get values of the properties:

```
$ gradle showProperties
:showProperties
Version: 4.0
Custom property: Property value from gradle.properties
BUILD SUCCESSFUL
Total time: 1.676 secs
```

Passing properties via the command line

Instead of defining the property directly in the build script or external file, we can use the –P command-line option to add an extra property to a build. We can also use the –P command-line option to set a value for an existing property. If we define a property using the –P command-line option, we can override a property with the same name defined in the external `gradle.properties` file.

The following build script has a `showProperties` task that shows the value of an existing property and a new property:

```
task showProperties {
    doLast {
        println "Version: $version"
        println "Custom property: $customProperty"
    }
}
```

Let's run our script and pass the values for the existing `version` property and the non-existent `customProperty`:

```
$ gradle –Pversion=1.1 –PcustomProperty=custom showProperties
:showProperties
Version: 1.1
Custom property: custom
BUILD SUCCESSFUL
Total time: 1.412 secs
```

Defining properties via system properties

We can also use Java system properties to define properties for our Gradle build. We use the –D command-line option just like in a normal Java application. The name of the system property must start with `org.gradle.project`, followed by the name of the property we want to set, and then by the value.

We can use the same build script that we created before:

```
task showProperties {
    doLast {
        println "Version: $version"
        println "Custom property: $customProperty"
    }
}
```

However, this time we use different command-line options to get a result:

```
$ gradle -Dorg.gradle.project.version=2.0 -
Dorg.gradle.project.customProperty=custom showProperties
:showProperties
Version: 2.0
Custom property: custom
BUILD SUCCESSFUL
Total time: 1.218 secs
```

Adding properties via environment variables

Using the command-line options provides much flexibility; however, sometimes we cannot use the command-line options because of environment restrictions or because we don't want to retype the complete command-line options each time we invoke the Gradle build. Gradle can also use environment variables set in the operating system to pass properties to a Gradle build.

The environment variable name starts with ORG_GRADLE_PROJECT_ and is followed by the property name. We use our build file to show the properties:

```
task showProperties {
    doLast {
        println "Version: $version"
        println "Custom property: $customProperty"
    }
}
```

Firstly, we set ORG_GRADLE_PROJECT_version
and ORG_GRADLE_PROJECT_customProperty environment variables, then we run
our showProperties task, as follows:

```
$ ORG_GRADLE_PROJECT_version=3.1 \
ORG_GRADLE_PROJECT_customProperty="Set by environment variable" \
gradle showProp
:showProperties
Version: 3.1
Custom property: Set by environment variable
BUILD SUCCESSFUL
Total time: 1.373 secs
```

Using logging

In `Chapter 1`, *Starting with Gradle,* we discussed several command-line options that we can use to show either more or fewer log messages when we run a Gradle build. These messages were from the Gradle internal tasks and classes. We used a `println` method in our Gradle build scripts to see some output, but we can also use Gradle's logging mechanisms to have a more customizable way to define logging messages.

Gradle supports several logging levels that we can use for our own messages. The level of our messages is important as we can use the command-line options to filter the messages for log levels.

The following table shows the log levels that are supported by Gradle:

Level	Used for
DEBUG	Debug messages
INFO	Information messages
LIFECYCLE	Progress information messages
WARNING	Warning messages
QUIET	Import information messages
ERROR	Error messages

Every Gradle build file and task has a `logger` object. The `logger` object is an instance of a Gradle-specific extension of the **Simple Logging Facade for Java (SLF4J) Logger interface**. SLF4J is a Java logging library. This library provides a logging API that is independent of the underlying logging framework. A specific logging framework can be used at deploy time or runtime to output the actual log message.

To use the `logger` object in our Gradle build files, we only have to reference `logger` and invoke the method for the logging level we want to use, or we can use the common `log()` method and pass the log level as a parameter to this method.

Let's create a simple task and use the different log levels:

```
// Simple logging sample.
task logLevels << {
    logger.debug 'debug: Most verbose logging level'
    logger.log LogLevel.DEBUG, 'debug: Most verbose logging level'

    logger.info 'info: Use for information messages'
    logger.log LogLevel.INFO, 'info: Use for information messages'
```

```
      logger.lifecycle 'lifecycle: Progress information messages'
      logger.log LogLevel.LIFECYCLE,
        'lifecycle: Progress information messages'

      logger.warn 'warn: Warning messages like invalid        configuration'
      logger.log LogLevel.WARN,
        'warn: Warning messages like invalid configuration'

      logger.quiet 'quiet: This is important but not an error'
      logger.log LogLevel.QUIET,
        'quiet: This is important but not an error'

      logger.error 'error: Use for errors'
      logger.log LogLevel.ERROR, 'error: Use for errors'
  }
```

When we run this `logLevels` task from the command line, we get the following output:

```
$ gradle logLevels
:logLevels
lifecycle: Progress information messages
lifecycle: Progress information messages
warn: Warning messages like invalid configuration
warn: Warning messages like invalid configuration
quiet: This is important but not an error
quiet: This is important but not an error
BUILD SUCCESSFUL
Total time: 1.523 secs
```

We notice that only the LIFECYCLE, WARN, QUIET, and ERROR log levels are shown if we don't add any extra command-line options. To see the INFO messages, we must use the --info command-line option. Then we get the following output:

```
$ gradle --info logLevels
...
Starting Build
Settings evaluated using empty settings script.
...
Selected primary task 'logLevels' from project :
Tasks to be executed: [task ':logLevels']
...
:logLevels (Thread[Daemon worker Thread 15,5,main]) started.
:logLevels Executing task ':logLevels' (up-to-date check took 0.0   secs)
due  to:
     Task has not declared any outputs.
  info: Use for information messages
  info: Use for information messages
  lifecycle: Progress information messages
```

```
lifecycle: Progress information messages
warn: Warning messages like invalid configuration
warn: Warning messages like invalid configuration
quiet: This is important but not an error
quiet: This is important but not an error
:logLevels (Thread[Daemon worker Thread 15,5,main]) completed. Took
0.001 secs.
BUILD SUCCESSFUL
Total time: 1.465 secs
```

Notice that we also get more messages from Gradle itself. Earlier, we only saw the log messages from our script, but this time a lot of extra logging is shown about the build process itself.

To get even more output and our DEBUG level logging messages, we must use the --debug command-line option to invoke the logLevels task, as follows:

```
$ gradle --debug logLevels
...
08:16:46.334 [DEBUG]
[org.gradle.initialization.buildsrc.BuildSourceBuilder] Starting to build
the build sources.
    08:16:46.335 [DEBUG]
[org.gradle.initialization.buildsrc.BuildSourceBuilder] Gradle source dir
does not exist. We leave.
    08:16:46.335 [DEBUG]
[org.gradle.initialization.DefaultGradlePropertiesLoader] Found env project
properties: []
    08:16:46.335 [DEBUG]
[org.gradle.initialization.DefaultGradlePropertiesLoader] Found system
project properties: []
    08:16:46.336 [DEBUG]
[org.gradle.initialization.ScriptEvaluatingSettingsProcessor] Timing:
Processing settings took: 0.001 secs
    08:16:46.338 [DEBUG]
[org.gradle.initialization.buildsrc.BuildSourceBuilder] Starting to build
the build sources.
    08:16:46.339 [DEBUG]
[org.gradle.initialization.buildsrc.BuildSourceBuilder] Gradle source dir
does not exist. We leave.
    08:16:46.339 [DEBUG]
[org.gradle.initialization.DefaultGradlePropertiesLoader] Found env project
properties: []
    08:16:46.339 [DEBUG]
[org.gradle.initialization.DefaultGradlePropertiesLoader] Found system
project properties: []
    08:16:46.340 [DEBUG]
[org.gradle.initialization.ScriptEvaluatingSettingsProcessor] Timing:
```

```
Processing settings took: 0.001 secs
    08:16:46.340 [INFO] [org.gradle.BuildLogger] Settings evaluated using
empty settings script.
    08:16:46.341 [DEBUG]
[org.gradle.model.internal.registry.DefaultModelRegistry] Transitioning
model element 'tasks' from state Known to Created
    08:16:46.341 [DEBUG]
[org.gradle.model.internal.registry.DefaultModelRegistry] Running model
element 'tasks' creator rule action Project.<init>.tasks()
    08:16:46.341 [DEBUG]
[org.gradle.model.internal.registry.DefaultModelRegistry] Creating tasks
using Project.<init>.tasks()
    ...
    08:16:46.355 [INFO]
[org.gradle.execution.taskgraph.AbstractTaskPlanExecutor] :logLevels
(Thread[Daemon worker Thread 16,5,main]) started.
    08:16:46.356 [LIFECYCLE] [class org.gradle.TaskExecutionLogger]
:logLevels
    08:16:46.356 [DEBUG]
[org.gradle.api.internal.tasks.execution.ExecuteAtMostOnceTaskExecuter]
Starting to execute task ':logLevels'
    08:16:46.356 [DEBUG]
[org.gradle.api.internal.tasks.execution.SkipUpToDateTaskExecuter]
Determining if task ':logLevels' is up-to-date
    08:16:46.356 [INFO]
[org.gradle.api.internal.tasks.execution.SkipUpToDateTaskExecuter]
Executing task ':logLevels' (up-to-date check took 0.0        secs) due to:
        Task has not declared any outputs.
    08:16:46.356 [DEBUG]
[org.gradle.api.internal.tasks.execution.ExecuteActionsTaskExecuter]
Executing actions for task ':logLevels'.
    08:16:46.357 [DEBUG] [org.gradle.api.Task] debug: Most verbose logging
level
    08:16:46.357 [DEBUG] [org.gradle.api.Task] debug: Most verbose logging
level
    08:16:46.357 [INFO] [org.gradle.api.Task] info: Use for information
messages
    08:16:46.357 [INFO] [org.gradle.api.Task] info: Use for information
messages
    08:16:46.357 [LIFECYCLE] [org.gradle.api.Task] lifecycle: Progress
information messages
    08:16:46.357 [LIFECYCLE] [org.gradle.api.Task] lifecycle: Progress
information messages
    08:16:46.357 [WARN] [org.gradle.api.Task] warn: Warning messages like
invalid configuration
    08:16:46.357 [WARN] [org.gradle.api.Task] warn: Warning messages like
invalid configuration
    08:16:46.357 [QUIET] [org.gradle.api.Task] quiet: This is important but
```

```
not an error
    08:16:46.358 [QUIET] [org.gradle.api.Task] quiet: This is important but
not an error
    08:16:46.358 [DEBUG]
[org.gradle.api.internal.tasks.execution.ExecuteAtMostOnceTaskExecuter]
Finished executing task ':logLevels'
    08:16:46.358 [INFO]
[org.gradle.execution.taskgraph.AbstractTaskPlanExecutor] :logLevels
(Thread[Daemon worker Thread 16,5,main]) completed. Took 0.002 secs.
    08:16:46.358 [DEBUG]
[org.gradle.execution.taskgraph.AbstractTaskPlanExecutor] Task worker
[Thread[Daemon worker Thread 16,5,main]] finished, busy: 0.002 secs, idle:
0.001 secs
    08:16:46.358 [DEBUG]
[org.gradle.execution.taskgraph.DefaultTaskGraphExecuter] Timing: Executing
the DAG took 0.004 secs
    08:16:46.358 [LIFECYCLE] [org.gradle.BuildResultLogger]
    08:16:46.359 [LIFECYCLE] [org.gradle.BuildResultLogger] BUILD
SUCCESSFUL
    08:16:46.359 [LIFECYCLE] [org.gradle.BuildResultLogger]
    08:16:46.359 [LIFECYCLE] [org.gradle.BuildResultLogger] Total time:
1.424 secs
```

This time, we get a lot of messages and we really have to look closely for our own messages. The output format of the logging has also changed, notice that while only the log message was shown before, now the time, log level, and originating class for the log message are also displayed.

So, we know that every Gradle project and task has a logger we can use. However, we can also explicitly create a `logger` instance with the `Logging` class. If, for example, we define our own class and want to use it in a Gradle build, we can use the `getLogger()` method of the `Logging` class to get a Gradle `logger` object. We can use the extra `lifecycle()` and `quiet()` methods on this `logger` instance, just like in projects and tasks.

We will now add a class definition in our build file and use an instance of this class to see the output:

```
class Simple {

    // Create new logger using the Gradle
    // logging support.
    private static final Logger logger = Logging.getLogger('Simple')

    int square(int value) {
        int square = value * value
        logger.lifecycle "Calculate square for ${value} = ${square}"
        return square
```

```
        }

    }

    logger.lifecycle 'Running sample Gradle build.'

    task useSimple {
        doFirst {
            logger.lifecycle 'Running useSimple'
        }
        doLast {
            new Simple().square(3)
        }
    }
```

We have used the `logger` of the project and task; in the class `Simple`, we use `Logging.getLogger()` to create a Gradle `logger` instance. When we run our script, we get the following output:

```
$ gradle useSimple
Running sample Gradle build.
:useSimple
Running useSimple
Calculate square for 3 = 9
BUILD SUCCESSFUL
Total time: 1.363 secs
```

To see the originating class of the logger, we can use the `--debug` (or `-d`) command-line option. Then, we will not only see the time when message was logged, but also see the name of the logger:

```
$ gradle useSimple -d
...
08:28:18.390 [LIFECYCLE] [org.gradle.api.Project] Running sample Gradle
build.
...
08:28:18.405 [LIFECYCLE] [org.gradle.api.Task] Running useSimple
08:28:18.406 [LIFECYCLE] [Simple] Calculate square for 3 = 9
...
```

Notice that our `logger` project is named `org.gradle.api.Project`, the `logger` task is named `org.gradle.api.Task`, and our `logger` in the `Simple` class is named `Simple`.

Controlling output

In the previous examples we used the `logger` instance and the `println()` method for logging messages. Gradle redirects the output sent to `System.out`—which is what we do when we use `println()`—to the logger with the `quiet` log level. This is why we get to see the `println()` output when we run a Gradle build. Gradle intercepts the output and uses its logging support.

When we run the following simple Gradle build with the `--debug` option, we can see that Gradle has redirected the output to the QUIET log level:

```
println 'Simple logging message'
```

Let's see the output if we run the build:

```
$ gradle --debug
...
08:34:13.497 [QUIET] [system.out] Simple logging message
...
```

Gradle redirects standard error to log messages, with the ERROR log level. This also applies to classes that we use from external libraries in our Gradle build. If the code in these libraries uses standard output and error, Gradle will capture the output and error messages and redirect them to the `logger` instance.

We can configure this ourselves if we want to change the log level that is used for the redirected output and error messages. Every project and task has an instance of the `org.gradle.api.logging.LoggingManager` class with the name logging. The `LoggingManager` class has the methods `captureStandardOutput()` and `captureStandardError()` that we can use to set the log level for output and error messages. Remember that Gradle will, by default, use the QUIET log level for output messages and ERROR log level for error messages. In the following script, we change the log level for output messages to INFO:

```
logging.captureStandardOutput LogLevel.INFO
println 'This message is now logged with log level info instead of quiet'

task redirectLogging {
    doFirst {
      // Use default redirect log level quiet.
      println 'Start task redirectLogging'
    }
    doLast {
      logging.captureStandardOutput LogLevel.INFO
```

```
        println 'Finished task redirectLogging'
    }
}
```

First we run the build without any extra command-line options:

```
$ gradle redirectLogging
:redirectLogging
Start task redirectLogging
BUILD SUCCESSFUL
Total time: 1.448 secs
```

Notice that the `println` statement that we have defined in the `doFirst` method of our task is shown, but the output of the other `println` statements is not shown. We redirected the output of these `println` statements to Gradle's logging with the `INFO` log level. The `INFO` log level is now shown by default.

Let's run the script again, but now we add the `--info` command-line option so that we can see all the output of our `println` statements:

```
$ gradle --info redirectLogging
...
Start task redirectLogging
Finished task redirectLogging
...
```

Using the Gradle Wrapper

Normally, if we want to run a Gradle build, we must have Gradle installed on our computer. Also, if we distribute our project to others and they want to build the project, they must have Gradle installed on their computers. The Gradle Wrapper can be used to allow others to build our project even if they don't have Gradle installed on their computers.

The wrapper is a batch script on the Microsoft Windows operating systems or shell script on other operating systems that will download Gradle and run the build using the downloaded Gradle.

By using the wrapper, we can make sure that the correct Gradle version for the project is used. We can define the Gradle version, and if we run the build via the wrapper script file, the version of Gradle that we defined is used.

Creating wrapper scripts

To create the Gradle Wrapper batch and shell scripts, we can invoke the built-in `wrapper` task. This task is already available if we have installed Gradle on our computer. Let's invoke the `wrapper` task from the command-line:

```
$ gradle wrapper
:wrapper
BUILD SUCCESSFUL
Total time: 0.61 secs
```

After the execution of the task, we have two script files—`gradlew.bat` and `gradlew`—in the root of our project directory. These scripts contain all the logic needed to run Gradle. If Gradle is not downloaded yet, the Gradle distribution will be downloaded and installed locally.

In the `gradle/wrapper` directory, relative to our project directory, we find the `gradle-wrapper.jar` and `gradle-wrapper.properties` files. The `gradle-wrapper.jar` file contains a couple of class files necessary to download and invoke Gradle. The `gradle-wrapper.properties` file contains settings, such as the URL, to download Gradle. The `gradle-wrapper.properties` file also contains the Gradle version number. If a new Gradle version is released, we only have to change the version in the `gradle-wrapper.properties` file and the Gradle Wrapper will download the new version so that we can use it to build our project.

All the generated files are now part of our project. If we use a version control system, then we must add these files to the version control. Other people that check out our project can use the `gradlew` scripts to execute tasks from the project. The specified Gradle version is downloaded and used to run the build file.

If we want to use another Gradle version, we can invoke the `wrapper` task with the `--gradle-version` option. We must specify the Gradle version that the Wrapper files are generated for. By default, the Gradle version that is used to invoke the `wrapper` task is the Gradle version used by the wrapper files.

To specify a different download location for the Gradle installation file, we must use the `--gradle-distribution-url` option of the `wrapper` task. For example, we could have a customized Gradle installation on our local intranet, and with this option, we can generate the Wrapper files that will use the Gradle distribution on our intranet.

In the following example, we generate the wrapper files for Gradle 2.12 explicitly:

```
$ gradle wrapper --gradle-version=2.12
:wrapper
BUILD SUCCESSFUL
Total time: 0.61 secs
```

Customizing the Gradle Wrapper

If we want to customize properties of the built-in `wrapper` task, we must add a new task to our Gradle build file with the `org.gradle.api.tasks.wrapper.Wrapper` type. We will not change the default `wrapper` task, but create a new task with new settings that we want to apply. We need to use our new task to generate the Gradle Wrapper shell scripts and support files.

We can change the names of the script files that are generated with the `scriptFile` property of the Wrapper task. To change the name and location of the generated JAR and properties files, we can change the `jarFile` property:

```
task createWrapper(type: Wrapper) {
    // Set Gradle version for wrapper files.
    gradleVersion = '2.12'

    // Rename shell scripts name to
    // startGradle instead of default gradlew.
    scriptFile = 'startGradle'

    // Change location and name of JAR file
    // with wrapper bootstrap code and
    // accompanying properties files.
    jarFile = "${projectDir}/gradle-bin/gradle-bootstrap.jar"
}
```

If we run the `createWrapper` task, we get a Windows batch file and shell script and the Wrapper bootstrap JAR file with the properties file is stored in the `gradle-bin` directory:

```
$ gradle createWrapper
:createWrapper
BUILD SUCCESSFUL
Total time: 0.605 secs
$ tree .

.
├── gradle-bin
│   ├── gradle-bootstrap.jar
│   └── gradle-bootstrap.properties
```

```
├── startGradle
├── startGradle.bat
└── build.gradle
2 directories, 5 files
```

To change the URL from where the Gradle version must be downloaded, we can alter the distributionUrl property. For example, we could publish a fixed Gradle version on our company intranet and use the distributionUrl property to reference a download URL on our intranet. This way we can make sure that all developers in the company use the same Gradle version:

```
task createWrapper(type: Wrapper) {
    // Set URL with custom Gradle distribution.
    distributionUrl = 'http://intranet/gradle/dist/gradle-custom-
2.12.zip'
}
```

Summary

In this chapter, we discussed the support that Gradle gives when working with files. We saw how to create a file or directory and a collection of files and directories. A file tree represents a hierarchical set of files.

We can add logging messages to our project and tasks and see the output when we run a Gradle build. We discussed how to use different log levels to influence how much information is shown in the output. We also used LoggingManager to capture the standard output and error messages and redirect them to custom log levels.

We discussed how to use the Gradle Wrapper to allow users to build our projects even if they don't have Gradle installed. We discussed how to customize the Wrapper to download a specific version of Gradle and use it to run our build.

In the next chapter, we will create a Java project and use the Java plugin to add a set of default tasks that we can use to compile, test, and package our Java code.

4
Using Gradle for Java Projects

We have seen how to write tasks in a Gradle build and how to execute them, but we haven't seen how to perform real-life tasks, such as compiling source code or testing with Gradle.

In this chapter, we will discuss how to use the Gradle Java plugin to get tasks for compiling and packaging a Java project. We will also see how Gradle's build-by-convention features make it very easy to start and work with a source code.

Why plugins?

In Gradle, we can apply plugins to our project. A plugin basically adds extra functionalities such as tasks and properties to our project. By using a plugin, functionality is decoupled from the core Gradle build logic. We can write our own plugins, but Gradle also ships with plugins that are ready out of the box. For example, Gradle has a Java plugin. This plugin adds tasks for compiling, testing, and packaging Java source code to our project.

The plugins that are packaged with a Gradle version are never updated or changed for this version, so if a new functionality is added to a plugin, a whole new Gradle version will be released. In the future versions of Gradle, this will change. This doesn't apply for the plugins that we write ourselves. We can release new versions of our own plugins, independent of the Gradle version. Let's start with the Java plugin that is a part of the Gradle distribution.

Getting started with the Java plugin

The Java plugin provides a lot of useful tasks and properties that we can use for building a Java application or library. If we follow the convention-over-configuration support of the plugin, we don't have to write a lot of code in our Gradle build file to use it. If we want to, we can still add extra configuration options to override the default conventions defined by the plugin.

Let's start with a new build file and use the Java plugin. We only have to apply the plugin for our build:

```
apply plugin: 'java'
```

That's it! Just by adding this simple line, we now have a lot of tasks that we can use to work with in our Java project. To see the tasks that have been added by the plugin, we run the `tasks` command on the command line and look at the output:

```
$ gradle tasks
:tasks
------------------------------------------------------------
All tasks runnable from root project
------------------------------------------------------------

Build tasks
-----------
assemble - Assembles the outputs of this project.
build - Assembles and tests this project.
buildDependents - Assembles and tests this project and all projects that
depend on it.
buildNeeded - Assembles and tests this project and all projects it depends
on.
classes - Assembles main classes.
clean - Deletes the build directory.
jar - Assembles a jar archive containing the main classes.
testClasses - Assembles test classes.
Build Setup tasks
-----------------
init - Initializes a new Gradle build. [incubating]
wrapper - Generates Gradle wrapper files. [incubating]
Documentation tasks
-------------------
javadoc - Generates Javadoc API documentation for the main source code.
Help tasks
----------
components - Displays the components produced by root project
'getting_started'. [incubating]
dependencies - Displays all dependencies declared in root project
'getting_started'.
```

```
dependencyInsight - Displays the insight into a specific dependency in root
project 'getting_started'.
help - Displays a help message.
model - Displays the configuration model of root project 'getting_started'.
[incubating]
projects - Displays the sub-projects of root project 'getting_started'.
properties - Displays the properties of root project 'getting_started'.
tasks - Displays the tasks runnable from root project 'getting_started'.
Verification tasks
------------------
check - Runs all checks.
test - Runs the unit tests.
Rules
-----
Pattern: clean<TaskName>: Cleans the output files of a task.
Pattern: build<ConfigurationName>: Assembles the artifacts of a
configuration.
Pattern: upload<ConfigurationName>: Assembles and uploads the artifacts
belonging to a configuration.
To see all tasks and more detail, run gradle tasks --all
To see more detail about a task, run gradle help --task <task>
BUILD SUCCESSFUL
Total time: 0.849 secs
```

If we look at the list of tasks, we can see the number of tasks that are now available to us, which we didn't have before; all this is done just by adding a simple line to our build file.

We have several task groups with their own individual tasks, which can be used. We have tasks related to building source code and packaging in the `Build tasks` section. The `javadoc` task is used to generate Javadoc documentation, and is in the `Documentation tasks` section. The tasks for running tests and checking code quality are in the `Verification tasks` section. Finally, we have several rule-based tasks to build, upload, and clean artifacts or tasks in our Java project.

The tasks added by the Java plugin are the visible part of the newly added functionality to our project. However, the plugin also adds the so-called `convention` object to our project.

A `convention` object has several properties and methods, which are used by the tasks of the plugin. These properties and methods are added to our project and can be accessed like normal project properties and methods. So, with the convention object, we can not only look at the properties used by the tasks in the plugin, but we can also change the value of the properties to reconfigure certain tasks.

Using the Java plugin

To work with the Java plugin, we are first going to create a very simple Java source file. We can then use the plugin's tasks to build the source file. You can make this application as complex as you want, but in order to stay on topic, we will make this as simple as possible.

By applying the Java plugin, we must now follow some conventions for our project directory structure. To build the source code, our Java source files must be in the `src/main/java` directory, relative to the project directory. If we have non-Java source files that need to be included in the JAR file, we must place them in the `src/main/resources` directory. Our test source files need to be in the `src/test/java` directory and any non-Java source files required for testing can be placed in `src/test/resources`. These conventions can be changed if we want or need it, but it is a good idea to stick with them so that we don't have to write any extra code in our build file, which could lead to errors.

Our sample Java project that we will write is a Java class that uses an external property file to get a welcome message. The source file with the name `Sample.java` is located in the `src/main/java` directory, as follows:

```
// File: src/main/java/gradle/sample/Sample.java
package gradle.sample;

import java.util.ResourceBundle;

/**
 * Read welcome message from external properties file
 * <code>messages.properties</code>.
 */
public class Sample {

    public Sample() {
    }

    /**
     * Get <code>messages.properties</code> file
     * and read the value for <em>welcome</em> key.
     *
```

```
 *  @return Value for <em>welcome</em> key
 *    from <code>messages.properties</code>
 */
public String getWelcomeMessage() {
    final ResourceBundle resourceBundle =
        ResourceBundle.getBundle("messages");
  final String message = resourceBundle.getString("welcome");
  return message;
  }
}
```

In the code, we use `ResourceBundle.getBundle()` to read our welcome message. The welcome message itself is defined in a `properties` file with the name `messages.properties`, which will go in the `src/main/resources` directory:

```
# File: src/main/resources/gradle/sample/messages.properties
welcome = Welcome to Gradle!
```

To compile the Java source file and process the properties file, we run the `classes` task. Note that the `classes` task has been added by the Java plugin. This is the so-called life cycle task in Gradle. The `classes` task is actually dependent on two other tasks—`compileJava` and `processResources`. We can see this task dependency when we run the `tasks` command with the `--all` command-line option:

```
$ gradle tasks --all
...
classes - Assembles main classes.
compileJava - Compiles main Java source.
processResources - Processes main resources.
...
```

Let's run the `classes` task from the command line:

```
$ gradle classes
:compileJava
:processResources
:classes
BUILD SUCCESSFUL
Total time: 1.08 secs
```

Here, we can see that `compileJava` and `processResources` tasks are executed because the `classes` task depends on these tasks. The compiled class file and properties file are now in the `build/classes/main` and `build/resources/main` directories. The `build` directory is the default directory that Gradle uses to build output files.

If we execute the `classes` task again, we will notice that the tasks support the incremental build feature of Gradle. As we haven't changed the Java source file or the properties file, and the output is still present, all the tasks can be skipped as they are up-to-date:

```
$ gradle classes
:compileJava UP-TO-DATE
:processResources UP-TO-DATE
:classes UP-TO-DATE
BUILD SUCCESSFUL
Total time: 0.595 secs
```

To package our class file and properties file, we invoke the `jar` task. This task is also added by the Java plugin and depends on the `classes` task. This means that if we run the `jar` task, the `classes` task is also executed. Let's try and run the `jar` task, as follows:

```
$ gradle jar
:compileJava UP-TO-DATE
:processResources UP-TO-DATE
:classes UP-TO-DATE
:jar
BUILD SUCCESSFUL
Total time: 0.585 secs
```

The default name of the resulting JAR file is the name of our project. So if our project is called `sample`, then the JAR file is called `sample.jar`. We can find the file in the `build/libs` directory. If we look at the contents of the JAR file, we see our compiled class file and the `messages.properties` file. Also, a manifest file is added automatically by the `jar` task:

```
$ jar tvf build/libs/sample.jar
0 Wed Oct 21 15:29:36 CEST 2015 META-INF/
25 Wed Oct 21 15:29:36 CEST 2015 META-INF/MANIFEST.MF
0 Wed Oct 21 15:26:58 CEST 2015 gradle/
0 Wed Oct 21 15:26:58 CEST 2015 gradle/sample/
685 Wed Oct 21 15:26:58 CEST 2015 gradle/sample/Sample.class
90 Wed Oct 21 15:26:58 CEST 2015  gradle/sample/messages.properties
```

We can also execute the `assemble` task to create the JAR file. The `assemble` task, another life cycle task, is dependent on the `jar` task and can be extended by other plugins. We could also add dependencies on other tasks that create packages for a project other than the JAR file, such as a WAR file or ZIP archive file:

```
$ gradle assemble
:compileJava UP-TO-DATE
:processResources UP-TO-DATE
:classes UP-TO-DATE
```

```
:jar UP-TO-DATE
:assemble UP-TO-DATE
BUILD SUCCESSFUL
Total time: 0.607 secs
```

To start again and clean all the generated output from the previous tasks, we can use the clean task. This task deletes the project build directory and all the generated files in this directory. So, if we execute the clean task from the command line, Gradle will delete the build directory:

```
$ gradle clean
:clean
BUILD SUCCESSFUL
Total time: 0.583 secs
```

Note that the Java plugin also added some rule-based tasks. One of them was clean<TaskName>. We can use this task to remove the output files of a specific task. The clean task deletes the complete build directory; but with clean<TaskName>, we only delete the files and directories created by the named task. For example, to clean the generated Java class files of the compileJava task, we execute the cleanCompileJava task. As this is a rule-based task, Gradle will determine that everything after clean must be a valid task in our project. The files and directories created by this task are then determined by Gradle and deleted:

```
$ gradle cleanCompileJava
:cleanCompileJava UP-TO-DATE
BUILD SUCCESSFUL
Total time: 0.578 secs
```

Working with source sets

The Java plugin also adds a new concept to our project—**source sets**. A source set is a collection of source files that are compiled and executed together. The files can be Java source files or resource files. Source sets can be used to group files together with a certain meaning in our project, without having to create a separate project. For example, we can separate the location of source files that describe the API of our Java project in a source set, and run tasks that only apply to the files in this source set.

Without any configuration, we already have the `main` and `test` source sets, which are added by the Java plugin. For each source set, the plugin also adds the following three tasks: `compile<SourceSet>Java`, `process<SourceSet>Resources`, and `<SourceSet>Classes`. When the source set is named `main`, we don't have to provide the source set name when we execute a task. For example, `compileJava` applies to the `main` source test, but `compileTestJava` applies to the `test` source set.

Each source set also has some properties to access the directories and files that make up the source set. The following table shows the properties that we can access in a source set:

Source set property	Type	Description
`java`	`SourceDirectorySet`	These are the Java source files for this project. Only files with the `.java` extension are in this collection.
`allJava`	`SourceDirectorySet`	By default, this is the same as the Java property, so it contains all the Java source files. Other plugins can add extra source files to this collection.
`resources`	`SourceDirectorySet`	These are all the resource files for this source set. This contains all the files in the resources source directory, excluding any files with the `.java` extension.
`allSource`	`SourceDirectorySet`	By default, this is the combination of the resources and Java properties. This includes all the source files of this source set, both resource and Java source files.
`output`	`SourceSetOutput`	These are the output files for the source files in the source set. This contains the compiled classes and processed resources.
`java.srcDirs`	`Set<File>`	These are the directories with Java source files.
`resources.srcDirs`	`Set<File>`	These are the directories with the resource files for this source set.
`output.classesDir`	`File`	This is the output directory with the compiled class files for the Java source files in this source set.

`output.resourcesDir`	File	This is the output directory with the processed resource files from the resources in this source set.
`name`	String	This is the read-only value with the name of the source set.

We can access these properties via the `sourceSets` property of our project. In the following example, we will create a new task to display values for several properties:

```
apply plugin: 'java'
task sourceSetJavaProperties << {
    sourceSets {
        main {
            println "java.srcDirs = ${java.srcDirs}"
            println "resources.srcDirs = ${resources.srcDirs}"
            println "java.files = ${java.files.name}"
            println "allJava.files = ${allJava.files.name}"
            println "resources.files = ${resources.files.name}"
            println "allSource.files = ${allSource.files.name}"
            println "output.classesDir = ${output.classesDir}"
            println "output.resourcesDir = ${output.resourcesDir}"
            println "output.files = ${output.files}"
        }
    }
}
```

When we run the `sourceSetJavaproperties` task, we get the following output:

```
$ gradle sourceSetJavaproperties
:sourceSetJavaProperties
java.srcDirs = [/gradle-book/Chapter4/Code_Files/sourcesets/src/main/java]
resources.srcDirs = [/gradle-
book/Chapter4/Code_Files/sourcesets/src/main/resources]
java.files = [Sample.java]
allJava.files = [Sample.java]
resources.files = [messages.properties]
allSource.files = [messages.properties, Sample.java]
output.classesDir = /gradle-
book/Chapter4/Code_Files/sourcesets/build/classes/main
output.resourcesDir = /gradle-
book/Chapter4/Code_Files/sourcesets/build/resources/main
output.files = [/gradle-
book/Chapter4/Code_Files/sourcesets/build/classes/main, /gradle-
book/Chapter4/Code_Files/sourcesets/build/resources/main]
BUILD SUCCESSFUL
Total time: 0.594 secs
```

Creating a new source set

We can create our own source set in a project. A source set contains all the source files that are related to each other. In our example, we will add a new source set to include a Java interface. Our `Sample` class will then implement the interface; however, as we use a separate source set, we can use this later to create a separate JAR file with only the compiled interface class. We will name the source set `api` as the interface is actually the API of our example project, which we can share with other projects.

To define this source set, we only have to put the name in the `sourceSets` property of the project, as follows:

```
apply plugin: 'java'

sourceSets {
    api
}
```

Gradle will create three new tasks based on this source set—`apiClasses`, `compileApiJava`, and `processApiResources`. We can see these tasks after we execute the `tasks` command:

```
$ gradle tasks --all
. . .
Build tasks
-----------
apiClasses - Assembles api classes.
compileApiJava - Compiles api Java source.
processApiResources - Processes api resources.
. . .
```

We have created our Java interface in the `src/api/java` directory, which is the source directory for the Java source files for the `api` source set. The following code allows us to see the Java interface:

```java
// File: src/api/java/gradle/sample/ReadWelcomeMessage.java
package gradle.sample;

/**
 * Read welcome message from source and return value.
 */
public interface ReadWelcomeMessage {

    /**
     * @return Welcome message
     */
```

```
    String getWelcomeMessage();

}
```

To compile the source file, we can execute the `compileApiJava` or `apiClasses` task:

```
$ gradle apiClasses
:compileApiJava
:processApiResources UP-TO-DATE
:apiClasses
BUILD SUCCESSFUL
Total time: 0.595 secs
```

The source file is compiled in the `build/classes/api` directory.

We will now change the source code of our `Sample` class and implement the `ReadWelcomeMessage` interface, as shown in the following code:

```
// File: src/main/java/gradle/sample/Sample.java
package gradle.sample;

import java.util.ResourceBundle;

/**
 * Read welcome message from external properties file
 * <code>messages.properties</code>.
 */
public class Sample implements ReadWelcomeMessage {

    public Sample() {
    }

    /**
     * Get <code>messages.properties</code> file
     * and read the value for <em>welcome</em> key.
     *
     * @return Value for <em>welcome</em> key
     *         from <code>messages.properties</code>
     */
    public String getWelcomeMessage() {
      final ResourceBundle resourceBundle =
          ResourceBundle.getBundle("messages");
      final String message = resourceBundle.getString("welcome");
      return message;
    }

}
```

Next, we run the `classes` task to recompile our changed Java source file:

```
$ gradle classes
:compileJava
/gradle-book/Chapter4/src/main/java/gradle/sample/Sample.java:10: error:
cannot find symbol
public class Sample implements ReadWelcomeMessage {
                               ^
symbol: class ReadWelcomeMessage
1 error
:compileJava FAILED
FAILURE: Build failed with an exception.
* What went wrong:
Execution failed for task ':compileJava'.
> Compilation failed; see the compiler error output for details.
* Try:
Run with --stacktrace option to get the stack trace. Run with --info or --
debug option to get more log output.
BUILD FAILED
Total time: 0.608 secs
```

We get a compilation error! The Java compiler cannot find the `ReadWelcomeMessage` interface. However, we just ran the `apiClasses` task and compiled the interface without errors.

To fix this, we must define a dependency between the `classes` and `apiClasses` tasks. The `classes` task is dependent on the `apiClasses` tasks. First, the interface must be compiled and then the class that implements the interface must be compiled .

Next, we must add the output directory with the compiled interface class file to the `compileClasspath` property of the `main` source set. Once we have done this, we know for sure that the Java compiler picks up the compiled class file to compile the `Sample` class.

To do this, we will change the build file and add the task dependency between the two tasks and the main source set configuration, as follows:

```
apply plugin: 'java'
n
sourceSets {
    api
    main {
       compileClasspath += files(api.output.classesDir)
    }
}

classes.dependsOn apiClasses
```

Now we can run the classes task again, without errors:

```
$ gradle classes
:compileApiJava
:processApiResources UP-TO-DATE
:apiClasses
:compileJava
:processResources
:classes
BUILD SUCCESSFUL
Total time: 0.648 secs
```

Custom configuration

If we use Gradle for an existing project, we might have a different directory structure than the default structure defined by Gradle, or it may be that we want to have a different structure for another reason. We can account for this by configuring the source sets and using different values for the source directories.

Consider that we have a project with the following source directory structure:

```
.
├── resources
│   ├── java
│   └── test
├── src
│   └── java
├── test
│   ├── integration
│   │   └── java
│   └── unit
│       └── java
└── tree.txt
```

We will need to reconfigure the `main` and `test` source sets, but we must also add a new `integration-test` source set. The following code reflects the directory structure for the source sets:

```
apply plugin: 'java'

sourceSets {
    main {
        java {
            srcDir 'src/java'
        }
        resources {
```

```
            srcDir 'resources/java'
        }
    }
    test {
        java {
            srcDir 'test/unit/java'
        }
        resources {
            srcDir 'resources/test'
        }
    }

    'integeration-test' {
        java {
            srcDir 'test/integration/java'
        }
        resources {
            srcDir 'resources/test'
        }
    }
}
```

Notice how we must put the name of the integration-test source set in quotes; this is because we use a hyphen in the name. Gradle then converts the name of the source set into integrationTest (without the hyphen and with a capital *T*). To compile, for example, the source files of the integration test source set, we use the compileIntegrationTestJava task.

Working with properties

We have already discussed that the Java plugin adds tasks and source sets to our Gradle project; however, we also get a lot of new properties that we can use. Custom properties of a plugin are set in a Convention object of the org.gradle.api.plugins.Convention type. A Convention object is used by a plugin to expose properties and methods that we can use in our project. The Convention object of the plugin is added to the convention property of a project. The convention property of a Gradle project is a container for all the Convention objects from the plugins.

We can access the properties from the plugin's Convention object directly as project properties or we can specify the complete path to the Convention object of the plugin in order to get to a property or invoke a method.

For example, the `sourceSets` property is a property of the `Convention` object of the Java plugin. With the following task, `showConvention`, we see the different ways that we have in order to access this property:

```
task showConvention << {
    println sourceSets.main.name
    println project.sourceSets.main.name
    println project.convention.plugins.java.sourceSets.main.name
}
```

To see all the properties available to us, we must invoke the `properties` task from the command line. The following output shows a part of the output from the `properties` task:

```
$ gradle properties
:properties
. . .
targetCompatibility: 1.8
tasks: [task ':buildDependents', task ':buildNeeded', task ':check', task
':classes', task ':compileJava', task ':compileTestJava', task ':jar', task
':javadoc', task ':processResources', task ':processTestResources', task
':properties', task ':test', task ':testClasses']
test: task ':test'
testClasses: task ':testClasses'
testReportDir: /gradle-book/Chapter4/Code_Files/props/build/reports/tests
testReportDirName: tests
testResultsDir: /gradle-book/Chapter4/Code_Files/props/build/test-results
testResultsDirName: test-results
version: unspecified
. . .
```

If we look through the list, we see a lot of properties that we can use to redefine the directories where output files of the `compile` or `test` tasks are stored. The following table shows the directory properties:

Property name	Default value	Description
distDirName	distributions	This is the directory name relative to the build directory to store distribution files
libsDirName	libs	This is the directory name to store generated JAR files; it is relative to the build directory
dependencyCacheDirName	dependency-cache	This is the name of the directory for storing cached information about dependencies; it is relative to the build directory

docsDirName	docs	This is the name of the directory for storing generated documentation; it is relative to the build directory
testReportDirName	tests	This is the directory name relative to the build directory to store test reports
testResultsDirName	test-results	This stores test result XML files; it is relative to the build directory

The Java plugin also adds other properties to our project. These properties can be used to set the source and target compatibility of the Java version for compiling the Java source files or set the base filename for the generated JAR files.

The following table shows the convention properties of the Java plugin:

Property name	Type	Default value	Description
archivesBaseName	Stringrce and target compatibility of the Java version for compili	Name of the project	This is the base filename to use for archives created by archive tasks, such as JAR
sourceCompatibility	String, Number, JavaVersion, Object	Java version of JDK used to run Gradle	This is the Java version compatibility to be used when compiling Java source files with the compile task
targetCompatibility	String,Number,JavaVersion,Object	Value of sourceCompatibility	This is the version of Java class files are generated for
sourceSets	SourceSetContainer	–	These are the source sets for the project
manifest	Manifest	Empty manifest	This is the manifest to be included in all JAR files
metaInf	List	Empty list	This is the list of files to be included in the META-INF directory of all the JAR files created in the project

In our example project, we already saw that the generated JAR file was named after the project name; but with the `archivesBaseName` property, we can change that. We can also change the source compatibility to Java 6 for our project. Finally, we can also change the manifest that is used for the generated JAR file. The following build file reflects all the changes:

```
apply plugin: 'java'

archivesBaseName = 'gradle-sample'
version = '1.0'
```

```
sourceCompatibility = JavaVersion.VERSION_1_8 // Or '1.8' or 8

jar {
    manifest {
      attributes(
        'Implementation-Version' : version,
        'Implementation-Title' : 'Gradle Sample'
      )
    }
}
...
```

Now if we invoke the `assemble` task to create our JAR file and look into the `build/libs` directory, we can see that the JAR file is now named `gradle-sample-1.0.jar`:

```
$ gradle assemble
:compileApiJava
:processApiResources UP-TO-DATE
:apiClasses
:compileJava
:processResources
:classes
:jar
:assemble
BUILD SUCCESSFUL
Total time: 0.657 secs
$ ls build/libs
gradle-sample-1.0.jar
```

To see the contents of the generated manifest file, we will first extract the file from the JAR file and then look at the contents:

```
$ cd build/libs
$ jar xvf gradle-sample-1.0.jar
created: META-INF/
inflated: META-INF/MANIFEST.MF
created: gradle/
created: gradle/sample/
inflated: gradle/sample/Sample.class
inflated: gradle/sample/messages.properties
$ cat META-INF/MANIFEST.MF
Manifest-Version: 1.0
Implementation-Version: 1.0
Implementation-Title: Gradle Sample
```

Creating Javadoc documentation

To generate a Javadoc documentation, we must use the `javadoc` task of the `org.gradle.api.tasks.javadoc.Javadoc` type. The task generates a documentation for the Java source files in the `main` source set. If we want to generate documentation for the source sets in our project, we must configure the `javadoc` task or add an extra `javadoc` task to our project.

Note that, in our project, we have an API and main source set with the Java source files. If we want to generate documentation for both the source sets, we have to configure the `javadoc` task in our project. The `source` property of the `javadoc` task is set to `sourceSets.main.allJava` by default. If we add `sourceSets.api.allJava` to the `source` property, our interface file is also processed by the `javadoc` task:

```
apply plugin: 'java'

javadoc {
    source sourceSets.api.allJava
}
...
```

Next, we can run the `javadoc` task and the documentation is generated and put into the `build/docs/javadoc` directory:

```
$ gradle javadoc
:compileApiJava
:processApiResources UP-TO-DATE
:apiClasses
:compileJava
:processResources
:classes
:javadoc
BUILD SUCCESSFUL
Total time: 1.503 secs
```

We can set more properties on the `javadoc` task. For example, we can set a title for the generated documentation with the `title` property. The default value is the name of the project followed by the project version number, if available.

To change the destination directory, we can set the `destinationDir` property of the `javadoc` task to the directory that we want.

We can also use the `options` property to define a lot of properties that we know from the Java SDK `javadoc` tool. The following example shows us how to set some of the options for the `javadoc` task in our project:

```
apply plugin: 'java'

javadoc {
    source sourceSets.api.allJava

    title = 'Gradle Sample Project'

    options.links = ['http://docs.oracle.com/javase/6/docs/api/']
    options.footer = "Generated on ${new Date().format('dd MMM yyyy')}"
    options.header = "Documention for version ${project.version}"
}
...
```

Assembling archives

If we want to package the output of the new API source set in our JAR file, we must define a new task ourselves. Gradle doesn't provide some magic to do this for us automatically; luckily, the task itself is very simple:

```
apply plugin: 'java'

archivesBaseName = 'gradle-sample'
version = '1.0'

sourceSets {
    api
    main {
        compileClasspath += files(api.output.classesDir)
    }
}

classes.dependsOn apiClasses

task apiJar(type: Jar) {
    // Define appendix that will be
    // appended to the archivesBaseName
    // for the JAR.
    appendix = 'api'

    // Define the input for the JAR file.
    from sourceSets.api.output
}
```

The `apiJar` task is a `Jar` task. We define the `appendix` property that is used to generate the final filename of the JAR file. We use the `from()` method to point the output directory of our API source set, so all the generated output is included in the JAR file. When we run the `apiJar` task, a new `gradle-sample-api-1.0.jar` JAR file is generated in the `build/libs` directory, as follows:

```
$ gradle apiJar
:compileApiJava
:processApiResources UP-TO-DATE
:apiClasses
 :apiJar
    BUILD SUCCESSFUL
    Total time: 3.242 secs
```

The base name of the JAR file is the project name, which is similar to one for the `jar` task. If we look at the contents, we see our compiled `ReadWelcomeMessage` class file:

```
$ jar tvf build/libs/sample-api.jar
    0 Thu Oct 22 16:38:56 CEST 2015 META-INF/
   25 Thu Oct 22 16:38:56 CEST 2015 META-INF/MANIFEST.MF
    0 Thu Oct 22 16:35:08 CEST 2015 gradle/
    0 Thu Oct 22 16:35:08 CEST 2015 gradle/sample/
  182 Thu Oct 22 16:38:56 CEST 2015
gradle/sample/ReadWelcomeMessage.class
```

Also note that we didn't define a task dependency between the `apiJar` and `apiClasses` tasks; but when we ran the `apiJar` task, Gradle automatically ran the `apiClasses` task. This happened because we used the `sourceSets.api.output` property to define the files that needed to be included in the JAR file; Gradle noticed this and determined the task that is responsible for creating the content in the `sourceSets.api.output` directory. The `apiClasses` task is the task that compiles the Java source files and processes the resources into the build directory, therefore, Gradle will first invoke the `apiClasses` task before the `apiJar` task.

Summary

In this chapter, we discussed the support for a Java project in Gradle. With a simple line needed to apply the Java plugin, we get masses of functionality, which we can use for our Java code. We can compile our source files, package the compiled code into a JAR file, and generate the documentation.

In the next chapter, we will see how to add dependencies to external libraries. We will also discuss how to configure repositories and organize our dependencies with configurations.

Dependency Management

5

When we develop our code, we usually use third-party or open source libraries. These libraries need to be available in the classpath of the compiler, otherwise we will get errors and our build will fail. Gradle provides support for dependency management, so we can define our dependencies in our build file. Gradle will then take care of the necessary configuration for our various tasks.

In this chapter, we will discuss how to use dependency management in our builds. We will see how to organize dependencies with configurations. We will also discuss repositories that host dependency artifacts, their dependencies, and how to handle different repository layouts.

Then, we will define dependencies using the Gradle syntax for modules with version information.

Dependency configuration

Java has no real support for working with versioned libraries as dependencies. We cannot express in Java whether our class depends on `lib-1.0.jar` or `lib- 2.0.jar`, for example. There are some open source solutions that deal with dependencies and allow us to express whether our Java code depends on `lib- 1.0.jar` or `lib-2.0.jar`. The most popular are **Maven** and **Apache Ivy**. Maven is a complete build tool and has a mechanism for dependency management. Ivy is only about dependency management.

Both tools support repositories where versioned libraries are stored together with metadata about these libraries. A library can have dependencies on other libraries and is described in the metadata of the library. The metadata is described in the descriptor XML files. Ivy fully supports Maven descriptor files and repositories; it also adds some extra functionality. Therefore with Ivy, you get what you would with Maven, and then some more. This is why Gradle uses the Ivy API under the hood to perform dependency management. Gradle also adds some extra sugar on top of Ivy, so we can define and use dependencies in a very flexible way.

In a Gradle build file, we group dependencies together in a configuration. A configuration has a name and configurations can extend each other. With a configuration, we can make logical groups of dependencies. For example, we can create a `javaCompile` configuration to include dependencies needed to compile the Java code. We can add as many configurations to our build as we want. We don't define our dependencies directly in the configuration. A configuration, as with a label, can be used when we define a dependency.

Every Gradle build has a `ConfigurationContainer` object. This object is accessible via the `Project` property with the name `containers`. We can use a closure to configure the container with `Configuration` objects. Each `Configuration` object has at least a name, but we can change more properties. We can set a resolution strategy, if a configuration has version conflicts with dependencies, or we can change the visibility of a configuration so that it will not be visible outside of our project. A `Configuration` object also has a hierarchy. So we can extend from the existing `Configuration` objects to inherit the settings.

In the following example, we will create a new configuration with the name `commonsLib` to hold our dependencies and a `mainLib` configuration that extends `commonsLib`. The extended `mainLib` configuration gets all settings and dependencies from `commonsLib`, and we can assign extra dependencies as well:

```
configurations {
    commonsLib {
        description = 'Common libraries'
    }
    mainLib {
        extendsFrom commonsLib
        description = 'Main libraries'
    }
}

// Reference mainLib configuration
// using [] syntax for the
// configuration container.
println configurations['mainLib'].name
```

```
// Reference commonsLib in another way,
// just use the name directly as property.
println configurations.commonsLib.name
```

The output of the build shows the names of the configurations, as follows:

```
$ gradle -q
mainLib
commonsLib
Welcome to Gradle 2.9.
To run a build, run gradle <task> ...
To see a list of available tasks, run gradle tasks
To see a list of command-line options, run gradle --help
To see more detail about a task, run gradle help --task <task>
```

Many plugins add new configurations to `ConfigurationContainer`. We used the Java plugin in the previous chapter, which added four configurations to our project. With the built-in `dependencies` task, we can get an overview of the defined dependencies and configurations for a project.

The following build script uses the Java plugin:

```
apply plugin: 'java'
```

We get the following output if we execute the `dependencies` task:

```
$ gradle -q dependencies
------------------------------------------------------------
Root project
------------------------------------------------------------

archives - Configuration for archive artifacts.
No dependencies
compile - Compile classpath for source set 'main'.
No dependencies
default - Configuration for default artifacts.
No dependencies
runtime - Runtime classpath for source set 'main'.
No dependencies
testCompile - Compile classpath for source set 'test'.
No dependencies
testRuntime - Runtime classpath for source set 'test'.
No dependencies
```

Notice how we already have six configurations in our project. The following table shows the configuration and the tasks that use the configuration:

Configuration	Extends	Used by task	Description
compile	–	compileJava	These are the dependencies needed at compile time to compile the source files
runtime	compile	–	These are the dependencies for runtime of the application, but are not needed for compilation
testCompile	compile	compileTestJava	These are the dependencies to compile test source files
testRuntime	testCompile	test	These are all the dependencies needed to run the tests
archives	–	uploadArchives	This contains artifacts, such as JAR files created by the project
default	runtime	–	This is the default configuration that contains all runtime dependencies

If our code has a dependency on a library, we can set the dependency with the compile configuration. The dependency is then automatically available in the runtime, testCompile, testRuntime, and default configurations.

Repositories

Dependencies are usually stored in some kind of repository. A repository has a layout that defines a pattern for the path of a versioned library module. Gradle knows, for example, the layout of a Maven repository. Ivy repositories can have customized layouts, and with Gradle, we can configure a customized layout. The repository can be accessible via the filesystem, HTTP, SSH, or other protocols.

We can declare several repository types in the Gradle build file. Gradle provides some preconfigured repositories, but it is also very easy to use a custom Maven or Ivy repository. We can also declare a simple filesystem repository to be used for resolving and finding dependencies. The following table shows the preconfigured and custom repositories that we can use:

Repository type	Description
Maven repository	This is the Maven layout repository on a remote computer or filesystem.
Bintray JCenter repository	This is the preconfigured Maven layout repository to search for dependencies in the Bintray JCenter repository. This is a superset of the Maven central repository.
Maven central repository	This is the preconfigured Maven layout repository to search for dependencies in the Maven central repository.
Maven local repository	This is the preconfigured Maven repository that finds dependencies in the local Maven repository.
Ivy repository	This is the Ivy repository that can be located on a local or remote computer.
Flat directory repository	This is a simple repository on the local filesystem of the computer or a network share.

We define a repository with the `repositories()` method. This method accepts a closure that is used to configure an `org.gradle.api.artifacts.dsl.RepositoryHandler` object.

Adding Maven repositories

A lot of Java projects use Maven as a build tool and for it's dependency management features. A Maven repository stores libraries with version information and metadata described in a descriptor XML file. The layout of a Maven repository is fixed and follows the `someroot/[organization]/[module]/[revision]/ [module]-[revision].[ext]` pattern. The `organization` section is split into subfolders based on the dots used in the organization name. For example, if the organization name is `org.gradle`, an `org` folder with the `gradle` subfolder needs to be in the Maven repository. A JAR library with the organization name, `org.gradle`; module name, `gradle-api`; and revision, `1.0`, is resolved via the `someroot/org/gradle/gradle-api/1.0/gradle-api-1.0.jar` path.

Bintray JCenter is a relatively new public Maven repository, where a lot of Maven open source dependencies are stored. It is a superset of the Maven central repository and also contains dependency artifacts published directly at JCenter. Also, it is very easy to deploy our own artifacts to Bintray JCenter. The URL to access the repository is `https://jcenter.bintray.com`. Gradle provides a shortcut for JCenter so that we don't have to type the URL ourselves in the `repositories` configuration block. The shortcut method is `jcenter()`.

The Maven central repository is located at `https://repo1.maven.org/maven2` and contains a lot of libraries. Many open source projects deploy their artifacts to Maven's central repository. We can use the `mavenCentral()` method in the configuration closure for the `repositories()` method. The following example is a build file, where we have defined the Maven central repository and Bintray JCenter:

```
repositories {
    // Define Bintray's JCenter
    // repository, to find
    // dependencies.
    jcenter()

    // Define Maven Central
    // as repository for
    // dependencies.
    mavenCentral()
}
```

If you have used Maven before on your computer, there is a good chance that you have a local Maven repository. Maven will use a hidden folder in our home directory to store the downloaded dependency libraries. We can add this local Maven repository with the `mavenLocal()` method to the list of repositories. We can add the Maven local repository to our build file, as follows:

```
repositories {
    mavenLocal()
}
```

The Bintray JCenter and Maven central and local repositories are preconfigured Maven repositories. We can also add a custom repository that follows the Maven layout. For example, our company can have a Maven repository available via the intranet. We define the URL of the Maven repository with the `maven()` or `mavenRepo()` method.

The example build file uses both methods to add two new Maven repositories, which are available through our intranet, as follows:

```
repositories {
    maven {
        // Name is optional. If not set url property is used
        name = 'Main Maven repository'
        url = 'http://intranet/repo'
    }

    // Alternative way for defining a custom
    // Maven repository.
    mavenRepo(
        name: 'Snapshot repository',
        url: 'http://intranet/snapshots')
}
```

Both methods configure a repository via a combination of a closure and method arguments. Sometimes we must access a Maven repository that stores the metadata in the descriptor XML files, but the actual JAR files are in a different location. To support this scenario, we must set the `artifactUrls` property and assign the addresses of the servers that store the JAR files:

```
repositories {
    maven {
        url: 'http://intranet/mvn'

        // Use a different location for
        // the artifacts.
        artifactUrls 'http://intranet/jars'
        artifactUrls 'http://intranet/snapshot-jars'
    }
}
```

To access a Maven repository with basic authentication, we can set the credentials when we define the repository, as follows:

```
repositories {
    maven(name: 'Secured repository') {

        // Set credentials to access
        // the repository. It is better
        // to store the values for username
        // and password outside the build file.
        credentials {
            username = 'username'
            password = 'password'
        }

        url = 'http://intranet/repo'
    }
}
```

It is not a good idea to store `username` and `password` as plain text in the build file as anyone can read our password if stored in plain text. It is better if we define the properties in a `gradle.properties` file in the Gradle user home directory, apply the correct security constraints on the property file, and use these properties in our build file.

Adding Ivy repositories

An Ivy repository has a customizable layout, this means that there is no single predefined layout as with a Maven repository. The default layout for an Ivy repository has the someroot/[organization]/[module]/[revision]/[type]s/[artifact].[ext] pattern. The name of the organization is not split into subfolders, as with the Maven layout. So, our gradle module with the org.gradle organization name and gradle-api artifact with revision 1.0 is resolved via the someroot/org.gradle/gradle/1.0/jars/gradle-api.jar path.

We use the same repositories() method to configure an Ivy repository. We use the ivy() method to configure the settings for an Ivy repository. We define the URL of the repository, and optionally, a name, as follows:

```
repositories {
    ivy(
        url: 'http://intranet/ivy-repo',
        name: 'Our repository')

    // Alternative way of defining
    // an Ivy repository.
    ivy {
        url = 'http://intranet/ivy-snapshots'
    }
}
```

If our Ivy repository has a Maven layout, we can set the layout property to maven. We can use the same property to define a custom layout for a repository. We will define the patterns that are used to resolve the descriptor XML files and the actual library files.

The following table shows the different layout names that we can use and the default patterns for the preconfigured layouts:

Layout name	Pattern Ivy descriptors	Pattern artifacts
gradle	someroot/[organization]/[module]/[revision]/ivy-[revision].xml	someroot/[organization]/[module]/[revision]/[artifact]-[revision](-[classifier])(.[ext])
pattern	someroot/[organization]/[module]/[revision]/ivy-[revision].xml	someroot/[organization]/[module]/[revision]/[artifact]-[revision](-[classifier])(.[ext])
gradle	Custom	Custom

The example build file uses the preconfigured layout names `gradle` and `maven` and also a custom pattern, as follows:

```
repositories {
    ivy {
        url = 'http://intranet/ivy-snapshots'
        // Repository follows the maven layout.
        layout = 'maven'
    }
    ivy {
        url = 'http://intranet/repository'
        // Repository follows the gradle layout.
        layout = 'gradle'
    }

    ivy {
        url = 'http://intranet/custom'
        layout('pattern') {
            // Pattern to resolve Ivy descriptor files.
            ivy '[module]/[revision]/ivy.xml'
            // Pattern to resolve files.
            artifact '[module]/[revision]/[artifact](.[ext])'
        }
    }
}
```

Instead of using the `layout()` method to define a custom pattern, we can use the `ivyPattern()` and `artifactPattern()` methods to define the patterns for the Ivy repository:

```
repositories {
    ivy {
        url = 'http://intranet/custom'
        ivyPatterns '[module]/[revision]/ivy.xml'
        artifactPatterns '[module]/[revision]/[artifact](.[ext])'
    }
}
```

To access an Ivy repository that is secured with basic authentication, we must pass our credentials. Just like with the secured Maven repository, it is best to store the username and password as properties in the `$USER_HOME/.gradle/gradle.properties` file:

```
repositories {
    ivy {
        credentials {
            // Username and password are from
            // external gradle.properties file.
```

```
            username = usernameFromGradleProperties
            password = passwordFromGradleProperties
        }
        url = 'http://intranet/custom'
        ivyPatterns '[module]/[revision]/ivy.xml'
        artifactPatterns '[module]/[revision]/[artifact](.[ext])'
        artifactPatterns '[module]/[revision]/[artifact](.[ext])'
    }
}
```

Adding a local directory repository

To use a simple repository on the local filesystem or a network share mapped as local storage, we must use the `flatDir()` method. The `flatDir()` method accepts arguments or a closure to configure the correct directory. We can assign a single directory or multiple directories.

Gradle will resolve files in the configured directory using the first match it finds with the following patterns:

- [artifact]-[version].[ext]
- [artifact]-[version]-[classifier].[ext]
- [artifact].[ext]
- [artifact]-[classifier].[ext]

The following example build file defines a flat directory repository:

```
repositories {
    flatDir(
        dir: '../lib',
        name: 'libs directory')

    // Alternative way to define
    // flat directory as repository.
    flatDir {
        dirs '../project-files', '/volumes/shared-libs'
        name = 'All dependency directories'
    }
}
```

Defining dependencies

We discussed how to use dependency configurations to group together dependencies; we also saw how we must define repositories so that the dependencies can be resolved, but we haven't discussed how to define the actual dependencies yet. We define dependencies in our build project with the `dependencies{}` script block. We define a closure to pass to the `dependencies{}` script block with the configuration of the dependency.

We can define different types of dependencies. The following table shows the types that we can use:

Dependency type	Method	Description
External module dependency	–	This is a dependency on an external module or library in a repository.
Project dependency	`project()`	This is a dependency on another Gradle project.
File dependency	`files()`, `fileTree()`	This is a dependency on a collection of files on the local computer.
Client module dependency	`module()`	This is a dependency on an external module, where the artifacts are stored in a repository, but the meta information about the module is in the build file. We can override meta information using this type of dependency.
Gradle API dependency	`gradleApi()`	This is a dependency on the Gradle API of the current Gradle version. We use this dependency when we develop Gradle plugins and tasks.
Local Groovy dependency	`localGroovy()`	This is a dependency on the Groovy libraries used by the current Gradle version. We use this dependency when we develop Gradle plugins and tasks.

Using external module dependencies

The most used dependency is the external module dependency. We can define a module dependency in different ways. For example, we can use arguments to set a group name, module name, and revision of the dependency. We can also use the `String` notation to set the group name, module name, and revision in a single string. We always assign a dependency to a specific dependency configuration. The dependency configuration must be defined by ourselves or a plugin that we have applied to our project.

In the following example build file, we will use the Java plugin so that we get a `compile` and `runtime` dependency configuration. We will also assign several external module dependencies to each configuration using the different syntax rules:

```
apply plugin: 'java'

repositories {
    jcenter()
}

dependencies {
    // Use attributes for the group, name and
    // version for the external module dependency.
    compile(group: 'org.springframework',
      name: 'spring-core',
      version: '4.2.3.RELEASE')

    // Use String notation with group, name and
    // version in a single String.
    runtime('org.springframework:spring-aop:4.2.3.RELEASE'
}
```

Remember that a Gradle build file is a Groovy script file, so we can define variables to set values and use them in the `dependencies{}` script block configuration closure. If we rewrite the previous build file, we get the following output:

```
apply plugin: 'java'

repositories {
    jcenter()
}

ext {
    springVersion = '4.2.3.RELEASE'
    springGroup = 'org.springframework'
}
```

```
dependencies {
    // Use attributes to define dependency and
    // refer to project properties.
    compile(group: springGroup,
      name: 'spring-core',
      version: springVersion)

    // Use String notation with expression support
    // for variables.
    runtime("$springGroup:spring-aop:$springVersion")
}
```

Gradle will look for the descriptor file in the JCenter repository. If the file is found, the artifact of the module and the dependencies of the module are downloaded and made available to the dependency configuration.

To see the dependencies and the transitive dependencies, we invoke the built-in `dependencies` task. We get the following output:

```
$ gradle -q dependencies
------------------------------------------------------------
Root project
------------------------------------------------------------
archives - Configuration for archive artifacts.
No dependencies
compile - Compile classpath for source set 'main'.
  \--- org.springframework:spring-core:4.2.3.RELEASE
       \--- commons-logging:commons-logging:1.2
  default - Configuration for default artifacts.
  +--- org.springframework:spring-core:4.2.3.RELEASE
  |    \--- commons-logging:commons-logging:1.2
  \--- org.springframework:spring-aop:4.2.3.RELEASE
       +--- aopalliance:aopalliance:1.0
       +--- org.springframework:spring-beans:4.2.3.RELEASE
       |    \--- org.springframework:spring-core:4.2.3.RELEASE (*)
       \--- org.springframework:spring-core:4.2.3.RELEASE (*)
  runtime - Runtime classpath for source set 'main'.
  +--- org.springframework:spring-core:4.2.3.RELEASE
  |    \--- commons-logging:commons-logging:1.2
  \--- org.springframework:spring-aop:4.2.3.RELEASE
       +--- aopalliance:aopalliance:1.0
       +--- org.springframework:spring-beans:4.2.3.RELEASE
       |    \--- org.springframework:spring-core:4.2.3.RELEASE (*)
       \--- org.springframework:spring-core:4.2.3.RELEASE (*)
  testCompile - Compile classpath for source set 'test'.
  \--- org.springframework:spring-core:4.2.3.RELEASE
       \--- commons-logging:commons-logging:1.2
  testRuntime - Runtime classpath for source set 'test'.
```

```
+--- org.springframework:spring-core:4.2.3.RELEASE
|     \--- commons-logging:commons-logging:1.2
\--- org.springframework:spring-aop:4.2.3.RELEASE
     +--- aopalliance:aopalliance:1.0
     +--- org.springframework:spring-beans:4.2.3.RELEASE
     |     \--- org.springframework:spring-core:4.2.3.RELEASE (*)
     \--- org.springframework:spring-core:4.2.3.RELEASE (*)
(*) - dependencies omitted (listed previously)
```

To download only the artifact of an external dependency and not the transitive dependencies, we can set the `transitive` property for the dependency to `false`. We can set the property with a closure or as an extra property in the argument list, as follows:

```
apply plugin: 'java'

repositories {
    jcenter()
}

dependencies {
    // Configure transitive property with closure.
    compile('org.slf4j:slf4j-simple:1.7.13') {
        transitive = false
    }

    // Or we can use the transitive property
    // as argument.
    compile(group: 'org.slf4j',
      name: 'slf4j-simple',
      version: '1.7.13',
      transitive: false)
}
```

We can also exclude some transitive dependencies with the `exclude()` method. Gradle will look at the descriptor file of the module and exclude any dependencies that we have added with the `exclude()` method.

For example, in the following build file, we exclude the `org.slf4j:sl4j-api` transitive dependency:

```
apply plugin: 'java'

repositories {
    jcenter()
}

dependencies {
    // Configure transitive property with closure.
    compile('org.slf4j:slf4j-simple:1.7.13') {
        exclude 'org.slf4j:slf4j-api'
    }
}
```

To get an artifact of only the external module dependency, we can use the artifact-only notation. We must also use this notation when a repository doesn't have a module descriptor file and we want to get the artifact. We must add an @ symbol before the extension of the artifact. Gradle will not look at the module descriptor file, if available, when we use this notation:

```
apply plugin: 'java'

repositories {
    jcenter()
}

dependencies {
    // Use artifact-only notation with @ symbol.
    runtime('org.slf4j:slf4j-simple:1.7.13@jar')

    // Or we can use the ext property
    // as method argument.
    runtime(group: 'org.slf4j',
      name: 'slf4j-simple',
      version: '1.7.13',
      ext: 'jar')
}
```

We can even set the transitive behavior on a complete configuration. Each configuration has a transitive property. We can set the value to true or false in order to change the transitive behavior for each dependency that we define in the configuration. In the following sample build file, we set the transitive property on the runtime configuration:

```
apply plugin: 'java'

repositories {
    jcenter()
}

dependencies {
    compile('org.slf4j:slf4j-simple:1.7.13')
}

// Make all dependencies for the compile
// configuration transitive.
configurations.compile.transitive = false
```

In a Maven repository, we can use classifiers for a dependency. For example, the module descriptor file defines the jdk16 and jdk15 classifiers for different JDK versions of the library. We can use classifier in a Gradle dependency definition to select the dependency with the given classifier, as follows:

```
apply plugin: 'java'

repositories {
    jcenter()
}

dependencies {
    // Use artifact-only notation with @ symbol
    // together with classifier jdk16.
    compile('sample:simple:1.0:jdk16@jar')

    // Or we can use the classifier property
    // as method argument.
    compile(
      group: 'sample',
      name: 'simple',
      version: '1.0',
      classifier: 'jdk16')
}
```

The module descriptor of a module in a Maven repository can only have one artifact; but in an Ivy repository, we can define multiple artifacts for a single module. Each set of artifacts is grouped together in a configuration. The default configuration contains all the artifacts belonging to the module. If we don't specify the configuration property when we define the dependency for an Ivy module, the `default` configuration is used. We must specify the `configuration` property if we want to use artifacts belonging to this specific configuration, as follows:

```
apply plugin: 'java'

repositories {
    ivy {
        url = 'http://intranet/custom'
        ivyPatterns '[module]/[revision]/ivy.xml'
        artifactPatterns '[module]/[revision]/[artifact](.[ext])'
    }
}

dependencies {
    // Use configuration property in method arguments.
    testCompile
      group: 'sample',
      name: 'logging',
      version: '1.0',
      configuration: 'test'

    // Or we use a closure to set the property.
    testCompile('sample:logging:1.0') {
        configuration = 'test'
    }
}
```

Using project dependencies

Gradle projects can be dependent on each other. To define such a dependency, we use the `project()` method and use the name of the other project as an argument. Gradle will look for a default dependency configuration in this project and use this dependency configuration. We can use the `configuration` property to use different dependency configurations as a dependency for each project:

```
apply plugin: 'java'

dependencies {
    // Define a dependency on projectA
    // for the code in our project.
```

```
        compile(project(':projectA'))

        // Define a dependency on projectB,
        // and use specifically the configuration
        // compile.
        compile(project(':projectB')) {
            configuration = 'compile'
        }
    }
```

Using file dependencies

We can add dependencies using `FileCollection`. We can use the `files()` and `fileTree()` methods to add dependencies to a configuration. The dependency must be resolved to an actual artifact.

The following example uses file dependencies for the compile configuration:

```
apply plugin: 'java'

dependencies {
    compile files('spring-core.jar', 'spring-aop.jar')
    compile fileTree(dir: 'deps', include: '*.jar')
}
```

Using client module dependencies

Normally, Gradle will use a descriptor XML file for dependencies found in the repository to see which artifacts and optional transitive dependencies need to be downloaded. However, these descriptor files can be misconfigured, and so, we may want to override the descriptors ourselves in order to ensure that the dependencies are correct. To do this, we must use the `module()` method to define the transitive dependencies of a dependency. Gradle will then use our configuration and not the one provided by the module in a repository, as follows:

```
apply plugin: 'java'

ext {
    springGroup = 'org.springframework'
    springRelease = '4.2.3.RELEASE'
}

dependencies {
    compile module("$springGroup:spring-context:$springRelease") {
        dependency("$springGroup:spring-aop:$springRelease") {
```

```
                    transitive = false
        }
    }
}
```

Using Gradle and Groovy dependencies

When we develop Grails plugins and tasks, we can define a dependency on the Gradle API and Groovy libraries used by the current Gradle version. We can use the `gradleApi()` and `localGroovy()` methods to do this.

The following example defines the dependencies in the compile dependency configuration of a project:

```
apply plugin: 'groovy'

// Dependency configuration for developing
// Gradle plugins and tasks with Groovy.
dependencies {
    // Gradle API available for compile task.
    compile gradleApi()

    // Groovy libraries used by Gradle version.
    groovy localGroovy()
}
```

Accessing configuration dependencies

We can access the dependencies for a dependency configuration in a build file or task through the `configurations` property of the `Project` object. We can use the `dependencies()` and `allDependencies()` methods to get a reference to the dependencies, as follows:

```
apply plugin: 'java'

repositories {
    jcenter()
}

dependencies {
    runtime "org.springframework:spring-aop:4.2.3.RELEASE"
}

task dependencyInfo << {
```

```
    println "-- Runtime dependencies --"
    configurations.runtime.dependencies.each {
        println "${it.group}:${it.name}:${it.version}"
    }

    println "-- Runtime allDependencies --"
    configurations.runtime.allDependencies.each {
        println "${it.group}:${it.name}:${it.version}"
    }
}
```

Setting dynamic versions

Until now, we have explicitly set a version for a dependency with a complete version number. To set a minimum version number, we can use a special dynamic version syntax. For example, to set the dependency version to a minimum of 2.1 for a dependency, we use a version value 2.1.+. Gradle will resolve the dependency to the latest version after version 2.1 or to version 2.1 itself. In the following example, we will define a dependency on a spring-core version of 3.1 at least:

```
apply plugin: 'java'

repositories {
    jcenter()
}

dependencies {
    compile(group: 'org.springframework',
        name: 'spring-core',
        version: '4.2.+')
}
```

We can also reference the latest released version of a module with latest.integration. We can also set a version range with a minimum and maximum version number. The following table shows the ranges that we can use:

Range	Description
[1.0, 2.0]	All versions greater than or equal to 1.0 and lower than or equal to 2.0
[1.0, 2.0[	All versions greater than or equal to 1.0 and lower than 2.0
]1.0, 2.0]	All versions greater than 1.0 and lower than or equal to 2.0
]1.0, 2.0[	All versions greater than 1.0 and lower than 2.0

[1.0,)	All versions greater than or equal to 1.0
]1.0,)	All versions greater than 1.0
(, 2.0]	All versions lower than or equal to 2.0
(, 2.0[	All versions lower than 2.0

The following example build file will use version `4.2.3.RELEASE` as the latest release, which is greater than `4.2` and less than `4.3`:

```
apply plugin: 'java'

repositories {
    jcenter()
}

dependencies {
    compile(group: 'org.springframework',
        name: 'spring-core',
        version: '[4.2, 4.3[')
}
```

Resolving version conflicts

If we have a project with a lot of dependencies and these dependencies have transitive dependencies, version conflicts can easily arise. If one module has a dependency on `sample:logging:1.0` and another on `sample:logging:2.0`, Gradle will use the newest version number by default.

To change the default behavior, we set the `resolutionStrategy` property of a dependency configuration. We can instruct Gradle to fail the build if a conflict arises. This is very useful for debugging version conflicts.

In the following example build file, we instruct Gradle to fail the build if a version conflicts arises for all configurations:

```
apply plugin: 'java'

configurations.all {
    resolutionStrategy {
        failOnVersionConflict()
    }
}
```

To force a certain version number to be used for all dependencies (even transitive dependencies), we can use the `force()` method of `resolutionStrategy`. With this method, we can make sure that the preferred version is always used for a given module:

```
apply plugin: 'java'

configurations.all {
    resolutionStrategy {
        force('org.springframework:spring-core:4.2.3.RELEASE')
    }
}
```

Adding optional ANT tasks

We can reuse existing **Another Neat Tool** (**ANT**) tasks in Gradle build files. Gradle uses Groovy's AntBuilder for ANT integration. However, if we want to use an optional ANT task, we must do something extra as the optional tasks and their dependencies are not in the Gradle classpath. Luckily, we only have to define our dependencies for the optional task in the `build.gradle` file and we can then define and use the optional ANT task.

In the following sample, we are using the `scp` ANT optional task. We define a new configuration with the name `sshAntTask` and assign the dependencies to this configuration. Then, we can define the task and set the `classpath` property to the `classpath` of the configuration. We use the `asPath` property to convert the `configurations` classpath for the ANT task. In the sample, we will also see how to ask for user input when the script is run. The `passphrase` for the SSH key file is a secret and we don't want to keep it in a file somewhere, so we ask the user for it. The `System.console()` Java method returns a reference to the console, and with the `readPassword()` method, we can get the value for the `passphrase`, as follows:

```
// We define a new configuration with the name 'sshAntTask'.
// This configuration is used to define our dependencies.
configurations {
    sshAntTask
}

repositories {
    jcenter()
}

// Assign dependencies to the sshAntTask configuration.
dependencies {
    sshAntTask('org.apache.ant:ant-jsch:1.7.1', 'jsch:jsch:0.1.29')
}
```

```
// Sample task which uses the scp ANT optional task.
task update {
    description = 'Update files on remote server.'

    // Get passphrase from user input.
    def console = System.console()

    def passphrase =
        console.readPassword(
            '%s: ',
            'Please enter the passphrase for the keyfile')

    // Redefine scp ANT task, with the classpath
    // property set to our newly defined
    // sshAntTask configuration classpath.
    ant.taskdef(
      name: 'scp',
      classname: 'org.apache.tools.ant.taskdefs.optional.ssh.Scp',
      classpath: configurations.sshAntTask.asPath)

    // Invoke the scp ANT task.
    // (Use gradle -i update to see the output of the ANT task.)
    ant.scp(
        todir: 'mrhaki@servername:/home/mrhaki',
        keyfile: '${user.home}/.ssh/id_rsa',
        // Use phassphrase entered by the user.
        passphrase: passphrase as String,
        verbose: 'true') {
        fileset(dir: 'work') {
          include(name: '**/**')
        }
    }
}
```

Using dependency configurations as files

Each dependency configuration implements the `FileCollection` interface of Gradle. This means that we can use a configuration reference if we need a list of files somewhere. The files that make up the resolved dependency configuration are then used.

Let's create a new build file and use a dependency configuration as the value for the `from()` method. We create a new task of the `Copy` type and copy all the dependencies of a new configuration, `springLibs`, to a directory:

```
repositories {
    jcenter()
```

```
}

configurations {
    springLibs
}

dependencies {
    springLibs('org.springframework:spring-web:4.2.3.RELEASE')
}

task copyCompileDeps(type: Copy) {
    from configurations.springLibs
    into "$buildDir/compileLibs"
}
```

Summary

In this chapter, we discussed dependency management support in Gradle. We also saw how to create a dependency configuration or use dependency configurations provided by a plugin.

To get the real dependency artifacts and their transitive dependencies, we must define repositories that store these files. Gradle allows very flexible repository configurations to be used.

Finally, we saw how to define the actual dependencies for a dependency configuration. We discussed how to resolve version conflicts between dependencies and use these dependencies in a Gradle build.

In the next chapter, we will look at how to run tests for our code and execute Java applications from our build. We will also discuss how to publish our own project to a repository.

6
Testing, Building, and Publishing Artifacts

An important part of developing software is writing tests for our code. In this chapter, we will discuss how to run our test code as part of the build process. Gradle supports both JUnit and TestNG testing frameworks. We can even run tests simultaneously to shorten the time of the build, resulting in quick builds.

We will also discuss how to run a Java application as part of a Gradle build. We can use the application plugin to automatically execute a Java application as part of the build.

After we have written and tested our code, it is time to publish the code so that others can use it. We will build a package and deploy our code to a company repository or any other repository.

Testing our projects

Gradle has a built-in support for running tests for our Java projects. When we add the Java plugin to our project, we will get new tasks to compile and run tests. We will also get the `testCompile` and `testRuntime` dependency configurations. We use these dependencies to set the class path for running the tests in our code base:

1. Let's write a simple JUnit test for a sample Java class. The implementation of `gradle.sample.Sample` has the `getWelcomeMessage()` method, where we read a text from the `file` property and then return the value. The following example contains the code for the `Sample` class:

   ```
   // File: src/main/java/gradle/sample/Sample.java
   package gradle.sample;
   ```

```
import java.util.ResourceBundle;

/**
 * Read welcome message from external properties file
 * <code>messages.properties</code>.
 */
```

2. Next, we must add the resource property file that is used by the `Sample` class. We will create the `messages.properties` file in the `src/main/resources/gradle/sample` directory with the following contents:

```
# File: src/main/resources/gradle/
  sample/messages.properties
welcome = Welcome to Gradle.
```

Our test is very simple. We will create a `Sample` object and invoke the `getWelcomeMessage()` method. We will compare the returned value with a value that we expect to be returned.

3. The following sample contains the test to check the value of the `getWelcomeMessage()` method with the expected `String` value, `Welcome to Gradle`. We need to create the `SampleTest.java` file in the `src/test/java/gradle/sample` directory:

```java
// File: src/test/java/gradle/sample/SampleTest.java
package gradle.sample;

import org.junit.Assert;
import org.junit.Test;

public class SampleTest {

  @Test
  public void readWelcomeMessage() {
    final Sample sample = new Sample();

    final String realMessage = sample.getWelcomeMessage();

    final String expectedMessage = "Welcome to Gradle.";
    Assert.assertEquals(
      "Get text from properties file",
      expectedMessage, realMessage);
  }

}
```

The Gradle build script for these files is very simple. We first apply the Java plugin, and as we are keeping to Gradle's configuration conventions, we don't have to configure or define anything else. Our test is written as a JUnit test. JUnit is one of the most used test frameworks for Java projects. To make sure that the required JUnit classes are available to compile and run the test class, we must add JUnit as a dependency to our project. The Java plugin adds `testCompile` and `testRuntime` configurations that we can use. We add the JUnit dependency to the `testCompile` configuration. All JUnit classes are now available to compile the test classes.

4. The following sample build file contains all the necessary code to execute the test:

```
apply plugin: 'java'

repositories {
    jcenter()
}

dependencies {
    testCompile('junit:junit:4.12')
}
```

5. To run our test, we only have to invoke the `test` task that is added by the Java plugin from the command line:

```
$ gradle test
:compileJava
:processResources
:classes
:compileTestJava
:processTestResources UP-TO-DATE
:testClasses
:test
 gradle.sample.SampleTest > readWelcomeMessage FAILED
 java.util.MissingResourceException at SampleTest.java:13
 1 test completed, 1 failed
 :test FAILED
FAILURE: Build failed with an exception.
* What went wrong:
Execution failed for task ':test'.
> There were failing tests. See the report  at:
file:///Users/mrhaki/Projects/
gradle-effective-implementation-guide-2/
gradle- impl-guide-
2/src/docs/asciidoc/Chapter6/Code_Files/testing/
sample/build/reports/tests/index.html
```

```
* Try:
Run with --stacktrace option to get the stack
trace. Run with --info
or --debug option to get more log output.
BUILD FAILED
Total time: 2.656 secs
```

If we look at the output, we will see that the test has failed, but we don't see why. One way to find it out is to rerun the `test` task with extra logging.

6. So, now we can enable the `info` logging level with `--info` (or `-i`) arguments, as shown in the following command:

```
$ gradle test --info
. . .
Gradle Test Executor 1 started executing tests.
Gradle Test Executor 1 finished executing tests.
gradle.sample.SampleTest > readWelcomeMessage FAILED
org.junit.ComparisonFailure: Get text from properties
file expected:<Welcome to Gradle[.]> but was:
<Welcome to Gradle[!]>
    at org.junit.Assert.assertEquals(Assert.java:115)
    at  gradle.sample.SampleTest.readWelcomeMessage
(SampleTest.java:16)
. . .
```

Now we can see why our test failed. In our test, we expected a dot (`.`) at the end of `String` instead of the exclamation mark (`!`) that we got from the property file. To fix our test, we must change the contents of the property file and replace the exclamation mark with a dot. Before we do this, we will use a different way to see the test results. Until now, we looked at the output on the command line after running the `test` task. In the `build/reports/tests` directory, there is an HTML file report available with the results of our test run.

7. If we open the `build/reports/tests/index.html` file in a web browser, we get a clear overview of the tests that have run and failed:

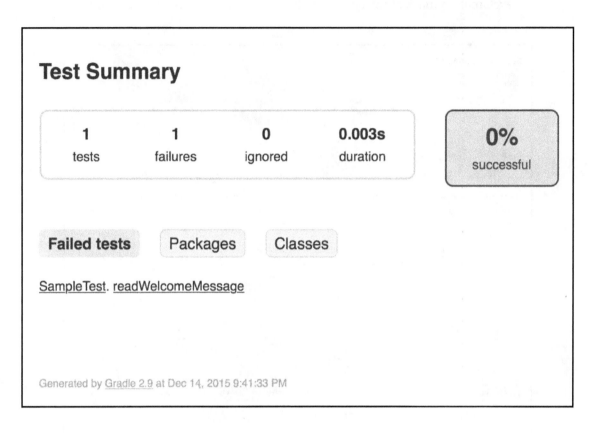

Generated HTML page with overview of tests

8. We can click on the method name of a failed test to see the details. Here we again see the message stating that the expected `String` value had a dot instead of an exclamation mark at the end of the line:

More detailed information about a test that has run

9. Let's change the contents of the `messages.properties` file and use a dot instead of an exclamation mark at the end of the line:

```
# File: src/main/resources/gradle/sample/
  messages.properties
welcome = Welcome to Gradle.
```

10. Now we run the `test` task again from the command line:

```
$ gradle test
:compileJava UP-TO-DATE
:processResources
:classes
:compileTestJava
:processTestResources UP-TO-DATE
:testClasses
:test
BUILD SUCCESSFUL
Total time: 1.174 secs
```

The Gradle build did not fail this time and is successful. Our test has run and we get the expected result from the `getWelcomeMessage()` method.

11. The following screenshot shows that the tests are 100 percent successful and are also documented in the generated test HTML reports:

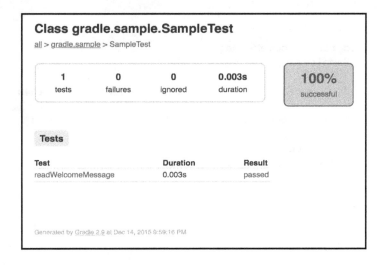

Generated HTML page with overview of test that have run

Using TestNG for testing

We have written a test with the JUnit test framework. Gradle also supports tests that are written with the TestNG test framework. Gradle scans the test class path for all class files and checks whether they have specific JUnit or TestNG annotations. If a test class or super class extends `TestCase` or `GroovyTestCase` or is annotated with the `@RunWith` annotation, the test class is also determined to be a JUnit test.

For Gradle to use either JUnit or TestNG tests when we run the `test` task, we invoke the `useJUnit()` or `useTestNG()` method, respectively, to force Gradle to use the correct testing framework. Gradle uses JUnit as a testing framework by default so that we don't have to use the `useJUnit()` method when we use JUnit or JUnit-compatible test frameworks to test our code.

Let's write a new test, but this time, we will use TestNG annotations and classes. The following sample class is the same test as we saw before, but it is written with the TestNG framework:

```java
// File: src/test/java/gradle/sample/SampleTestNG.java
package gradle.sample;


import org.testng.AssertJUnit;
import org.testng.annotations.Test;

public class SampleTestNG {

    @Test
    public void readWelcomeMessage() {
        final Sample sample = new Sample();

        final String realMessage = sample.getWelcomeMessage();

        final String expectedMessage = "Welcome to Gradle.";
        AssertJUnit.assertEquals(
                "Get text from properties file",
                expectedMessage, realMessage);
    }

}
```

We need to add the TestNG dependency to the `testCompile` dependency configuration. Furthermore, we invoke the `useTestNG()` method on our `test` task so that Gradle will pick up our new test. We will create a new build file and add the following code:

```
apply plugin: 'java'

repositories {
    jcenter()
}

dependencies {
    testCompile('org.testng:testng:6.5.1')
}

test.useTestNG()
```

Now we can run the `test` task again; but this time, Gradle will use our TestNG test:

```
$ gradle test
:compileJava
:processResources
:classes
:compileTestJava
:processTestResources UP-TO-DATE
:testClasses
:test
BUILD SUCCESSFUL
Total time: 1.262 secs
```

The generated HTML test report is in the `build/reports/tests` directory. We can open the `index.html` file in our web browser and see the output that is generated by the TestNG framework. The following screenshot shows an example of the output that we can view:

Generated HTML page with overview of run tests

Gradle cannot use the `test` task to run both the JUnit and TestNG tests at the same time. If we have both types of tests in our project and want to run them, we must add a new task of the `Test` type. This new task can run the specific tests for one of the frameworks.

We add a new task of the `Test` type to run the TestNG tests in our build file:

```
apply plugin: 'java'

repositories {
    jcenter()
}

dependencies {
    testCompile('junit:junit:4.12')
    testCompile('org.testng:testng:6.5.1')
}

// New task of type Test
// for running TestNG classes.
task testNG(type: Test) {
```

```
    useTestNG()
}

// Make sure testNG is executed,
// when the test task is executed.
test.dependsOn(testNG)
```

To add configuration options for TestNG, we can pass a closure to the `useTestNG()` method. The closure has an argument of the `org.gradle.api.tasks.testing.testng.TestNGOptions` type. The following table shows the options that we can set:

Option name	Type	Description
excludeGroups	Set	This is the set of groups to exclude
includeGroups	Set	This is the set of groups to include
javadocAnnotations	boolean	When `true`, Javadoc annotations are used for these tests
listeners	Set	This is the set of qualified classes that are TestNG listeners
parallel	String	This is the parallel mode to use for running tests; `method` or `tests` are valid options
suiteName	String	This sets the default name of the test suite, if one is not specified in a `suite.xml` file or source code
suiteXmlBuilder	MarkupBuilder	`MarkupBuilder` to create a suite XML
suiteXmlWriter	StringWriter	`StringWriter` to write out XML
testName	String	This sets the default name of the test, if one is not specified in a `suite.xml` file or source code
testResources	List	This is the list of all the directories containing test sources
threadCount	int	These are the number of threads to use for this run
useDefaultListeners	boolean	This states whether the default listeners and reporters should be used

The following sample build file uses some of the following options to configure TestNG:

```
apply plugin: 'java'

repositories {
    jcenter()
}

dependencies {
    testCompile('org.testng:testng:6.5.1')
}

test {
    useTestNG { options ->
        options.excludeGroups = ['functional'] as Set
        options.parallel = 'method'
        options.threadCount = 4
    }
}
```

Configuring the test process

The tests that are executed by the test task run in a separate isolated JVM process. We can use several properties to control this process. We can set system properties and JVM arguments and we can configure the Java class that needs to be executed to run the tests.

To debug the tests, we can set the debug property of the test task. Gradle will start the test process in the debug mode and listen on port 5005 for a debug process to attach to. This way we can run our tests and use an IDE debugger to step through the code.

By default, Gradle will fail the build if any test fails. If we want to change this setting, we must set the ignoreFailures property to true. Our build will not fail then, even if we have errors in our tests. The generated test reports will still have the errors. It is bad practice to ignore failures, but it is good to know that there is an option for it if we need.

The following build file configures the test task with the properties just discussed:

```
apply plugin: 'java'

repositories {
    jcenter()
}

dependencies {
    testCompile('junit:junit:4.12')
```

```
}

test {
    // Add System property to running tests.
    systemProperty 'sysProp', 'value'

    // Use the following JVM arguments for each test process.
    jvmArgs '-Xms256m', '-Xmx512m'

    // Enable debugging mode.
    debug = true

    // Ignore any test failues and don't fail the build.
    ignoreFailures = true

    // Enable assertions for test with the assert keyword.
    enableAssertions = true
}
```

Gradle can execute tests simultaneously. This means that Gradle will start multiple test processes concurrently. A test process only executes a single test at a time. By enabling parallel test execution, the total execution time of the `test` task can drastically decrease if we have a lot of tests. We must use the `maxParallelForks` property to set the number of test processes that we want to run in parallel. The default value is `1`, which means that the tests don't run simultaneously.

Each test process sets a `org.gradle.test.worker` system property with a unique value. We could use this value to generate unique files for a test process.

If we have a lot of tests that are executed by a single test process, we might get heap size or PermGen problems. With the `forkEvery` property, we can set the number of tests that need to run in a single test process before a new test process is started to execute more tests. Therefore, if Gradle sees that the number of tests exceeds the given number assigned to the `forkEvery` property, the test process restarts and the following set of tests is executed.

Let's create a new build file and configure it such that we can run four test processes simultaneously and relaunch the test process after `10` tests:

```
apply plugin: 'java'

repositories {
    jcenter()
}

dependencies {
    testCompile('junit:junit:4.12')
```

```
    }

test {
    // Run four tests in parallel.
    maxParallelForks = 4



    // Restart proces after
    // 10 executions.
    forkEvery = 10
}
```

Determining tests

To determine the files that are tests, Gradle will inspect the compiled class files. If a class or its methods have the @Test annotation, Gradle will treat it as a JUnit or TestNG test. If the class extends TestCase or GroovyTestCase or is annotated with @RunWith, Gradle will handle it as a JUnit test. Abstract classes are not inspected.

We can disable this automatic inspection with the scanForTestClasses property of the test task. If we set the property to false, Gradle will use the implicit /Tests.class and /*Test.class include rules and the */Abstract*.class exclude rule.

We can also set our own include and exclude rules to find tests. We can use the include() method of the test task to define our own rule for test classes. If we want to exclude certain class files, we can use the exclude() method to define the exclude rules. Alternatively, we can use the includes and excludes properties.

In the following build file, we will disable the automatic class inspection for test classes and set the include and exclude rules for test classes, explicitly:

```
apply plugin: 'java'

repositories {
    jcenter()
}

dependencies {
    testCompile('junit:junit:4.12')
}

test {
    // Disable automatic scanning
```

```
    // for test classes.
    scanForTestClasses = false

    // Include test classes.
    include('**/*Test.class', '**/*Spec.class')

    // Exclude test classes.
    exclude('**/Abstract*.class', '**/Run*.class')
}
```

Logging test output

We have already noticed that the output that is shown on the command line isn't much if we simply run the `test` task in the *Testing our projects* section. We must set the logging level to `info` or `debug` to get more information about the output that is generated by the tests. We can configure the `test` task to show more output with the `testLogging` property. This property is of the `org.gradle.api.tasks.testing.logging.TestLoggingContainer` type. We can set different options for each log level. If we don't specify a log level, the `lifecyle` log level is implied.

`TestLoggingContainer` has the `showStandardStreams` option, which we can be set to `true` or `false`. If we set the value of the property to `true`, we will get the output from `System.out` and `System.err` when we run the `test` tasks. The default value is `false`, and then we don't see the output from tests that are executed.

We can also use the `events()` method to set the events that are logged on the command-line output. For example, we can configure that we also want to see the passed tests, with the `String` value passed as an argument. We can use the `standardOut` and `standardError` arguments to get the same effect as with the `showStandardStreams` property. Other valid arguments are `failed`, `started`, and `skippedrr`.

If a test fails, we only see the line number of the test that failed. To get more output for a failed test, we can set the `exceptionFormat` option to `full`. Then we get the exception message with, for example, the assertion-failed message. The default value is `short`, which only shows the line number. With the `stackTraceFilters` property, we can determine how much of the stack trace is logged.

We can also set the `maximum` and `minimum` granularity of the log messages with the `minGranularity` and `maxGranularity` properties. We use the value for the Gradle-generated test suite, 1 for the generated test suite per test JVM, 2 for a test class, and 3 for a `test` method.

The following sample build file sets some of the options that are available:

```
apply plugin: 'java'

repositories {
    jcenter()
}

dependencies {
    testCompile('junit:junit:4.12')
}

test {
    // Set exception format to full
    // instead of default value 'short'.
    testLogging.exceptionFormat 'full'

    // We can also use a script block to configure
    // the testLogging property.
    testLogging {

        // No log level specified so the
        // property is set on LIFECYCLE log level.
        // We can pass arguments to determine
        // which test events we want to see in the
        // command-line output.
        events 'passed'

        // Show logging events for test methods.
        minGranularity = 3

        // All valid values for the stackTrace output.
        stackTraceFilters 'groovy', 'entry_point', 'truncate'

        // Show System.out and System.err output
        // from the tests.
        showStandardStreams = true

        // Configure options for DEBUG log level.
        debug {
            events 'started'
        }
    }
}
```

Changing the test report directory

We have already seen the HTML reports that are generated when we run the tests in the `build/reports/tests` directory. To change the directory name, we can set the `testReportDir` property as part of the `Project` object.

Besides the generated HTML report, we have XML files that are generated by the `test` task with the results of the tests. These XML files are actually the input for the generated HTML report. There are a lot of tools available that can use the XML files generated by JUnit or TestNG and perform an analysis on them. We can find the files in the `build/test-results` directory. If we want to generate the HTML reports in a different directory, we must create a new `TestReport` task. The `TestReports` task has properties for changing the output directories for the HTML reports. To change the HTML output directory, we set the `destinationDir` property. We use the `testResultsDir` property to refer to the directory or directories with the XML output.

To disable the generation of the test reports, we set the `reports.enabled` property to `false`.

The following build file shows how to change the report directory:

```
apply plugin: 'java'

repositories {
    jcenter()
}

dependencies {
    testCompile('junit:junit:4.12')
}

task testReport(type: TestReport) {
    destinationDir = file("$buildDir/test-reports")
    testResultDirs = files("$buildDir/test-results")
    reportOn(test)
}

// If the test task is finished,
// we want the testReport to be executed.
test.finalizedBy(testReport)
```

When we execute the `test` task from the command line, we can see the order of the tasks that are executed:

```
:clean
:compileJava
:processResources
:classes
:compileTestJava
:processTestResources UP-TO-DATE
:testClasses
:test
:testReport
BUILD SUCCESSFUL
Total time: 1.285 secs
```

Running Java applications

If we want to execute a Java executable from a Gradle build, we have several options. Before we explore these options, we will first create a new Java class with a `main()` method in our project. We will execute this Java class from our build file.

In the `src/main/java/gradle/sample` directory, we need to create a new `SampleApp.java` file. The following code listing shows the contents of the file. We will use our `Sample` class to print the value of the `getWelcomeMessage()` method to `System.out`:

```java
// File: src/main/java/gradle/sample/SampleApp.java
package gradle.sample;

public class SampleApp {

    public SampleApp() {
    }

    public static void main(String[] args) {
        final SampleApp app = new SampleApp();
        app.welcomeMessage();
    }

    public void welcomeMessage() {
        final String welcomeMessage = readMessage();
        showMessage(welcomeMessage);
    }

    private String readMessage() {
```

```
        final Sample sample = new Sample();
        final String message = sample.getWelcomeMessage();
        return message;
    }

    private void showMessage(final String message) {
        System.out.println(message);
    }
}
```

To run our `SampleApp` class, we can use the `javaexec()` method, which is part of Gradle's `Project` class. We can also use the `JavaExec` task in our build file. Finally, we can use the application plugin to run our `SampleApp` class. In the next chapter, we will discuss how to use the `javaexec` method.

Running an application from a project

The `Project` class that is always available in our build file has the `javaexec()` method. With this method, we can execute a Java class. The method accepts a closure that is used to configure the `org.gradle.process.JavaExecSpec` object. `JavaExecSpec` has several methods and properties that we can use to configure the main class that needs to be executed, optional arguments, and system properties. A lot of the options are same as the ones for running tests.

We will create a new build file and use the `javaexec()` method to run our `SampleApp` class with some extra options:

```
apply plugin: 'java'

task runJava(dependsOn: classes,
    description: 'Run gradle.sample.SampleApp') << {

    javaexec {
        // Java main class to execute.
        main = 'gradle.sample.SampleApp'

        // We need to set the classpath.
        classpath sourceSets.main.runtimeClasspath

        // Extra options can be set.
        maxHeapSize = '128m'
        systemProperty 'sysProp', 'notUsed'
        jvmArgs '-client'
    }
```

```
}
repositories {
    jcenter()
}
```

To run our Java class, we will execute the `runJava` task from the command line and get the following output:

```
$ gradle runJava
:compileJava
:processResources
:classes
:runJava
Welcome to Gradle.
BUILD SUCCESSFUL
Total time: 0.761 secs
```

Running an application as a task

Besides the `javaexec()` method, we can define a new `org.gradle.api.tasks.JavaExec` task. To configure the task, we can use the same methods and properties as with the `javaexec()` method.

In the following sample build file, we will create the `runJava` task of the `JavaExec` type. We will configure the task to set the class path and main class. Also, we will see how to add other properties and invoke other methods to further configure the execution of the Java class, as follows:

```
apply plugin: 'java'

task runJava(type: JavaExec) {
    dependsOn classes
    description = 'Run gradle.sample.SampleApp'

    // Java main class to execute.
    main = 'gradle.sample.SampleApp'

    // We need to set the classpath.
    classpath sourceSets.main.runtimeClasspath

    // Extra options can be set.
    systemProperty 'sysProp', 'notUsed'
    jvmArgs '-client'

    // We can pass arguments to the main() method
```

```
    // of gradle.sample.SampleApp.
    args 'mainMethodArgument', 'notUsed'
}
```

If we run the task, we get the following output:

```
$ gradle runJava
:compileJava UP-TO-DATE
:processResources UP-TO-DATE
:classes UP-TO-DATE
:runJava
Welcome to Gradle.
BUILD SUCCESSFUL
Total time: 0.686 secs
```

Running an application with the application plugin

Another way to run a Java application is with the application plugin. The application plugin adds functionality to our build file in order to run Java applications and also to bundle the Java application for distribution.

To use the application plugin, we must add the plugin to our build file with the apply() method. Once we have added the plugin, we can set the main class to be executed with the mainClassName property. This time, we don't have to create a new task ourselves. The plugin has added the run task that we can invoke to run the Java application.

The sample build file uses the application plugin to run our SampleApp class, as follows:

```
apply plugin: 'application'

mainClassName = 'gradle.sample.SampleApp'

// Extra configuration for run task if needed.
run {
    // Extra options can be set.
    systemProperty 'sysProp', 'notUsed'
    jvmArgs '-client'

    // We can pass arguments to the main() method
    // of gradle.sample.SampleApp.
    args 'mainMethodArgument', 'notUsed'
}
```

We can invoke the `run` task and check the output of the `SampleApp` class:

```
$ gradle run
:compileJava UP-TO-DATE
:processResources UP-TO-DATE
:classes UP-TO-DATE
:run
Welcome to Gradle.
BUILD SUCCESSFUL
Total time: 0.816 secs
```

Note that we don't have to set the `classpath` property anymore. The plugin automatically includes the `runtimeClasspath` object of the project to execute the Java class.

Creating a distributable application archive

With the application plugin, we can also build a distribution with our Java application. This means that we can distribute the application, and people can run the Java application without Gradle. The plugin will create the necessary operating system-specific start scripts and package all the necessary classes and dependencies.

The following table shows the extra tasks that we can use with the application plugin to build a distribution:

Task	Depends on	Type	Description
startScripts	jar	CreateStartScripts	This creates operating system-specific scripts to run the Java application
installDist	jar, startScripts	Sync	This installs the application into a directory
distZip	jar, startScripts	Zip	This creates a full distribution ZIP archive, including all the necessary files to run the Java application
distTar	jar, startScripts	Tar	This creates a full distribution TAR archive, including all the necessary files to run the Java application

All tasks depend on the `Jar` task. In order to get a meaningful JAR filename, we set
the `archivesBaseName` and `version` properties in our build file, as follows:

```
apply plugin: 'application'

mainClassName = 'gradle.sample.SampleApp'

archivesBaseName = 'gradle-sample'
version = '1.0'
```

To create the start scripts, we invoke the `createScript` task. After we have executed the
task, we have two files, `sample` and `sample.bat`, in the `build/scripts` directory.
The `sample.bat` file is for the Windows operating system and `sample` is for other
operating systems, such as Linux or OS X.

To have all files that are needed to run the application in a separate directory, we must run
the `installDist` task. When we execute the task, we get a `sample` directory in
the `build/install` directory. The sample directory has a `bin` directory with the start
scripts and a `lib` directory with the JAR file, containing the `SampleApp` application. We can
change to the `build/install/sample` directory and then invoke `bin/sample`
or `bin/sample.bat` to run our application:

```
$ gradle installDist
:compileJava UP-TO-DATE
:processResources UP-TO-DATE
:classes UP-TO-DATE
:jar UP-TO-DATE
:startScripts UP-TO-DATE
:installDist
BUILD SUCCESSFUL
Total time: 0.629 secs
$ cd build/install/sample
$ bin/sample
Welcome to Gradle.
```

To create a ZIP archive with all the necessary files, which would enable others to run the
application, we run the `distZip` task. The resulting ZIP archive can be found in
the `build/distributions` directory. We can distribute this ZIP file and people can unzip
the archive on their computers to run the Java application, as follows:

```
$ gradle distZip
:compileJava UP-TO-DATE
:processResources UP-TO-DATE
:classes UP-TO-DATE
:jar UP-TO-DATE
:startScripts UP-TO-DATE
```

```
:distZip
BUILD SUCCESSFUL
Total time: 0.602 secs
$ jar tvf build/distributions/sample-1.0.zip
    0 Wed Dec 16 10:23:42 CET 2015 app-1.0/
    0 Wed Dec 16 10:23:42 CET 2015 app-1.0/lib/
    2064 Wed Dec 16 10:18:54 CET 2015 app-1.0/lib/gradle-sample-1.0.jar
    0 Wed Dec 16 10:23:42 CET 2015 app-1.0/bin/
    4874 Wed Dec 16 10:18:54 CET 2015 app-1.0/bin/sample
    2329 Wed Dec 16 10:18:54 CET 2015 app-1.0/bin/sample.bat
```

To create a Tar archive, we use the distTar task.

If we want to add other files to the distribution, we can create the src/dist directory and place the files in there. Any files in the src/dist directory are included in the distribution ZIP archive. To include files from another directory, we can use the applicationDistribution copy specification.

The following sample build file uses the applicationDistribution copy specification to include the output of the docs task. Gradle will automatically execute the docs task before invoking the distZip task:

```
apply plugin: 'application'

archivesBaseName = 'gradle-sample'
version = '1.0'

mainClassName = 'gradle.sample.SampleApp'

task docs {
    ext {
        docsDir = 'docs'
        docsResultDir = file("$buildDir/$docsDir")
    }

    // Assign directory to task outputs.
    outputs.dir docsResultDir

    doLast {
        docsResultDir.mkdirs()
        new File(docsResultDir, 'README').write('Please read me.')
    }

}

applicationDistribution.from(docs) {
    // Directory in distribution ZIP archive.
```

```
        into 'docs'
    }
```

Publishing artifacts

A software project can contain artifacts that we want to publish. An artifact can be a ZIP or JAR archive file or any other file. In Gradle, we can define more than one artifact for a project. We can publish these artifacts in a central repository so that other developers can use our artifacts in their projects. These central repositories can be available on the company intranet, network drive, or via the Internet.

In Gradle, we group artifacts through configurations, just like dependencies. A configuration can contain both dependencies and artifacts. If we add the Java plugin to our project, we also have two extra tasks per configuration to build and upload the artifacts belonging to the configuration. The task to build the artifacts is called `build<configurationName>` and the task to upload the artifacts is called `upload<configurationName>`.

The Java plugin also adds the `archives` configuration that can be used to assign artifacts. The default JAR artifact for a Java project is already assigned to this configuration. We can assign more artifacts to this configuration for our project. We can also add new configurations to assign artifacts in a project.

For our Java project, we will define the following sample build file:

```
apply plugin: 'java'

archivesBaseName = 'gradle-sample'
version = '1.0'
```

As we use the Java plugin, we have the `archives` configuration available. When we execute the `buildArchives` task, our Java code is compiled and a JAR file is created in the `build/libs` directory, called `gradle-sample-1.0.jar`.

To publish our JAR file, we can execute the `uploadArchives` task, but we must first configure where to publish the artifact. The repositories that we have defined for the dependencies are not used to upload the artifacts. We have to define the upload repository in the `uploadArchives` task. We can reference a repository that is already defined in our project or define the repositories in the task.

The following sample build file defines an upload repository at project level and task level:

```
apply plugin: 'java'
```

```
archivesBaseName = 'gradle-sample'
version = '1.0'

repositories {
    flatDir {
        name 'uploadRepository'
        dirs 'upload'
    }
}

uploadArchives {
    repositories {
        // Use repository defined in project
        // for uploading the JAR file.
        add project.repositories.uploadRepository

        // Extra upload repository defined in
        // the upload task.
        flatDir {
            dirs 'libs'
        }
    }
}
```

If we invoke the uploadArchives task, the JAR file is created and copied to the libs and upload directories in our project root directory. An ivy.xml configuration file is also created and copied to the directories, as follows:

```
$ gradle uploadArchives
:compileJava
:processResources
:classes
:jar
:uploadArchives
BUILD SUCCESSFUL
Total time: 0.753 secs
$ ls libs/
gradle-sample-1.0.jar
gradle-sample-1.0.jar.sha1
ivy-1.0.xml
ivy-1.0.xml.sha1
$ ls upload/
gradle-sample-1.0.jar
gradle-sample-1.0.jar.sha1
ivy-1.0.xml
ivy-1.0.xml.sha1
```

We can use all the Ivy resolvers to define upload repositories.

Uploading our artifacts to a Maven repository

If we want to upload to a Maven repository, we must create a **Maven Project Object Model (POM)** file. The Maven POM file contains all the necessary information about our artifact. Gradle can generate the POM file for us. We must add the Maven plugin to our project in order to make this work.

We must configure the repository for our `uploadArchives` task via a closure argument of the `mavenDeployer()` method. In the following sample build file, we will define a Maven repository with the `file` protocol:

```
apply plugin: 'java'
apply plugin: 'maven'

archivesBaseName = 'gradle-sample'
group = 'gradle.sample'
version = '1.0'

uploadArchives {
    repositories {
        mavenDeployer {
            repository(url: 'file:./maven')
        }
    }
}
```

Note that we set the `group` property of our project so that it can be used as `groupId` of the Maven POM. The `version` property is used as `version` and the `archivesBaseName` property is used as the artifact ID. We can invoke the `uploadArchives` task to deploy our artifact, as follows:

```
$ gradle uploadArchives
:compileJava UP-TO-DATE
:processResources UP-TO-DATE
:classes UP-TO-DATE
:jar UP-TO-DATE
:uploadArchives
BUILD SUCCESSFUL
Total time: 1.121 secs
$ ls maven/gradle/sample/gradle-sample/1.0/
gradle-sample-1.0.jar
gradle-sample-1.0.jar.md5
gradle-sample-1.0.jar.sha1
gradle-sample-1.0.pom
gradle-sample-1.0.pom.md5
gradle-sample-1.0.pom.sha1
```

The contents of the generated `gradle-sample-1.0.pom` POM file are as follows:

```
<?xml version="1.0" encoding="UTF-8"?>
<project xsi:schemaLocation="http://maven.apache.org/POM/4.0.0
http://maven.apache.org/xsd/maven-4.0.0.xsd"
xmlns="http://maven.apache.org/POM/4.0.0"
    xmlns:xsi="http://www.w3.org/2001/XMLSchema-instance">
  <modelVersion>4.0.0</modelVersion>
  <groupId>gradle.sample</groupId>
  <artifactId>gradle-sample</artifactId>
  <version>1.0</version>
</project>
```

Gradle uses the native Maven ANT tasks to deploy the artifacts to a Maven repository. The `file` protocol is supported without any extra configuration; but if we want to use other protocols, we must configure the libraries on which these protocols depend on:

Protocol	Library
http	org.apache.maven.wagon:wagon-http:1.0-beta-2
ssh	org.apache.maven.wagon:wagon-ssh:1.0-beta-2
ssh-external	org.apache.maven.wagon:wagon-ssh-external:1.0-beta-2
scp	org.apache.maven.wagon:wagon-scp:1.0-beta-2
ftp	org.apache.maven.wagon:wagon-ftp:1.0-beta-2
webdav	org.apache.maven.wagon:wagon-webdav-jackrabbit:1.0-beta-2
file	−

In the following sample build file, we will use the `scp` protocol to define a Maven repository and use it to upload the project's artifact:

```
apply plugin: 'java'
apply plugin: 'maven'

archivesBaseName = 'gradle-sample'
group = 'gradle.sample'
version = '1.0'

configurations {
    mavenScp
}
```

```
repositories {
    jcenter()
}

dependencies {
    mavenScp 'org.apache.maven.wagon:wagon-scp:1.0-beta-2'
}

uploadArchives {
    repositories {
      mavenDeployer {
        configuration = configurations.mavenScp
          repository(url: 'scp://localhost/mavenRepo') {
            authentication(userName: 'user', privateKey: 'id_sha')
            }
        }
      }
    }
}
```

The Maven plugin also adds the `install` task to our project. With the `install` task, we can install the artifact to our local Maven repository. Gradle will use the default location of the local Maven repository or the location that is defined in a `settings.xml` Maven file.

Working with multiple artifacts

Until now, we have uploaded a single artifact to a repository. In a Gradle project, we can define multiple artifacts and deploy them. We need to define an archive task and assign it to a configuration. We will use the `artifacts{}` script block to define a configuration closure in order to assign an artifact to a configuration. The artifact is then deployed to a repository when we execute the `upload` task.

In the following sample build, we will create JAR files with the source code and Javadoc documentation. We will assign both JAR files as artifacts to the `archives` configuration:

```
apply plugin: 'java'

archivesBaseName = 'gradle-sample'
version = '1.0'

// New task to archive the source files.
task sourcesJar(type: Jar) {
    classifier = 'sources'
    from sourceSets.main.allSource
}
```

```
// New task to archive the documentation.
task docJar(type: Jar, dependsOn: javadoc) {
    classifier = 'docs'
    from javadoc.destinationDir
}

artifacts {
    // Assign the output of the sourcesJar
    // task to the archives configuration.
    archives sourcesJar

    // Assign the output of the docJar
    // task to the archives configuration.
    archives docJar
}

uploadArchives {
    repositories {
        flatDir {
            dirs 'upload'
        }
    }
}
```

Signing artifacts

We can digitally sign artifacts in Gradle with the signing plugin. The plugin only has support to generate the **Pretty Good Privacy (PGP)** signature, which is the signature format required for publication to the **Maven Central Repository**. To create a PGP signature, we must install some PGP tools on our computers. Installation of the tools is different for each operating system. With the PGP software, we need to create a key pair that we can use to sign our artifacts.

We need to configure the signing plugin with the information about our key pair. We need the hexadecimal representation of the public key, the path to the secret key ring file with our private key, and the passphrase used to protect the private key. The values of these properties are assigned to the `signing.keyId`, `signing.secretKeyRingFile`, and `signing.password` Gradle project properties. The values of these properties are best kept secret, so it is better to store them in our `gradle.properties` file in the Gradle user directory and apply secure file permissions to the file. It is best to make the file read-only for a single user.

The following `gradle.properties` sample file has the signing properties set. The values of the properties shown are sample values. These will be different for other users:

```
signing.keyId=4E12C354
signing.secretKeyRingFile=/Users/current/.gnupg/secring.gpg
signing.password=secret phassphrase
```

We are ready to sign our artifacts. We need to configure the artifacts that we want signed. The signing plugin has a DSL that we can use to define the tasks or configurations that we want signed.

In our sample Java project, we have the `archives` configuration with artifacts of our project. To sign the artifacts, we can use the `signing()` method and a closure to configure that all artifacts of the `archives` configuration need to be signed. The following sample build file shows how we can do this:

```
apply plugin: 'java'
apply plugin: 'signing'

archivesBaseName = 'gradle-sample'
version = '1.0'

signing {
    sign configurations.archives
}
```

The signing plugin adds a new `signArchives` task to our project as we have configured that we want the `archives` configuration to be signed. The signing plugin adds tasks with the `sign<configurationName>` pattern to our project, for each configuration we configure to be signed.

We can invoke the `signArchives` task to sign our JAR artifact or use the `Jar` task, which is automatically dependent on the `signArchives` task, as follows:

```
$ gradle signArchives
:compileJava UP-TO-DATE
:processResources UP-TO-DATE
:classes UP-TO-DATE
:jar UP-TO-DATE
:signArchives
BUILD SUCCESSFUL

Total time: 1.649 secs
$ ls build/libs/gradle-sample-1.0.jar*
build/libs/gradle-sample-1.0.jar
build/libs/gradle-sample-1.0.jar.asc
```

Note that the `gradle-sample-1.0.jar.asc` signature file is placed next to the artifact.

If the artifact we want to sign is not part of a configuration, we can use the signing DSL to configure a task to be signed. The task must create an archive file in order to be used for signing. After we have configured the task to be signed, the signing plugin adds a new task with the `sign<taskName>` naming pattern. We can execute this task to sign the output of the configured task.

The following build file has the `sourcesJar` task to create a new archive with the source files of our project. We will use the signing DSL to configure our task for signing:

```
apply plugin: 'java'
apply plugin: 'signing'

archivesBaseName = 'gradle-sample'
version = '1.0'

task sourcesJar(type: Jar) {
    classifier = 'sources'
    from sourceSets.main.allSource
}

signing {
    sign sourcesJar
}
```

We can invoke the `signSourcesJar` task to digitally sign our JAR file with the sources of our project. The generated signature file is placed next to the JAR file in the `build/libs` directory. We can also invoke the `assemble` task to create the digitally-signed JAR file as this task is made dependent on all our archive tasks, including the signing tasks:

```
$ gradle signSourcesJar
:sourcesJar
:signSourcesJar
BUILD SUCCESSFUL
Total time: 0.87 secs
$ ls build/libs/gradle-sample-1.0-sources.jar*
build/libs/gradle-sample-1.0-sources.jar
build/libs/gradle-sample-1.0-sources.jar.asc
```

Packaging Java Enterprise Edition applications

We have discussed how to create ZIP, TAR, and JAR archives with Gradle in this chapter and the previous one. In a Java project, we can also package our applications as **Web application Archive** (**WAR**) or **Enterprise Archive** (**EAR**) files. For a web application, we would like to package our application as a WAR file, while a **Java Enterprise Edition** application can be packaged as an EAR file. Gradle also supports these types of archives with plugins and tasks.

Creating a WAR file

To create a WAR file, we can add a new task of the `War` type to our Java project. The properties and methods of the `War` task are the same as for the other archive tasks, such as `Jar`. In fact, the `War` task extends the `Jar` task.

The `War` task has an extra `webInf()` method to define a source directory for the `WEB-INF` directory in a WAR file. The `webXml` property can be used to reference a `web.xml` file that needs to be copied to the WAR file. This is just another way to include a `web.xml` file, we can also place the `web.xml` file in the `WEB-INF` directory of the root source directory that we defined for the WAR file.

With the `classpath()` method, we can define a dependency configuration or directory with libraries or class files that we want copied to our WAR file. If the file is a JAR or ZIP file, it is copied to the `WEB-INF/lib` directory and other files are copied in the `WEB-INF/classes` directory.

In the following sample build file, we will define a new `War` task. We set the root of the WAR file contents to the `src/main/webapp` directory. We use the `webInf()` and `classpath()` methods to customize the contents of the WEB-INF, `WEB-INF/classes`, and `WEB-INF/lib` folders. We also set a custom `web.xml` file with the `webXml` property of the task, as follows:

```
apply plugin: 'java'

version = '1.0'

// Custom archive task with
// specific properties for a WAR archive.
task war(type: War) {
    dependsOn classes

    from 'src/main/webapp'

    // Files copied to WEB-INF.
    webInf {
        from 'src/main/webInf'
    }

    // Copied to WEB-INF/classes.
    classpath sourceSets.main.runtimeClasspath

    // Copied to WEB-INF/lib.
    classpath fileTree('libs')

    // Custom web.xml.
    webXml = file('  ')
    baseName = 'gradle-webapp'
}

assemble.dependsOn war
```

To create the WAR file, we can execute the War or assemble task. The War task is added to the assemble task as a task dependency. This is why if we invoke the assemble task, Gradle will execute the War task. Once we have executed the task, the gradle-webapp-1.0.war WAR file is created in the build/libs directory:

```
$ gradle war
:compileJava
:processResources
:classes
:war
BUILD SUCCESSFUL
Total time: 0.727 secs
$ ls build/libs
gradle-webapp-1.0.war
```

Creating an EAR file

To create an EAR file, we can create a new task of the Ear type. This task has the same properties and methods as the Jar task. The Ear task extends the Jar task.

With the lib() method, we can define the files that need to be copied to the lib directory in the EAR file.

The following build file has a simple Ear task:

```
apply plugin: 'java'

version = '1.0'

// Create custom archive task
// with specific properties to
// create an EAR archive file.
task ear(type: Ear) {
    from 'src/main/application'

    lib {
        from fileTree('earLibs')
    }

    baseName = 'gradle-enterprise-app'
}

assemble.dependsOn ear
```

We can execute the `Ear` task and look in the `build/libs` directory to see the resulting `gradle-enterprise-app-1.0.ear` file:

```
$ gradle ear
:ear
BUILD SUCCESSFUL
Total time: 0.694 secs
$ ls build/libs
gradle-enterprise-app-1.0.ear
```

Summary

In this chapter, we discussed how to run JUnit or TestNG tests from a Gradle build. We also saw how to get the test results and reports that are generated by executing the tests.

With the application plugin, we discussed how to create a distributable ZIP file with all the code and scripts necessary to run the Java application that we have built.

We have also discussed how to upload our project artifacts to a repository so that other projects can use our code. We have seen that we can use Gradle to create an artifact that is ready to be uploaded to a Maven repository.

To digitally sign our artifacts, we saw how to use the signing plugin together with locally-installed PGP tools.

Also, we saw how we can use the `war` and `ear` plugins to create web and enterprise applications with Gradle. We can use tasks, methods, and configuration properties to configure the packaging output.

In the next chapter, we will look at how to run and create a multi-module project with Gradle. We will also discuss how to create dependencies between projects and apply a common configuration to multiple projects at once.

7
Multi-project Builds

When applications and projects get bigger, we usually split up several parts of the application into separate projects. Gradle has great support for multi-project builds. We can configure multiple projects in an easy way. Gradle is also able to resolve dependencies between projects and can build the necessary projects in the right order, so we don't have to switch to a specific directory to build the code; Gradle will resolve the correct project order for us.

In this chapter, we will discuss about multi-project configuration and dependencies. First, we will look at how to configure projects and tasks. Then we will use a multi-project Java application to learn how to have inter-project dependencies and how Gradle resolves them for us.

Working with multi-project builds

Let's start with a simple multi-project structure. We have a root project called garden with two other projects, tree and flower. The project structure is as follows:

```
└─ garden
   ├─ flower
   └─ tree
```

We learn how we can invoke tasks in a multi-project build as follows:

1. We will add a new `printInfo` task to each of these projects. The task will print the name of the project to `System.out`. We must add a `build.gradle` file to each project with the following contents:

```
task printInfo << {
    println "This is ${project.name}"
}
```

2. To execute the task for each project, we must first enter the correct directory and then invoke the task with Gradle. We can also run `build.gradle` for a specific project with the `-b` argument of Gradle. We will get the following output if we run the `printInfo` task for each project:

```
garden $ gradle -q printInfo
This is garden
garden $ cd tree
tree $ gradle -q printInfo
This tree
tree $ cd ..
garden $ gradle -b flower/build.gradle -q printInfo
This is flower
garden $
```

We have multiple projects, but we haven't used Gradle's support for multi-project builds yet.

3. Let's reconfigure our projects and use Gradle's multi-project support. We need to add a new file, `settings.gradle`, in the `garden` directory. In this file, we will define the projects that are part of our multi-project build. We use the `include()` method to set the projects that are part of our multi-project build. The project with the `settings.gradle` file is automatically part of the build. We will use the following line in the `settings.gradle` file to define our multi-project build:

```
include('tree', 'flower')
```

4. Now, we can execute the `printInfo` task for each project with a single command. We will get the following output if we execute the task:

```
garden $ gradle printInfo
:printInfo
This is garden
:flower:printInfo
This is flower
```

```
:tree:printInfo
This is tree
BUILD SUCCESSFUL
Total time: 0.684 secs
```

Executing tasks by project path

We see the output of each invocation of the `printInfo` task. The path of the `project` task is also displayed. The root project is denoted by a colon (`:`) and has no explicit name. The `flower` project is referenced as `:flower`, and the `printInfo` task of the `flower` project is referenced as `:flower:printInfo`. The path of a task is the name of the project, with a colon (`:`) followed by the task name. The colon separates the project and task name. We can also reference a specific task in a project using this syntax from the command line. If we want to invoke the `printInfo` task of the `flower` project, we can run the following command:

```
garde $ gradle :flower:printInfo
:flower:printInfo
This is flower
BUILD SUCCESSFUL
Total time: 0.649 secs
```

This also works for executing tasks in a root project from another project directory. If we first go to the `flower` project directory and want to execute the `printInfo` task of the root project, we must use the `:printInfo` syntax. We get the following output if we execute the `printInfo` task of the root project, current project, and `flower` project from the `tree` project directory:

```
tree $ gradle :printInfo printInfo :flower:printInfo
:printInfo
This is garden
:tree:printInfo
This is tree
:flower:printInfo
This is flower
BUILD SUCCESSFUL
Total time: 0.632 secs
```

Gradle takes a couple of steps to determine whether a project must be executed as a single or multi-project build, as follows:

1. First, Gradle looks for a `settings.gradle` file in a directory with the name `master` at the same level as the current directory.

2. If `settings.gradle` is not found, the parent directories of the current directory are searched for a `settings.gradle` file.

3. If `settings.gradle` is still not found, the project is executed as a single-project build.

4. If a `settings.gradle` file is found, and the current project is part of the multi-project definition, the project is executed as part of the multi-project build. Otherwise, the project is executed as a single-project build.

We can force Gradle to not look for a `settings.gradle` file in the parent directories with the `--no-search-upward` (or `-u`) command-line argument.

Using a flat layout

In our current project setup, we have defined a hierarchical layout of the projects. We placed the `settings.gradle` file in the parent directory, and with the `include()` method, we added the `tree` and `flower` projects to our multi-project build.

We can also use a flat layout to set up our multi-project build, which can be done as follows:

1. We must first create a `master` directory in the `garden` directory.

2. We must move our `build.gradle` and `settings.gradle` files from the `garden` directory to the `master` directory.

3. As we don't have a hierarchical layout anymore, we must replace the `include()` method with the `includeFlat()` method. Our `settings.gradle` file now looks similar to the following code:

```
// Include tree and flower projects
// as part of the build.
includeFlat('tree', 'flower')
```

The projects are referenced via the parent directory of the `master` directory. So, if we define `tree` as an argument for the `includeFlat()` method, the actual path that is used to resolve the project directory is `master/../tree`.

4. To invoke the `printInfo` task for each project, we run Gradle from the `master` directory with the following command:

```
master $ gradle printInfo
Unresolved directive in
Gradle-Effective-Implementation-Guide_07_
1stDraft.adoc -include::/Users/mrhaki/Projects/
gradle-effective-implementation-guide-2/
gradle-impl-guide-  2/src/docs/asciidoc/Chapter7/Code_Files/
multi-project/garden-proj/flat-master/printinfo.output.txt[]
```

Ways of defining projects

We have added a `build.gradle` file to the `tree` and `flower` projects with an implementation of the `printInfo` task. However, with the multi-project support of Gradle, we don't have to do this. We can define all project tasks and properties in the root `build.gradle` file. We can use this to define the common functionality for all projects in a single place.

We can reference a project with the `project()` method and use the complete name of the project as an argument. We must use a closure to define the tasks and properties of the project.

For our example project, we will first remove the `build.gradle` files from the `tree` and `flower` directories. Next, we will change the `build.gradle` file in the `master` directory. Here, we will define the `printInfo` tasks with the `project()` method for the `tree` and `flower` projects, as follows:

```
task printInfo << {
    println "This is ${project.name}"
}

project(':flower') {
    // Add an extra action to the printInfo task.
    task printInfo << {
        println "This is ${project.name}"
    }
}

project(':tree') {
```

```
    // Add an extra action to the printInfo task.
    task printInfo << {
        println "This is ${project.name}"
    }
}
```

If we execute the printInfo task from the master directory, we can see that all printInfo tasks of the projects are invoked:

```
master $ gradle printInfo
:printInfo
This is master
:flower:printInfo
This is flower
:tree:printInfo
This is tree
BUILD SUCCESSFUL
Total time: 0.674 secs
```

Gradle also has the allprojects{} script block to apply project tasks and properties to all projects that are part of the multi-project build. We can rewrite our build.gradle file and use the allprojects{} script block to get a clean definition of the task without repeating ourselves:

```
allprojects {
    // Add task printInfo to all projects:
    // master, flower and tree
    task printInfo << {
        println "This is ${project.name}"
    }
}
```

If we invoke the printInfo task from the master directory, we can see that each project has the newly added task:

```
master $ gradle -q printInfo
This is master
This is flower
This is tree
```

If we only want to configure the `tree` and `flower` subprojects, we must use the `subprojects{}` script block. With this script block, only tasks and properties of the subprojects of a multi-project build are configured. In the following example build file, we will only configure `subprojects`:

```
subprojects {
    // Add task printInfo to all sub projects:
    // flower and tree
    task printInfo << {
        println "This is ${project.name}"
    }
}
```

If we invoke the `printInfo` task, we can see that our `master` project no longer has the `printInfo` task:

```
master $ gradle -q printInfo
This is flower
This is tree
```

Gradle will not throw an exception if the `printInfo` task is not defined for a single project. Gradle will first build a complete task graph for all the projects that are part of the multi-project build. If any of the projects contains the task that we want to run, the task for that project is executed. Only when none of the projects has the task will Gradle fail the build.

We can combine the `allprojects{}` and `subprojects{}` script blocks and the `project()` method to define the common behavior and apply specific behavior for specific projects. In the following sample build file, we add extra functionality to the `printInfo` task at different levels:

```
allprojects {
    task printInfo << {
        println "This is ${project.name}"
    }
}

subprojects {
    // Add an extra action to the printInfo task.
    printInfo << {
        println "Can be planted"
    }
}

project(':tree') {
    // Add an extra action to the printInfo task.
    printInfo << {
```

```
            println "Has leaves"
        }
    }

    project(':flower') {
        // Add an extra action to the printInfo task.
        printInfo << {
            println "Smells nice"
        }
    }
```

Now when we execute the `printInfo` task, we will get the following output:

```
master $ gradle printInfo
:printInfo
This is master
:flower:printInfo
This is flower
Can be planted
Smells nice
:tree:printInfo
This is tree
Can be planted
Has leaves
BUILD SUCCESSFUL
Total time: 0.631 secs
```

We have added a specific behavior to the `tree` and `flower` projects with the `project()` method. However, we could have also added a `build.gradle` file to the `tree` and `flower` projects and added the extra functionality there.

Filtering projects

To apply specific configuration to more than one project, we can also use project filtering. In our `build.gradle` file, we must use the `configure()` method. We will define a filter based on the project names as an argument of the method. In a closure, we define the configuration for each found project.

In the following sample build file, we use a project filter to find the projects that have names that start with `f` and then apply a configuration to the project, as follows:

```
allprojects {
    task printInfo << {
        println "This is ${project.name}"
    }
}

// Find all projects that start with an f.
    ext {
    projectsWithF =
        allprojects.findAll { project ->
            project.name.startsWith('f')
        }
}

// Configure the found projects.
configure(projectsWithF) {
    printInfo << {
        println 'Smells nice'
    }
}
```

When we execute the `printInfo` task, we get the following output:

```
master $ gradle printInfo
:flower:printInfo
This is flower
Smells nice
BUILD SUCCESSFUL
Total time: 0.231 secs
```

We have used the project name as a filter. We can also use project properties to define a filter. As project properties are only set after the build is defined, either with a `build.gradle` file or with the `project()` method, we must use the `afterEvaluate()` method. This method is invoked once all projects are configured and the project properties are set. We will pass our custom configuration as a closure to the `afterEvaluate()` method.

In the following example build file, we read the `hasLeaves` project property for the `tree` and `flower` projects. If the property is `true`, we customize the `printInfo` task for this project:

```
allprojects {
    task printInfo << {
        println "This is ${project.name}"
```

```
        }
    }

    subprojects {
        // After all projects have been evaluated
        // the properties are set and we can check
        // the value.
        afterEvaluate { project ->
            if (project.hasLeaves) {
                printInfo << {
                    println "Has leaves"
                }
            }
        }
    }

    project(':tree') {
        ext.hasLeaves = true
    }

    project(':flower') {
        ext.hasLeaves = false
    }
```

When we execute the printInfo task from the master directory, we get the following output:

```
master $ gradle printInfo
:printInfo
This is master
:flower:printInfo
This is flower
:tree:printInfo
This is tree

as leaves
BUILD SUCCESSFUL
Total time: 0.667 secs
```

Defining task dependencies between projects

If we invoke the printInfo task, we see that the printInfo task of the flower project is executed before the tree project. Gradle uses the alphabetical order of the projects, by default, to determine the execution order of the tasks. We can change this execution order by defining explicit dependencies between tasks in different projects.

If we first want to execute the printInfo task of the tree project before the flower project, we can define that the printInfo task of the flower project depends on the printInfo task of the tree project. In the following example build file, we will change the dependency of the printInfo task in the flower project. We will use the dependsOn() method to reference the printInfo task of the tree project, as follows:

```
allprojects {
    task printInfo << {
        println "This is ${project.name}"
    }
}

project(':flower') {
    printInfo.dependsOn(':tree:printInfo')
}
```

If we execute the printInfo task, we will see in the output that the printInfo task of the tree project is executed before the printInfo task of the flower project:

```
master $ gradle printInfo
:printInfo
This is master
:tree:printInfo
This is tree
:flower:printInfo
This is flower
BUILD SUCCESSFUL
Total time: 0.637 secs
```

Defining configuration dependencies

Besides task dependencies between projects, we can also include other configuration dependencies. For example, we could have a project property set by one project that is used by another project. Gradle will evaluate the projects in alphabetical order. In the following example, we will create a new `build.gradle` file in the `tree` directory and set a property on the root project:

```
rootProject.ext.treeMessage = 'I am a tree'
```

We will also create a `build.gradle` file in the `flower` project and set a project property with a value based on the root project property set by the `tree` project, as follows:

```
ext.message = rootProject.hasProperty('treeMessage') ?
 rootProject.treeMessage : 'is not set'

printInfo << {
    println "Tree say ${message}"
}
```

When we execute the `printInfo` task, we get the following output:

```
master $ gradle printInfo
:printInfo
This is master
:flower:printInfo
This is flower
Tree say I am a tree
:tree:printInfo
This is tree
BUILD SUCCESSFUL
Total time: 0.578 secs
```

Note that the `printInfo` task in the `flower` project cannot display the value of the root project property as the value is not yet set by the `tree` project. To change the evaluation order of the project, we can explicitly define that the `flower` project depends on the `tree` project with the `evaluationDependsOn()` method. We can change the `build.gradle` file in the `flower` directory and add `evaluationDependsOn(':tree')` to the top of the file:

```
evaluationDependsOn(':tree')

ext.message = rootProject.hasProperty('treeMessage') ?
  rootProject.treeMessage : 'is not set'

printInfo << {
    println "Tree say ${message}"
}
```

When we execute the `printInfo` task again, we see in the output that the value of the root project property is available in the `flower` project:

```
master $ gradle printInfo
:printInfo
This is master
:flower:printInfo
This is flower
Tree say I am a tree
:tree:printInfo
This is tree
BUILD SUCCESSFUL
Total time: 0.578 secs
```

Working with Java multi-project builds

In a Java project, we usually have compile or runtime dependencies between projects. For example, the output of one project is a compile dependency for another project. This is very common in Java projects. Let's create a Java project with a `common` project that contains a Java class used by other projects. We will add a `services` project that references the class in the `common` project. Finally, we will add a `web` project with a Java servlet class that uses classes from the `services` project.

We have the following directory structure for our project:

```
.
├── build.gradle
├── common
│   └── src
```

```
|          └── main
|               └── java
|                    └── sample
|                         └── gradle
|                              └── util
|                                   └── Logger.java
├── services
|    └── sample
|         └── src
|              ├── main
|              |    └── java
|              |         └── sample
|              |              └── gradle
|              |                   ├── api
|              |                   |    └── SampleService.java
|              |                   └── impl
|              |                        └── SampleImpl.java
|              └── test
|                   └── java
|                        └── sample
|                             └── gradle
|                                  └── impl
|                                       └── SampleTest.java
├── settings.gradle
└── web
     └── src
          └── main
               ├── java
               |    └── gradle
               |         └── sample
               |              └── web
               |                   └── SampleServlet.java
               └── webapp
                    └── WEB-INF
                         └── web.xml
```

In the root directory, we will create a settings.gradle file. We will use the include()
method to add the common, web, and services/sample projects to the build:

```
include('common', 'services:sample', 'web')
```

Next, we will create a `build.gradle` file in the root directory. We will apply the Java plugin for each subproject and add a `testCompile` dependency on the JUnit libraries. This configuration is applied to each subproject in our build. Our `:services:sample` project has a dependency on the `common` project. We will configure this dependency in the project configuration of `:services:sample`. We will use the `project()` method to define this inter-project dependency. Our web project uses classes from both `:common` and `:services:sample` projects. We only have to define the dependency on the `:services:sample` project. Gradle will automatically add the dependencies for this project to the `:web` project. In our project, this means that the `:common` project is also added as a transitive project dependency and we can use the `Logger` class from this project in our `SampleServlet` class. We will add another external dependency for the servlet API to our `:web` project and also apply the `war` plugin to our `:web` project, as follows:

```
subprojects {
    apply plugin: 'java'

    repositories {
        mavenCentral()
    }

    dependencies {
        testCompile 'junit:junit:4.8.12'
    }
}

project(':services:sample') {
    dependencies {
        // Dependency on the common project classes.
        compile project(':common')
    }
}

project(':web') {
    apply plugin: 'war'

    dependencies {
        // Dependency on the sample classes.
        compile project(':services:sample')
        compile 'javax.servlet:servlet-api:2.5'
    }
}
```

The project dependencies are also called lib dependencies. These dependencies are used to evaluate the execution order of the projects. Gradle will analyze the dependencies and then decide the project that needs to be built first so that the resulting classes can be used by dependent projects.

Let's build our project with the following command from the root directory:

```
$ gradle build
:common:compileJava
:common:processResources UP-TO-DATE
:common:classes
:common:jar
:common:assemble
:common:compileTestJava UP-TO-DATE
:common:processTestResources UP-TO-DATE
:common:testClasses UP-TO-DATE
:common:test UP-TO-DATE
:common:check UP-TO-DATE
:common:build
:services:compileJava UP-TO-DATE
:services:processResources UP-TO-DATE
:services:classes UP-TO-DATE
:services:jar
:services:assemble
:services:compileTestJava UP-TO-DATE
:services:processTestResources UP-TO-DATE
:services:testClasses UP-TO-DATE
:services:test UP-TO-DATE
:services:check UP-TO-DATE
:services:build
:services:sample:compileJava
:services:sample:processResources UP-TO-DATE
:services:sample:classes
:services:sample:jar
:web:compileJava
:web:processResources UP-TO-DATE
:web:classes
:web:war

web:assemble
:web:compileTestJava UP-TO-DATE
:web:processTestResources UP-TO-DATE
:web:testClasses UP-TO-DATE
:web:test UP-TO-DATE
:web:check UP-TO-DATE
:web:build
:services:sample:assemble
:services:sample:compileTestJava
```

```
:services:sample:processTestResources UP-TO-DATE
:services:sample:testClasses
:services:sample:test
:services:sample:check
:services:sample:build
BUILD SUCCESSFUL
Total time: 3.786 secs
```

A lot of tasks are executed, but we don't have to worry about their dependencies. Gradle will make sure that the correct order of tasks is executed.

We can also have project dependencies based on a configuration in a project. Suppose we define a separate JAR artifact with only the SampleService class in the :services:sample project. We can add this as a separate dependency to our :web project. In the following example build file, we will create a new JAR file with the SampleService class and then use this as a lib dependency in the :web project:

```
subprojects {
    apply plugin: 'java'

    repositories {
        mavenCentral()
    }

    dependencies {
        testCompile 'junit:junit:4.8.2'
    }
}

project(':services:sample') {
    configurations {
        api
    }

    task apiJar(type: Jar) {
        baseName = 'api'
        dependsOn classes
        from sourceSets.main.output
        include 'sample/gradle/api/SampleService.class'
    }

    artifacts {
        api apiJar
    }

    dependencies {
        compile project(':common')
```

```
    }
}

project(':web') {
    apply plugin: 'war'

    dependencies {
        compile project(path: ':services:sample', configuration: 'api')
        compile project(':services:sample')
        compile 'javax.servlet:servlet-api:2.5'
    }
}
```

Using partial builds

Due to the lib dependencies between projects, we can execute partial builds in Gradle. This means that we don't have to be in the root directory of our project to build the necessary projects. We can change to a project directory and invoke the build task from there and Gradle will build all the necessary projects first and then the current project.

Let's change to the `services/sample` directory, invoke the build task from there, and check the output:

```
$ cd services/sample
sample $ gradle build
:common:compileJava
:common:processResources UP-TO-DATE
:common:classes
:common:jar
:services:sample:compileJava
:services:sample:processResources UP-TO-DATE
:services:sample:classes
:services:sample:jar
:services:sample:assemble
:services:sample:compileTestJava
:services:sample:processTestResources UP-TO-DATE
:services:sample:testClasses
:services:sample:test
:services:sample:check
:services:sample:build
BUILD SUCCESSFUL
Total time: 1.676 secs
```

The `:common` project is built before our `:services:sample` project. If we don't want the projects that we are dependent on to be built, we must use the `--no-rebuild` (or `-a`) command-line argument. Gradle will then skip the building the projects that our project depends on and will use cached versions of the dependencies.

When we use the `-a` argument while invoking the `build` task, we get the following output:

```
sample $ gradle -a build
:services:sample:compileJava UP-TO-DATE
:services:sample:processResources UP-TO-DATE
:services:sample:classes UP-TO-DATE
:services:sample:jar UP-TO-DATE
:services:sample:assemble UP-TO-DATE
:services:sample:compileTestJava UP-TO-DATE
:services:sample:processTestResources UP-TO-DATE
:services:sample:testClasses UP-TO-DATE
:services:sample:test UP-TO-DATE
:services:sample:check UP-TO-DATE
:services:sample:build UP-TO-DATE
BUILD SUCCESSFUL
Total time: 0.638 secs
```

If we invoke the `build` task on our `:services:sample` project, the `:common` project is also built. However, there is a catch as only the `jar` task of the `:common` project is executed. Normally, the `build` task also runs tests and executes the `check` task. Gradle will skip these tasks only if the project is built as a lib dependency.

If we want to execute the tests and checks for the dependency projects, we must execute the `buildNeeded` task. Gradle will then perform a complete build of all the dependent projects. Let's execute the `buildNeeded` task from the `services/sample` directory and look at the output:

```
sample $ gradle buildNeeded
:common:compileJava UP-TO-DATE
:common:processResources UP-TO-DATE
:common:classes UP-TO-DATE
:common:jar UP-TO-DATE
:common:assemble UP-TO-DATE
:common:compileTestJava UP-TO-DATE
:common:processTestResources UP-TO-DATE
:common:testClasses UP-TO-DATE
:common:test UP-TO-DATE
:common:check UP-TO-DATE
:common:build UP-TO-DATE
:common:buildNeeded UP-TO-DATE
:services:sample:compileJava UP-TO-DATE
```

```
:services:sample:processResources UP-TO-DATE
:services:sample:classes UP-TO-DATE
:services:sample:jar UP-TO-DATE
:services:sample:assemble UP-TO-DATE
:services:sample:compileTestJava UP-TO-DATE
:services:sample:processTestResources UP-TO-DATE
:services:sample:testClasses UP-TO-DATE
:services:sample:test UP-TO-DATE
:services:sample:check UP-TO-DATE
:services:sample:build UP-TO-DATE
:services:sample:buildNeeded UP-TO-DATE
BUILD SUCCESSFUL
Total time: 0.651 secs
```

If we have made changes to our `:services:sample` project, we may also want projects that are dependent on the `sample` project to be built. We can use this to make sure that we have not broken any code that depends on our project. Gradle has a `buildDependents` task to do this. For example, let's execute this task from our `:services:sample` project, our `:web` project is also built as it has a dependency on the `:services:sample` project. We will get the following output when we execute the `buildDependents` task:

```
sample $ gradle buildDependents
:common:compileJava UP-TO-DATE
:common:processResources UP-TO-DATE
:common:classes UP-TO-DATE
:common:jar UP-TO-DATE
:services:sample:compileJava UP-TO-DATE
:services:sample:processResources UP-TO-DATE
:services:sample:classes UP-TO-DATE
:services:sample:apiJar
:services:sample:jar UP-TO-DATE
:web:compileJava
:web:processResources UP-TO-DATE
:web:classes
:web:war
:web:assemble
:web:compileTestJava UP-TO-DATE
:web:processTestResources UP-TO-DATE
:web:testClasses UP-TO-DATE
:web:test UP-TO-DATE
:web:check UP-TO-DATE
:web:build
:web:buildDependents
:services:sample:assemble UP-TO-DATE
:services:sample:compileTestJava UP-TO-DATE
:services:sample:processTestResources UP-TO-DATE
:services:sample:testClasses UP-TO-DATE
```

```
:services:sample:test UP-TO-DATE
:services:sample:check UP-TO-DATE
:services:sample:build UP-TO-DATE
:services:sample:buildDependents
 BUILD SUCCESSFUL
Total time: 0.709 secs
```

Using the Jetty plugin

In the previous section, we created a Java project with a `web` subproject. The `web` project has a simple servlet. To execute the servlet, we must create a WAR file and deploy the WAR file to a servlet container, such as Tomcat or Jetty. You can learn more about Jetty at `http://www.eclipse.org/jetty/`. With the Jetty plugin, we can run our `web` project from the command line in a Jetty web container. We don't have to install Jetty on our computer, we only need to apply the Jetty plugin to our project. The plugin will take care of configuring Jetty and starting the web container. If everything is okay, we can open a web browser and access our servlet.

To add the Jetty plugin to our `web` project, let's create a new `build.gradle` file in the web directory. Here, we will use the `apply()` method to add the Jetty plugin to the project:

```
apply plugin: 'jetty'
```

The plugin adds the following tasks to our project: `jettyRun`, `jettyRunWar`, and `jettyStop`. The following table shows the different tasks:

Task	Depends on	Type	Description
jettyRun	classes	JettyRun	This is to start a Jetty web container and deploy the exploded web application
jettyRunWar	war	JettyRunWar	This is to start a Jetty web container and deploy the WAR file
jettyStop	–	JettyStop	This is to stop a running Jetty web container

We can test our servlet in a web browser after we execute the `jettyRun` or `jettyWar` task. We get the following output when we execute the `jettyRun` task from the root of the multi-project build:

```
$ gradle :web:jettyRun
:common:compileJava
```

```
:common:processResources UP-TO-DATE
:common:classes
:common:jar
:services:sample:compileJava
:services:sample:processResources UP-TO-DATE
:services:sample:classes
:services:sample:apiJar
:services:sample:jar
:web:compileJava
:web:processResources UP-TO-DATE
:web:classes
> Building 92% > :web:jettyRun > Running at http://localhost:8080/web
```

Gradle will keep running, and at the end, we will see that the application is running at `http://localhost:8080/web`. We can open a web browser and access our web application. In the following screenshot, we can see the output of the servlet:

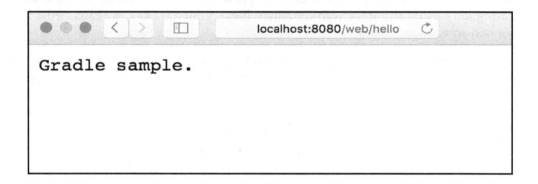

Results of web application in web browser

To stop the Jetty web container, press *Ctrl + C* at the command line to return to our prompt.

We can change the port number via the `httpPort` project convention property added by the Jetty plugin or the `httpPort` task property of the `jettyRun` and `jettyRunWar` tasks. To change the context path, we can set the `contextPath` property of the `jettyRun` and `jettyRunWar` tasks.

If we want the Jetty container to automatically scan for changes, we can set the `reload` property to `automatic`. If the property is set to `manual`, we must press *Enter* on the command line to reload changes. We can set the scan interval in seconds with the `scanIntervalSeconds` property.

In the following sample build file, we will customize the Jetty web container with another HTTP port, context path, and automatic reloading:

```
apply plugin: 'jetty'

httpPort = 8090

jettyRun {
    contextPath = 'sample'
    reload = 'automatic'
    scanIntervalSeconds = 10
}
```

We can even customize the Jetty container further with custom Jetty configuration files. We could use the jettyRun task property, jettyConfig, to use configuration files. We can also add extra runtime libraries with the additionalRuntimeJars property.

If we want to use the jettyStop task, we must also define the stopPort and stopKey properties in either our project or task. If we have defined these properties, we can open a new command-line prompt and invoke the jettyStop task to stop a running Jetty web container.

In the following example build file, we will apply some of these properties and methods to customize the Jetty configuration:

```
apply plugin: 'jetty'
configurations {
    // Extra configuration to
    // be used in the jettyRun task.
    jettyAdditionalLibs
}
dependencies {
    jettyAdditionalLibs 'org.slf4j:slf4j-simple:1.7.3'
}
// Properties for stopping Jetty with jettyStop
stopPort = 8109
stopKey = 'JettyStop'
jettyRun {
    // External Jetty configuration file.
    jettyConfig = file('src/jetty/jetty.xml')
    // Extra libraries for Jetty runtime.
    additionalRuntimeJars configurations.jettyAdditionalLibs
}
```

Summary

Multi-project builds are very common in software projects. Gradle has great support for multi-project builds. We can use a hierarchical layout as the project structure, but we can easily customize this and use other layouts.

Configuring projects is easy and can be done in one place—at the root of the projects. We can also add project configurations at the project level itself. Not only can we define the dependencies between projects on a project-library level, but we can also do so via configuration or task dependencies. Gradle will resolve the correct way to build the complete project so that we don't have to worry too much about that.

As Gradle knows the projects that will be involved before a task is executed, we can do partial multi-project builds. Gradle will automatically build project dependencies, which are necessary for our current project, and we can use a single task to build the projects that depend on our current project.

We also saw how to run our web application code in a Jetty web container with the Jetty plugin. We applied the plugin and executed the `jettyRun` or `jettyRunWar` tasks to run our code as a web application. We can now open a web browser and execute our code.

In the next chapter, we will take a look at how to use other languages, besides Java, with Gradle.

8
Mixed Languages

We have seen how to use Gradle for projects with Java code. Gradle has support for other languages as well. In the last couple of years, other languages for JVM have emerged. In this chapter, we will take a look at Gradle's support for Groovy and Scala languages. Both languages are supported by JVM.

We will see how to apply the correct plugin and configuration to our Gradle build files to work with the different languages.

Gradle also supports C. The C plugin adds support to compile source files. JavaScript and Closure plugins are available as third-party plugins, which add support for these languages. We will not cover this support in this book. We will focus on the JVM languages-Groovy and Scala.

Using the Groovy plugin

To use Groovy sources in our project, we can apply the Groovy plugin. The Groovy plugin makes it possible to compile Groovy source files to class files. The project can contain both Java and Groovy source files. The compiler that Gradle uses is a joint compiler that can compile Java and Groovy source files.

The plugin also adds new tasks to our build. To compile the Groovy source files, we can invoke the `compileGroovy` task. Test sources written in Groovy can be compiled with the `compileTestGroovy` task. Also, a `compile<SourceSet>Groovy` task is added for each extra source set in our build definition. So, if we create a new source set with the name `api`, there will be a `compileApiGroovy` task.

In the following example build file, we apply the Groovy plugin:

```
apply plugin: 'groovy'
```

If we invoke the `tasks` task to see what is available, we get the following output:

```
$ gradle tasks
:tasks
-----------------------------------------------------------------
All tasks runnable from root project
-----------------------------------------------------------------
Build tasks
-----------
assemble - Assembles the outputs of this project.
build - Assembles and tests this project.
buildDependents - Assembles and tests this project and all projects that
depend on it.
buildNeeded - Assembles and tests this project and all projects it depends
on.
classes - Assembles main classes.
clean - Deletes the build directory.
jar - Assembles a jar archive containing the main classes.
testClasses - Assembles test classes.
Build Setup tasks
-----------------
init - Initializes a new Gradle build. [incubating]
wrapper - Generates Gradle wrapper files. [incubating]
Documentation tasks
-------------------
groovydoc - Generates Groovydoc API documentation for the main source code.
javadoc - Generates Javadoc API documentation for the main source code.
Help tasks
----------
buildEnvironment - Displays all buildscript dependencies declared in root
project 'groovy'.
components - Displays the components produced by root project 'groovy'.
[incubating]
dependencies - Displays all dependencies declared in root project 'groovy'.
dependencyInsight - Displays the insight into a specific dependency in root
project 'groovy'.
help - Displays a help message.
model - Displays the configuration model of root project 'groovy'.
[incubating]
projects - Displays the sub-projects of root project 'groovy'.
properties - Displays the properties of root project 'groovy'.
tasks - Displays the tasks runnable from root project 'groovy'.
Verification tasks
------------------
```

```
check - Runs all checks.
test - Runs the unit tests.
Rules
-----
Pattern: clean<TaskName>: Cleans the output files of a task.
Pattern: build<ConfigurationName>: Assembles the artifacts of a
configuration.
Pattern: upload<ConfigurationName>: Assembles and uploads the artifacts
belonging to a configuration.
To see all tasks and more detail, run gradle tasks --all
To see more detail about a task, run gradle help --task <task>
BUILD SUCCESSFUL
Total time: 1.378 secs
```

Note that we also got all the tasks from the Java plugin. This is because the Groovy plugin automatically includes the Java plugin. So, even though we only defined the Groovy plugin in our build file, the Java plugin is applied as well.

The extra `compileGroovy` and `compileTestGroovy` tasks are visible in the command output. The new tasks are dependency tasks for the `classes` and `testClasses` tasks. If we invoke the `classes` task, the `compileGroovy` task is also executed.

The plugin adds the groovy configuration. The Groovy compiler uses this configuration. Therefore, to compile Groovy source files in our project, we must set a dependency on the `compile` configuration.

To compile Groovy source files, we must add a dependency with the Groovy library that we want to use to the `compile` configuration. We might expect that Gradle will use the Groovy version that is used by Gradle, but the compilation task is independent of the Groovy version used by Gradle. We have to define the Groovy library ourselves.

It is good to be independent of the Groovy libraries shipped with Gradle as we can then use the Groovy version we really need. When we want to use the Groovy libraries shipped with Gradle, we can use the `localGroovy()` special dependency. For a normal Groovy project, this is not advised; but for plugin development, it is useful.

First, we create a Groovy source file so that we can compile it with Gradle. The default source directory for Groovy source files is `src/main/groovy`. Let's create a new file in the `src/main/groovy/gradle/sample` directory, with the name `Sample.groovy`. The following code shows the contents of this file:

```
// File: src/main/groovy/gradle/sample/Sample.groovy
package gradle.sample

import groovy.transform.ToString
```

```
@ToString
class Sample {
    String name
}
```

Next, we create a Gradle build file and apply the Groovy plugin. We add the Bintray JCenter repository and a Groovy dependency to the `compile` configuration, as follows:

```
apply plugin: 'groovy'

repositories {
    jcenter()
}

dependencies {
    // Define dependency for Groovy libraries.
    compile group: 'org.codehaus.groovy',
        name: 'groovy',
        version: '2.4.5'
}
```

When we run the `build` task, we get the following output:

```
$ gradle build
:compileJava UP-TO-DATE
:compileGroovy
:processResources UP-TO-DATE
:classes
:jar
:assemble
:compileTestJava UP-TO-DATE
:compileTestGroovy UP-TO-DATE
:processTestResources UP-TO-DATE
:testClasses UP-TO-DATE
:test UP-TO-DATE
:check UP-TO-DATE
:build
BUILD SUCCESSFUL
Total time: 6.081 secs
```

When we don't have the specified Groovy library in our cache, it is downloaded by Gradle from the Bintray JCenter repository. The source code file is compiled, and if we look in the `build/classes` directory, we can see the compiled class file.

The Groovy plugin also adds new source set properties. The following table shows the extra properties:

Property name	Type	Description
groovy	org.gradle.api.file.SourceDirectorySet	These are the Groovy source files for this project. This contains both .java and .groovy source files if they are in the groovy directory.
groovy.srcDirs	java.util.Set<java.io.File>	These are the directories with the Groovy source files. They can also contain Java source files for joint compilation.
allGroovy	org.gradle.api.file.FileTree	These consist of only the Groovy source files. All files with extension .groovy are part of this collection.

We extend our previous build file and add the groovySourceSetsProperties task. We print the extra properties and their values with this task. The build now looks similar to the following code:

```
apply plugin: 'groovy'

repositories {
    jcenter()
}

dependencies {
    // Use String notation to define dependency.
    compile 'org.codehaus.groovy:groovy:2.4.5'
}

// New task to print out source set properties
```

```
// added by the Groovy plugin.
task groovySourceSetProperties << {
    sourceSets.main.with { sourceSet ->
        println "groovy.srcDirs = ${sourceSet.groovy.srcDirs}"
        println "groovy.files = ${sourceSet.groovy.files.name}"
        println "allGroovy.files = ${sourceSet.allGroovy.files.name}"
    }
}
```

When we run the `groovySourceSetProperties` task on the command line, we see the following output:

```
$ gradle groovySourceSetProperties
:groovySourceSetProperties
groovy.srcDirs = [/gradle-
book/samples/Chapter8/Code_Files/groovy/src/main/groovy]
groovy.files = [Sample.groovy]
allGroovy.files = [Sample.groovy]
BUILD SUCCESSFUL
Total time: 0.729 secs
```

When our Java code uses Groovy classes, and vice versa, we can use the joint compilation feature. We must make sure that both Java and Groovy source files are in the `src/main/groovy` directory.

Creating documentation with the Groovy plugin

The Groovy plugin also adds the `groovydoc` task. The `groovydoc` task is like the `javadoc` task from the Java plugin. Gradle uses the `GroovyDoc` tool, which is available from the Groovy version that we have defined as a dependency of the `compile` configuration.

The task has several properties that we can change. For example, we can set the header and footer to be used in the generated documentation.

In the following build file, we will configure the `groovydoc` task:

```
apply plugin: 'groovy'

// Set version for project, we use
// it in the configuration for groovydoc.
version = 1.0

repositories {
    jcenter()
}
```

```
dependencies {
    compile 'org.codehaus.groovy:groovy:2.4.5'
}

// Configure groovydoc task.
groovydoc {
    header = 'GroovyDoc for sample project'
    footer = "Generated documentation - $version"
    docTitle = 'GroovyDoc Title'
    windowTitle = docTitle
    use = true // Create class and package usage pages

    // Exclude files, use include to include files
    exclude '**/*Doc.groovy'
}
```

When we run the `groovydoc` task, we can see the generated documentation in the `build/docs/groovydoc` directory. We must open the `index.html` file in our web browser to see the result.

Using the Scala plugin

We can also use Gradle to work with Scala source files. We can have a Scala-only project or both Java and Scala source files in our project. We must apply the Scala plugin to enable the Scala support for our build. The plugin adds new tasks to compile the Scala source files. With the `compileScala` task, we compile our main Scala source files. The source files must be in the `src/main/scala` directory. The `compileTestScala` task compiles all Scala source code files that are in the `src/test/scala` directory. The plugin also adds a `compile<SourceSet>Scala` task for custom-defined source sets in our build.

The compile tasks support both Java and Scala source files with joint compilation. We can place our Java source files in say the `src/main/java` directory of our project and the Scala source files in the `src/main/scala` directory. The compiler will compile both types of files. To be able to compile the files, we must add dependencies to the Scala library in our build file. We must assign the correct dependencies from a Maven repository to the `compile` configuration so that Gradle can invoke the compiler to compile the source files.

Let's create a simple Scala source file in the `src/main/scala/gradle/` directory sample and save it as `Sample.scala`:

```
package gradle.sample

class Sample(val name: String) {
    def getName() = name
}
```

In the following example build file, we apply the Scala plugin. Also, in the `dependencies` section, we set the correct dependencies for the compiler, as follows:

```
apply plugin: 'scala'

repositories {
    jcenter()
}

dependencies {
    // Define dependency on Scala library
    // for compilation and Scala tools.
    compile group: 'org.scala-lang',
      name: 'scala-library',
      version: '2.11.4'
}
```

To build the project, we invoke the `build` task and get the following output:

```
$ gradle build
:compileJava UP-TO-DATE
:compileScala
:processResources UP-TO-DATE
:classes
:jar
:assemble
:compileTestJava UP-TO-DATE
:compileTestScala UP-TO-DATE
:processTestResources UP-TO-DATE
:testClasses UP-TO-DATE
:test UP-TO-DATE
:check UP-TO-DATE
:build

BUILD SUCCESSFUL
Total time: 2.656 secs
```

Note how the `compileScala` and `compileTestScala` tasks are dependency tasks for the `classes` and `testClasses` tasks, respectively. So, the newly added tasks are automatically part of the normal build tasks that we know from our Java projects. The Scala plugin will automatically include the Java plugin if we don't apply the Java plugin ourselves.

We can define a custom source set in our project. The Scala plugin adds a `compile` task for each source set to our project. In the following Gradle build file, we add a new source set with the name `actors`, as follows:

```
apply plugin: 'scala'

repositories {
    jcenter()
}

dependencies {
    compile "org.scala-lang:scala-library:2.11.4"
}

sourceSets {
    // Extra source set actors.
    actors
}
```

When we invoke the `tasks` command, we see that Gradle added `compileActorsScala` to the list of available tasks:

```
$ gradle tasks --all
:tasks
------------------------------------------------------------
All tasks runnable from root project
------------------------------------------------------------

Build tasks
-----------
actorsClasses - Assembles actors classes.
compileActorsJava - Compiles actors Java source.
compileActorsScala - Compiles the actors Scala source.
processActorsResources - Processes actors resources.
assemble - Assembles the outputs of this project. [jar]
build - Assembles and tests this project. [assemble, check]
buildDependents - Assembles and tests this project and all projects that
depend on it. [build]
buildNeeded - Assembles and tests this project and all projects it depends
on. [build]
classes - Assembles main classes.
compileJava - Compiles main Java source.
```

```
compileScala - Compiles the main Scala source.
processResources - Processes main resources.
clean - Deletes the build directory.
jar - Assembles a jar archive containing the main classes. [classes]
testClasses - Assembles test classes. [classes]
compileTestJava - Compiles test Java source.
compileTestScala - Compiles the test Scala source.
processTestResources - Processes test resources.
...
BUILD SUCCESSFUL
Total time: 0.76 secs
```

The `actorsClasses` task is added and has all the compile tasks for the `actors` source set. When we want the `actorsClasses` task to be part of the build task, we can assign it as a task dependency to the `jar` task. In the following example build file, we use the `from()` method of the `jar` task to assign the output of the `actors` source set as part of the JAR file contents.

When we execute the `build` task, our source files in the `actors` source set are compiled and added to the JAR file.

The Scala plugin also adds several new properties to a source set. The following table shows the extra properties:

Property name	Type	Description
scala	org.gradle.api.file.SourceDirectorySet	This is the Scala source files for this project; it contains both .java and .scala source files if they are in the Scala directory.
scala.srcDirs	java.util.Set<java.io.File>	These are the directories with the Scala source files; they can also contain Java source files for joint compilation.
allScala	org.gradle.api.file.FileTree	These are only the Scala source files. All files with the .scala extension are part of this collection.

Let's create a new task, scalaSourceSetsProperties, to see the contents of each of these properties:

```
apply plugin: 'scala'

repositories {
    jcenter()
}

dependencies {
    compile "org.scala-lang:scala-library:2.11.4"
}

// New task to show properties on the
// main source set added by the Scala plugin.
task scalaSourceSetsProperties << {
    sourceSets.main.with { sourceSet ->
        println "scala.srcDirs = ${sourceSet.scala.srcDirs}"
        println "scala.files = ${sourceSet.scala.files.name}"
        println "allScala.files = ${sourceSet.allScala.files.name}"
    }
}
```

When we invoke the scalaSourceSetsProperties task from the command line, we get the following output:

```
$ gradle scalaSourceSetsProperties
:scalaSourceSetsProperties
scala.srcDirs = [/gradle-
book/samples/Chapter8/Code_Files/scala/src/main/scala]
scala.files = [Sample.scala]
allScala.files = [Sample.scala]
BUILD SUCCESSFUL
Total time: 0.627 secs
```

Creating documentation with the Scala plugin

The Scala plugin also adds a scaladoc task to our build. We can use this task to generate documentation from the source files. This is like the javadoc task from the Java plugin. We can configure the scaladoc task to provide extra options.

In the following example build file, we add a title to the generated documentation by configuring the `scaladoc` task:

```
import org.gradle.api.tasks.scala.*

apply plugin: 'scala'

version = 2.1

repositories {
    jcenter()
}

dependencies {
    compile "org.scala-lang:scala-library:2.11.4"
}

// Configure ScalaDoc task.
scaladoc {
    title = 'Scala documentation'
}
```

When we invoke the `scaladoc` task, Gradle will generate the documentation and the result is in `build/docs/scaladoc`. We can open the `index.html` file in our web browser to see the generated documentation.

Summary

In this chapter, we discussed how to work with Groovy and Scala sources in a Gradle project. We applied the either Groovy or Scala plugins to our project and saw that Gradle added the tasks to compile the source files to the project. We also discussed that we must add a dependency to the correct Groovy or Scala version of the dependency configuration added by the plugin. Both plugins will include the Java plugin as well.

We also discussed that the plugins also provide some new properties for source sets so that we can, for example, find all Groovy or Scala source files in a source set.

In the next chapter, we will take a look at how to add code quality tools to our Gradle builds.

9
Maintaining Code Quality

While working on a project, we want to have some kind of tooling or process in place, which we can use to see whether our code follows certain standards; either our code has no common coding problems or it calculates the complexity of the code.

We need these tools to write better code. Better code means that it will be easier to maintain, and this lowers the cost of maintaining the code. In a project team, we want to make sure that the code follows the same standards defined by the project team. A company could define a set of standards that developers need to follow as a condition for the project to be started.

There tools are already available for Java and Groovy projects to analyze and check the source code, such as **Checkstyle**, **JDepend**, **PMD**, **FindBugs**, and **CodeNarc**. Gradle has plugins for each of these tools. In this chapter, we will take a look at the following plugins and discuss how to use them in our projects:

- Checkstyle
- PMD
- FindBugs
- JDepend
- CodeNarc

Using the Checkstyle plugin

If we are working on a Java project, and we apply the Java plugin to our project, we will get an empty task, named `check`. This is a dependency task for the `build` task. This means that when we execute the `build` task, the `check` task is executed as well. We can write our own tasks to check something in our project and make it a dependency task for the `check` task.

So if the `check` task is executed, our own task is executed as well. Not only the tasks that we write ourselves, but also the plugins can add new dependency tasks to the `check` task.

In this chapter, we will see that most plugins will add one or more tasks as a dependency task to the `check` task. This means that we can apply a plugin to our project, and when we invoke the `check` or `build` task, the extra tasks of the plugin are executed automatically.

Also, the `check` task is dependent on the `test` task. Gradle will always make sure that the `test` task is executed before the `check` task, so we know that all source files and test source files are compiled, and tests are run before the code is checked. To add the Checkstyle analysis to our project, we simply have to apply the `checkstyle` plugin, as follows:

```
apply plugin: 'java'
apply plugin: 'checkstyle'
```

If we invoke the `tasks` task from the command line, we can see that new tasks have been added by the plugin:

```
$ gradle tasks --all
:tasks
------------------------------------------------------------
All tasks runnable from root project
------------------------------------------------------------

. . .
Verification tasks
------------------
check - Runs all checks. [classes, test, testClasses]
    checkstyleMain - Run Checkstyle analysis for main classes
    checkstyleTest - Run Checkstyle analysis for test classes
test - Runs the unit tests. [classes, testClasses]
. . .
BUILD SUCCESSFUL
Total time: 1.194 secs
```

The `checkstyleMain` and `checkstyleTest` tasks are added as dependencies for the `check` task. The tasks run the Checkstyle analysis for the main and test classes.

We cannot execute these tasks yet as we have to add a Checkstyle configuration file to our project. This file contains the rules that we want to apply to our code. The plugin will look for a `checkstyle.xml` file in the `config/checkstyle` directory in our project. This is the default location and filename, but we can change it.

Let's create a configuration file with the following content:

```
<?xml version="1.0"?>
<!DOCTYPE module PUBLIC
    "-//Puppy Crawl//DTD Check Configuration 1.3//EN"
    "http://www.puppycrawl.com/dtds/configuration_1_3.dtd">
<module name="Checker">
    <module name="JavadocPackage"/>
    <module name="NewlineAtEndOfFile"/>
    <module name="RegexpSingleline">
        <property name="format" value="\s+$"/>
        <property name="minimum" value="0"/>
        <property name="maximum" value="0"/>
        <property name="message" value="Line has trailing spaces."/>
    </module>

    <module name="TreeWalker">
        <module name="IllegalImport"/>
        <module name="RedundantImport"/>
        <module name="UnusedImports"/>
        <module name="AvoidNestedBlocks"/>
        <module name="EmptyBlock"/>
        <module name="LeftCurly"/>
        <module name="NeedBraces"/>
        <module name="RightCurly"/>
        <module name="DesignForExtension"/>
        <module name="FinalClass"/>
        <module name="HideUtilityClassConstructor"/>
        <module name="InterfaceIsType"/>
        <module name="VisibilityModifier"/>
    </module>

</module>
```

The `checkstyle` plugin does not add the required library dependencies to our project automatically. We need to add an appropriate repository to our project so that the `checkstyle` plugin can download all the dependencies.

Let's create the following example build file and add the repository definition:

```
apply plugin: 'java'
apply plugin: 'checkstyle'

repositories {
    // Add repository so Checkstyle
    // dependencies can be downloaded.
    jcenter()
}
```

Now we can run the check task and see the output:

```
$ gradle check
:compileJava
:processResources UP-TO-DATE
:classes
:checkstyleMain
[ant:checkstyle] /Projects/gradle-
bookChapter9/Code_Files/checkstyle/src/main/java/gradle/sample/JavaSample.j
ava:0: File does not end with a newline.
[ant:checkstyle] /Projects/gradle-
bookChapter9/Code_Files/checkstyle/src/main/java/gradle/sample/JavaSample.j
ava:0: Missing package-info.java file.
[ant:checkstyle] /Projects/gradle-
bookChapter9/Code_Files/checkstyle/src/main/java/gradle/sample/JavaSample.j
ava:9: Line has trailing spaces.
[ant:checkstyle] /Projects/gradle-
bookChapter9/Code_Files/checkstyle/src/main/java/gradle/sample/JavaSample.j
ava:14: Line has trailing spaces.
[ant:checkstyle] /Projects/gradle-
bookChapter9/Code_Files/checkstyle/src/main/java/gradle/sample/JavaSample.j
ava:15: Line has trailing spaces.
[ant:checkstyle] /Projects/gradle-
bookChapter9/Code_Files/checkstyle/src/main/java/gradle/sample/JavaSample.j
ava:17:5: Method 'setGreeting' is not designed for extension - needs to be
abstract, final or empty.
[ant:checkstyle] /Projects/gradle-
bookChapter9/Code_Files/checkstyle/src/main/java/gradle/sample/JavaSample.j
ava:21:5: Method 'getGreeting' is not designed for extension - needs to be
abstract, final or empty.
[ant:checkstyle] /Projects/gradle-
bookChapter9/Code_Files/checkstyle/src/main/java/gradle/sample/JavaSample.j
ava:25:5: Method 'greet' is not designed for extension - needs to be
abstract, final or empty.
[ant:checkstyle] /Projects/gradle-
bookChapter9/Code_Files/checkstyle/src/main/java/gradle/sample/JavaSample.j
ava:29:5: Method 'equals' is not designed for extension - needs to be
abstract, final or empty.
:checkstyleMain FAILED
FAILURE: Build failed with an exception.
* What went wrong:
Execution failed for task ':checkstyleMain'.
> Checkstyle rule violations were found. See the report at:
file:///Projects/gradle-
book/Chapter9/Code_Files/checkstyle/build/reports/checkstyle/main.html
* Try:
Run with --stacktrace option to get the stack trace. Run with --info or --
debug option to get more log output.
```

```
BUILD FAILED
Total time: 1.296 secs
```

The `checkstyleMain` task has been executed and the build has failed because our code doesn't follow our Checkstyle rules. In the output, we can see all the violations of the rules. Gradle will also create an XML and HTML file with the violations in the `build/reports/checkstyle` directory.

If we don't want the build to fail, we can use the `ignoreFailures` property of the `checkstyle` tasks. The checks are still executed and the report files are generated, but the build will not fail.

We can configure the checkstyle plugin with the `checkstyle{}` script block or `checkstyle` property in a Gradle build. The script block accepts a configuration closure, where we can change the properties. In the following build file, we will set the `ignoreFailures` property to true, so the build will not fail even after Checkstyle finds errors:

```
apply plugin: 'java'
apply plugin: 'checkstyle'

repositories {
    jcenter()
}

// Configuration for Checkstyle.
checkstyle {
    // The build will not fail if there
    // are violations found.
    ignoreFailures = true
}
```

To change the version of Checkstyle that is used by Gradle is setting the `toolVersion` property in the `checkstyle{}` configuration block. We can assign a different version than the one that is available by default in Gradle.

In the following sample build file, we will use the `toolVersion` property to use Checkstyle version 5.7:

```
apply plugin: 'java'
apply plugin: 'checkstyle'

repositories {
    jcenter()
}
```

```
checkstyle {
    // Use version 5.7 of Checkstyle.
    toolVersion = '5.7'
}
```

The plugin also adds a new dependency configuration, named `checkstyle`. We will use this configuration to add dependencies that are needed by the Checkstyle tool.

To change the Checkstyle configuration file, we can set the `configFile` property to a different value in the `checkstyle{}` configuration block. The default value is `config/checkstyle/checkstyle.xml`. We can, for example, copy the `sun_checks.xml` configuration file from a Checkstyle distribution to the `config/checkstyle` directory. We will set the `configFile` property with the value of this new file and our code is checked using the rules from the `sun_checks.xml` configuration file.

The following sample build file shows that we have referenced another Checkstyle configuration file:

```
apply plugin: 'java'
apply plugin: 'checkstyle'

repositories {
    jcenter()
}

// Configuration for Checkstyle.
checkstyle {
    // Use a different configuration file.
    configFile = file('config/checkstyle/sun_checks.xml')
}
```

A Checkstyle configuration supports property expansion. This means that the configuration file has variable property values with the `${propertyName}` syntax. We can set the value for such a property using the `configProperties` property of the Checkstyle configuration closure. This property accepts a map, where the keys are the property names from the Checkstyle configuration file and the values are the property values. If the Checkstyle configuration file has a property, named `tabWidth`; for example, we can set the value with the following example build file:

```
apply plugin: 'java'
apply plugin: 'checkstyle'

repositories {
    jcenter()
```

```
}

// Configuration for Checkstyle.
checkstyle {
    // Define key-value pairs to replace properties
    // in the configuration file.
    configProperties = [tabWidth: 10]
}
```

We use the `checkstyle{}` script block to change the properties for all the `checkstyle` tasks in a project. However, we can also configure individual `checkstyle` tasks in our build file. We have the `checkstyleMain` and `checkstyleTest` tasks and we can alter their configuration just like any other task.

Let's create the following example build file and change the properties of the `checkstyleTest` task, which will override the properties set in the `checkstyle{}` script block:

```
apply plugin: 'java'
apply plugin: 'checkstyle'

repositories {
    jcenter()
}

// Set checkstyle options, that are used by
// all checkstyle tasks.
checkstyle {
    configFile = file('config/checkstyle/sun_checks.xml')
}

// Reconfigure the checkstyleTest task.
checkstyleTest {
    configFile = file('config/checkstyle/test.xml')
    ignoreFailures = true
}
```

If we have defined custom source sets in our build, then the `checkstyle` plugin automatically adds a `checkstyle<SourceSet>` task to the project. If our source set is named `api`, then we can invoke the `checkstyleApi` task to only check this source set. The `checkstyleApi` task is also added as a dependency task for the `check` task. Therefore, once we run the `check` task, Gradle will invoke the `checkstyleApi` task as well.

In the following example build file, we will create a new source set, named `api`:

```
apply plugin: 'java'
apply plugin: 'checkstyle'

repositories {
    jcenter()
}

sourceSets {
    // Add new source set with
    // the name api. This will
    // add a task checkstyleApi.
    api
}
```

If we invoke the `tasks` task, we can see in the output that a newly created task `checkstyleApi` is added, which is a dependency task for the `check` task:

```
$ gradle tasks --all
:tasks
------------------------------------------------------------
All tasks runnable from root project
------------------------------------------------------------

. . .
Verification tasks
------------------
check - Runs all checks. [apiClasses, classes, test, testClasses]
    checkstyleApi - Run Checkstyle analysis for api classes
    checkstyleMain - Run Checkstyle analysis for main classes
    checkstyleTest - Run Checkstyle analysis for test classes
test - Runs the unit tests. [classes, testClasses]
. . .
```

The report XML files that are generated are placed in the `build/reports/checkstyle` directory. The name of the files is based on the source set name. So the `checkstyleMain` task will generate the `build/reports/checkstyle/main.xml` report file. We can configure this in our build file. We can change the directory containing the reports with the `reportsDir` property. We can change the destination file for a specific `checkstyle` task with the `destination` property. We can also disable the report generation with the `enabled` property for a given task.

The following sample build file changes the reporting directory and the destination file for the `checkstyleMain` task and disables report generation for the `checkstyleTest` task:

```
apply plugin: 'java'
```

```
apply plugin: 'checkstyle'

repositories {
    jcenter()
}

checkstyle {
    // Change the output directory.
    reportsDir = file("${buildDir}/checkstyle-output")
}

checkstyleTest {
    // Disable running CheckStyle for the test classes.
    reports.xml.enabled = false
}

// Configure the checkstyle task for the main source set.
checkstyleMain {
    reports {
        xml {
            // Change the destination and filename of the
            // XML file with results generated by CheckStyle.
            destination = file("${checkstyle.reportsDir}/checkstyle.xml")
        }
    }
}
```

Using the PMD plugin

Another tool to analyze the Java source code is PMD. It finds unused variables, empty catch blocks, unnecessary object creation, and so on. We can configure our own rule sets and even define our own rules. To use PMD with Gradle, we have to apply the PMD plugin to our build. After we have added the plugin, we have the `pmdMain` and `pmdTest` tasks already installed. These tasks will run PMD rules for the main and test source sets. If we have a custom source set, then the plugin adds a `pmd<SourceSet>` task as well. These tasks are also dependency tasks of the `check` task. So if we invoke the `check` task, all the `pmd` tasks are executed as well.

This plugin only defines a structure to work with PMD, but it doesn't contain the actual PMD library dependencies. Gradle will download the PMD dependencies the first time that we invoke the `pmd` tasks. We have to define a repository that contains the PMD libraries, such as the Bintray JCenter repository or a corporate intranet repository.

In the following build file, we apply the `pmd` plugin and define a custom source set:

```
apply plugin: 'java'
apply plugin: 'pmd'

repositories {
    // We need a repository, so the
    // PMD dependencies can be downloaded.
    jcenter()
}

sourceSets {
    // New source set with
    // the name util.
    util
}
```

When we invoke the `check` task, we get the following output if there are no rule violations:

```
$ gradle check
:pmdMain
:compileJava
:processResources UP-TO-DATE
:classes
:pmdTest UP-TO-DATE
:pmdUtil
:compileTestJava UP-TO-DATE
:processTestResources UP-TO-DATE
:testClasses UP-TO-DATE
:test UP-TO-DATE
:check
BUILD SUCCESSFUL
Total time: 1.735 secs
```

Note the `pmdMain`, `pmdTest`, and `pmdUtil` tasks that are executed.

If one of the files has a violation, then the build will fail by default. We can set the `ignoreFailures` property for the `pmd` tasks to true so that the build does not fail. The following sample build shows how to set the `ignoreFailures` property to true:

```
apply plugin: 'java'
apply plugin: 'pmd'

repositories {
    jcenter()
}

sourceSets {
```

```
        util
    }

pmd {
    // Don't fail the build process when
    // rule violations are found.
    ignoreFailures = true
}
```

Rule violations will be reported in an XML and HTML file in the `build/reports/pmd` directory. The name of the file is the same as the source set name. We can change the name of the reporting directory and output filename or we can also disable the report generation.

The following example build file changes several properties of the reporting with the `pmd` tasks:

```
apply plugin: 'java'
apply plugin: 'pmd'

repositories {
    jcenter()
}

sourceSets {
    util
}

pmd {
    // Change base reporting dir for PDM reports.
    reportsDir = file("${reporting.baseDir}/pmd-output")
}

configure(tasks.withType(Pmd)) {
    // Disable HTML report generation for all PDM tasks.
    reports.html.enabled = false
}

// Special configuration for the pmd task
// that runs for the source set main.
pmdMain {
    reports {
        xml {
            // Change output file for XML report.
            destination = file("${pmd.reportsDir}/pmd.xml")
        }
    }
}
```

Only the basic rule set of PMD is applied if we don't define anything else in the build file. To change the rule sets that are applied, we can use the `ruleSets` property and `ruleSets()` method. With the `ruleSets()` method, we have a convenient way to add new rules. With the `ruleSets` property, we have to define all the rules that we want to use as a property assignment.

Besides configuring the rule sets, we can also assign rule set files for pmd tasks. A rule set file contains several rules and allows customization of the rules. To add a rule set file, we can use the `ruleSetFiles` property or `ruleSetFiles()` method. We need to reference a file to set the property or pass it as a method argument.

The following sample build file shows how to set rules and rule set files:

```
apply plugin: 'java'
apply plugin: 'pmd'

repositories {
    jcenter()
}

pmd {
    // Add rule sets with the ruleSets method.
    ruleSets 'design', 'braces'

    // Or use property syntax.
    // ruleSets = ['design', 'braces']

    // Set rule set files via the task
    // property ruleSetFiles.
    ruleSetFiles = files('config/pmd/customRules.xml')

    // Or use ruleSetFiles method to add new file
    // to existing collection of files.
    //ruleSetFiles file('config/pmd/customRules.xml')
}
```

To change the version of PMD that we want to use, we must set the `toolVersion` property of the PMD plugin. At the time of writing this book, this was set to version 5.2.3, but we can change it to other versions if required. In the following example build file, we will simply change the version to 5.2.3 with the `toolVersion` property:

```
apply plugin: 'java'
apply plugin: 'pmd'

repositories {
    jcenter()
```

```
}

pmd {
    // Use a different version of PMD.
    toolVersion = '5.4.1'
}
```

Using the FindBugs plugin

FindBugs is another library that we can use to analyze our source code. To use FindBugs in our Gradle builds, we will simply have to apply the `findbugs` plugin. We can either apply one source code analysis plugin to our project or we can apply multiple plugins. Each tool has different features. It just depends on what we want to check or what is prescribed per company policy. The plugin will add the `findbugsMain` and `findbugsTest` tasks to analyze the source code from the main and test source sets. If we have a custom source set, then the `findbugs<SourceSet>` task is also added to the plugin. These tasks are all dependency tasks for the `check` task.

Just as with the other code quality plugins, the FindBugs dependencies are not included with Gradle, but they will be downloaded the first time we use `findbugs` tasks. We must include a repository definition that will enable Gradle to find the FindBugs dependencies. To change the FindBugs version that is being used, we can set the `toolVersion` property of the `findbugs` plugin extension added to our project by the `findbugs` plugin.

In the following build file, we will apply the `findbugs` plugin and configure an extra source set, named `webservice`:

```
apply plugin: 'java'
apply plugin: 'findbugs'

repositories {
    // We need to set a repository where the
    // Findbugs dependencies can be downloaded from.
    jcenter()
}

findbugs {
    // Default version with Gradle 2.10 is 3.0.1.
    toolVersion = '3.0.0'
}

sourceSets {

    // New source set with the name webservice.
```

```
            webservice
    }
```

When we execute the `tasks` task, we will see that the `findbugsMain`, `findbugsTest`, and `findbugsWebservice` tasks are dependencies for the `check` task:

```
$ gradle tasks --all
:tasks
------------------------------------------------------------
All tasks runnable from root project
------------------------------------------------------------
...
Verification tasks
------------------
check - Runs all checks. [classes, test, testClasses, webserviceClasses]
    findbugsMain - Run FindBugs analysis for main classes
    findbugsTest - Run FindBugs analysis for test classes
    findbugsWebservice - Run FindBugs analysis for webservice classes
test - Runs the unit tests. [classes, testClasses]
...
```

If FindBugs finds violations of the rules in our source, then the build will fail. We can set the `ignoreFailures` property to true, as shown in the following lines of code, in order to make sure that the build will continue even if violations are found:

```
apply plugin: 'java'
apply plugin: 'findbugs'

repositories {
    jcenter()
}

// Global setting for all findbugs tasks.
findbugs {
    ignoreFailures = true
}

// We can change ignoreFailures property also per task.
findbugsMain {
    ignoreFailures = false
}
```

The plugin generates an XML report with the result of the FindBugs analysis in the `build/reports/findbugs` directory. The name of the XML file is the same as the name of the source set that is analyzed. We can also configure the plugin so that an HTML report is generated. In the following build file, we will configure the reporting in the `findbugs` plugin:

```
apply plugin: 'java'
apply plugin: 'findbugs'

repositories {
    jcenter()
}

findbugs {
    // Change base directory for FindBugs reports.
    reportsDir = file("${reporting.baseDir}/findbugs-output")
}

// Configure the findbugs task for the main source set.
findbugsMain {
    reports {
        html {
            enabled = true

            // Change output file name.
            destination = "${findbugs.reportsDir}/findbugs.html"
        }

        // Only one report (xml or html) can be active.
        xml {
            enabled = !html.enabled
        }
    }
}
```

If we want to use `findbugs` plugins, we can define them as dependencies. The `findbugs` plugin adds a `findbugs` dependency configuration. We can assign plugin dependencies to this configuration, and the `findbugs` tasks will use these plugins to analyze the code.

Using the JDepend plugin

To get quality metrics for our code base, we can use JDepend. JDepend traverses the generated class files in our project and generates design quality metrics. To use JDepend, we will simply have to apply the `jdepend` plugin in our project. This will add `jdependMain` and `jdependTest` tasks. For each extra source set in our project, a `jdepend<SourceSet>` task is added. These tasks are all dependency tasks of the `check` task.

We must configure a repository so that Gradle can fetch the JDepend dependencies. Gradle doesn't provide the JDepend libraries in the Gradle distribution. This means that we can easily use another version of JDepend, independent of the Gradle version that we are using. We see this behavior in the other code quality plugins as well. To change a version number, we will simply have to set the `toolVersion` property of the `jdepend` plugin extension.

In the following example build file, we will apply the `jdepend` plugin and create an extra source set:

```
apply plugin: 'java'
apply plugin: 'jdepend'

repositories {
    // Repository is need to the JDepend dependencies
    // can be downloaded.
    jcenter()
}

// We can change the version of JDepend to be used.
jdepend{
    // Default version with Gradle 2.10 is JDepend 2.9.1
    toolVersion = '2.9.1'
}

// Custom source set so jdependRestApi task is created.
sourceSets {
    restApi
}
```

When we invoke the `tasks` task, we will see that three `jdepend` tasks are created as a dependency for the `check` task:

```
$ gradle tasks --all
:tasks

------------------------------------------------------------
All tasks runnable from root project
```

```
----------------------------------------------------------
. . .
Verification tasks
------------------
check - Runs all checks. [classes, restApiClasses, test, testClasses]
    jdependMain - Run JDepend analysis for main classes
    jdependRestApi - Run JDepend analysis for restApi classes
    jdependTest - Run JDepend analysis for test classes
test - Runs the unit tests. [classes, testClasses]
. . .
```

The jdepend tasks create statistics about our code. The results are stored in an XML file in the build/reports/jdepend directory. We can configure the jdepend plugin so that the directory that we store the reports in is different than the default directory. For each jdepend task, we can also alter the output format. Instead of XML, we can generate a text file with the statistics about our code. We have to choose between XML and text; we cannot choose both report outputs for a single jdepend task.

The following sample build file shows several options on how to change the reports with information about our source code:

```
apply plugin: 'java'
apply plugin: 'jdepend'

repositories {
    // Repository is need to the JDepend dependencies
    // can be downloaded.
    jcenter()
}

// We can change the version of JDepend to be used.
jdepend{
    reportsDir = file("${reporting.baseDir}/jdepend-output")
}

// Configure JDepend for the main source set.
jdependMain {
    reports {
        // Configure text output.
        text {
            enabled = true

            // Set destination file.
            destination = file("${jdepend.reportsDir}/jdepend.txt")
        }
        xml {
            // Only text or XML output can be enabled.
```

```
                    enabled = !text.enabled
            }
        }
    }
```

Using the CodeNarc plugin

To check code written in the Groovy language, we can use CodeNarc. CodeNarc has several rules to do a static analysis of Groovy code. Gradle has a `codenarc` plugin, so we can apply the rules from CodeNarc to our Groovy code base. If we apply the plugin, we automatically get a `codenarcMain` and `codenarcTest` target. Also, for each custom source set, we get a new `codenarc<SourceSet>` task. All these tasks are dependency tasks of the `check` task.

The CodeNarc library is not included with Gradle. We need to define a repository in our build file that contains CodeNarc. If we invoke a `codenarc` task, then Gradle sets CodeNarc dependencies. We can change the version of CodeNarc that we want to use by setting `toolVersion` of the `codenarc` property of the plugin extension.

The plugin defines that we provide a CodeNarc configuration file with the name `codenarc.xml` in the `config/codenarc` directory. We can change the reference to the configuration file with the `configFile` property of the plugin extension.

Let's create the following example build file and apply the `codenarc` plugin for a Groovy project. We will change the version of CodeNarc to what we want to use. We will also redefine the location of the CodeNarc configuration file to `config/codenarc/custom.xml`:

```
apply plugin: 'groovy'
apply plugin: 'codenarc'

repositories {
    // Define repository for downloading
    // Codenarc dependencies.
    jcenter()
}

codenarc {
    // Change version of CodeNarc.
    toolVersion = '0.24.1'

    // Change name of configuration file. Default value
    // is file('config/codenarc/codenarc.xml')
    configFile = file('config/codenarc/rules.groovy')
}
```

When we run the check task and our Groovy code base starts violating the configured
CodeNarc rules, the build will fail. If we don't want the build to fail on a violation, we can
set the `ignoreFailures` property to true. We can set this for all `codenarc` tasks with
the `codenarc.ignoreFailures` property. We can also set this property for
individual `codenarc` tasks.

The following build file shows that we can set the `ignoreFailures` property for all
the `codenarc` tasks:

```
apply plugin: 'groovy'
apply plugin: 'codenarc'

repositories {
    jcenter()
}

codenarc {
    // Keep running the build even
    // if there are violations. We can
    // check the reports for violations.
    ignoreFailures = true
}
```

The `codenarc` tasks create an HTML report with the found results and place it in
the `build/reports/codenarc` directory. The name of the file is defined by the source set
name for which the task is executed. We can also choose different output formats. We can
set the output to XML or text file formats. We can change the format of the reports with
the `reports()` method of `codenarc` tasks. To change the output directory, we can set
the `codenarc.reportsDir` property in our project, as follows:

```
apply plugin: 'groovy'
apply plugin: 'codenarc'

repositories {
    jcenter()
}

codenarc {
    configFile = file('config/codenarc/rules.groovy')

    // Change output directory for reports.
    reportsDir = file("${reporting.baseDir}/codenarc-output")
}

tasks.withType(CodeNarc) { task ->
    reports {
```

```
        // Enable text format.
        text {
            enabled = true
        }

        // Configure XML output.
        xml {
            enabled = true

            // Change destination file.
            destination = file("${codenarc.reportsDir}/${task.name}.xml")
        }
    }
}
```

Summary

In this chapter, we discussed that it is easy to use code analysis tools in a Gradle project. We can use Checkstyle, PMD, JDepend, and FindBugs for Java projects. For Groovy projects, we can use CodeNarc. All the plugins of these tools add new tasks to our project for each source set to do the analysis. Each of these tasks is a dependency task for the check task. So when we apply the plugin in a normal build, the code analysis will take place. We also discussed that the usage and syntax are mostly identical for each plugin.

In the next chapter, we will take a look at how to write our own custom task and plugin. We'll also discuss how to make it reusable in other Gradle builds.

10
Writing Custom Tasks and Plugins

In Gradle, we can either write a simple task in a build file, where we add actions with a closure, or we can configure an existing task that is included in Gradle. The process of writing our own task is easy. There are different ways to create a custom task, which we will cover in this chapter:

- We will see how to create a new task class in our build file and use it in our project.
- We will discuss how to create custom tasks in a separate source file. We will also discuss how to make our task reusable in other projects.
- We will discuss how to write a plugin for Gradle. Similar to writing custom tasks, we will cover the different ways to write a plugin. We will also see how to publish our plugin and discuss how to use it in a new project.
- We can write our tasks and plugins in Groovy, which works very well with the Gradle API, but we can also use other languages, such as Java and Scala. As long as the code is compiled into bytecode, we are fine.

Creating a custom task

When we create a new task in a build and specify a task with the `type` property, we actually configure an existing task. The existing task is called **enhanced task** in Gradle. For example, the `Copy` task type is an enhanced task. We will configure the task in our build file, but the implementation of the `Copy` task is in a separate class file. It is good practice to separate the task usage from task implementation. It improves the maintainability and reusability of the task. In this section, we will create our own enhanced tasks.

Creating a custom task in the build file

First, let's see how to create a task to display the current Gradle version in our build by simply adding a new task with a simple action. We have seen these types of tasks earlier in other sample build files. In the following sample build, we will create a new `info` task:

```
task info(description: 'Show Gradle version') << {
    println "Current Gradle version: $project.gradle.gradleVersion"
}
```

When we invoke the `info` task from the command line, we will see the following output:

```
$ gradle info
:info
Current Gradle version: 2.10
BUILD SUCCESSFUL
Total time: 0.829 secs
```

Now, we are going to create a new task definition in our build file and make it an enhanced task. We will create a new class in our build file and this class extends `org.gradle.api.DefaultTask`. We will write an implementation for the class by adding a new method. To indicate that the method is the action of the class, we will use the `@TaskAction` annotation.

After we have defined our task class, we can use it in our build file. We will add a task to the `tasks` project container and use the `type` property to reference our new task class.

In the following sample build file, we have a new `InfoTask` task class and the `info` task that uses this new task class:

```
/**
 * New class that defines a Gradle task.
 */
class InfoTask extends DefaultTask {

    /**
     * Method that has the logic for the task.
     * We tell this to Gradle with the @TaskAction annotation.
     */
    @TaskAction
    def info() {
        // Show current Gradle version.
        println "Current Gradle
        version:$project.gradle.gradleVersion"
    }
}
```

```
// Define new task in our Gradle build file
// with name info and of type InfoTask.
// InfoTask implementation is at the top.
task info(type: InfoTask)
```

Next, we will run our build file with the `info` task. In the following output, we can see our current Gradle version:

```
$ gradle info
:info
Current Gradle version:2.10
BUILD SUCCESSFUL
Total time: 0.6 secs
```

To customize our simple task, we can add properties to our task. We can assign values to these properties when we configure the task in our build file.

For our sample task, we will first add a `prefix` property. This property is used when we print the Gradle version instead of the `'Current Gradle version'` text. We give it a default value, so when we use the task and don't set the property value, we still get a meaningful prefix. We can mark our property as optional because of the default value, with the `@Optional` annotation. This way we have documented that our property doesn't need to be configured when we use the task.

If we want another prefix in our output, we can configure the `info` task in our build file. We will assign the `'Running Gradle'` value to the prefix property of our `InfoTask`:

```
/**
 * New class that defines a Gradle task.
 */
class InfoTask extends DefaultTask {

    /**
     * An optional property for our task.
     */
    @Optional
    String prefix = 'Current Gradle version'

    /**
     * Method that has the logic for the task.
     * We tell this to Gradle with the @TaskAction annotation.
     */
    @TaskAction
    def info() {
        // Show current Gradle version.
        println "$prefix: $project.gradle.gradleVersion"
    }
```

```
    }

    // Define new task in our Gradle build file
    // with name info and of type InfoTask.
    // InfoTask implementation is at the top.
    // We give the optional property prefix a value.
    task info(type: InfoTask) {
        prefix = 'Running Gradle'
    }
```

Now, if we run our build file, we can see our new prefix value in the output:

```
$ gradle info
:info
Running Gradle: 2.10
BUILD SUCCESSFUL
Total time: 0.588 secs
```

Using incremental build support

We know Gradle supports incremental builds. This means that Gradle can check whether a task has any dependencies for input or output on files, directories, and properties. If none of these have changed since the last build, the task is not executed. We will discuss how to use annotations with our task properties to make sure that our task supports Gradle's incremental build feature.

We have seen how to use the `inputs` and `outputs` properties of tasks that we have created so far. To indicate the properties of our new enhanced tasks that are input and output properties, the ones used by Gradle's incremental support, we must add certain annotations to our class definition. We can assign the annotation to the `field` property or the `getter` method for the property.

In a previous chapter, we created a task that reads a XML source file and converts the contents to a text file. Let's create a new enhanced task for this functionality. We will use the `@InputFile` annotation for the property that holds the value for the source XML file. The `@OutputFile` annotation is assigned to the property that holds the output file, as follows:

```
    class ConvertTask extends DefaultTask {

        /**
         * Input file for this task and by
         * using the @InputFile annotation we
         * tell Gradle the file can be used
```

```
 * for determining incremental build support.
 */
@InputFile
File source

/**
 * Output file for this task and by
 * using the @OutputFile annotation we
 * tell Gradle the file can be used
 * for determining incremental build support.
 */
@OutputFile
File output

/**
 * Method with the real implementation of the task.
 * We convert the source file and save the output.
 */
@TaskAction
void convert() {
    def xml = new XmlSlurper().parse(source)
    output.withPrintWriter { writer ->
        xml.person.each { person ->
            writer.println "${person.name},${person.email}"
        }
    }
    println "Converted ${source.name} to ${output.name}"
    }
}

// Configure task for this build
task convert(type: ConvertTask) {
    source = file("src/people.xml")
    output = file("$buildDir/convert-output.txt")
}
```

Let's create an XML file with the name `people.xml` in the current directory, with the following code:

```
<?xml version="1.0"?>
<people>
    <person>
        <name>mrhaki</name>
        <email>hubert@mrhaki.com</email>
    </person>
</people>
```

Now, we can invoke the `convert` task in our build file. We can see in the output that the file is converted:

```
$ gradle convert
:convert
Converted people.xml to convert-output.txt
BUILD SUCCESSFUL
Total time: 0.99 secs
```

If we look at the contents of the `convert-output.txt` file, we will see the following values from the source file:

```
$ cat build/convert-output.txt
mrhaki,hubert@mrhaki.com
```

When we invoke the `convert` task for the second time, we can see that Gradle's incremental build support has noticed that the input and output file haven't changed, so our task is up to date:

```
$ gradle convert
:convert UP-TO-DATE
BUILD SUCCESSFUL
Total time: 0.621 secs
```

The following table shows the annotations that we can use to indicate the input and output properties of our enhanced task:

Annotation Name	Description
`@Input`	Indicates that property specifies an input value. When the value of this property changes, the task is not longer up to date.
`@InputFile`	Indicates that property is an input file. Use this for properties that reference a single file of the `File` type.
`@InputFiles`	Marks property as input files for a property that holds a collection of `File` objects.
`@InputDirectory`	Indicates that property is an input directory. Use this for a `File` type property that references a directory structure.
`@OutputFile`	Indicates that property is an output file. Use this for properties that reference a single file of the `File` type.
`@OutputFiles`	Marks property as output files for a property that holds a collection of `File` objects.

@OutputDirectory	Indicates that property is an output directory. Use this for a `File` type property that references a directory structure. If the output directory doesn't exist, it will be created.
@OutputDirectories	Marks property as an output directory Use this for a property that references a collection of `File` objects, which are references to directory structures.
@Optional	If applied to any of the preceding annotations, we will mark it as optional. The value doesn't have to be applied for this property.
@Nested	We can apply this annotation to a JavaBean property. The bean object is checked for any of the preceding annotations. This way, we can use arbitrary objects as input or output properties.

Creating a task in the project source directory

In the previous section, we defined and used our own enhanced task in the same build file. Now we are going to extract the class definition from the build file and put it in a separate file. We are going to place the file in the `buildSrc` project source directory.

Let's move our `InfoTask` to the `buildSrc` directory of our project. We will first create the `buildSrc/src/main/groovy/sample` directory. We will create an `InfoTask.groovy` file in this directory, with the following code:

```
package sample

import org.gradle.api.DefaultTask
import org.gradle.api.tasks.TaskAction

class InfoTask extends DefaultTask {
    /**
    * Task property can be changed by user
    * of this task.
    */
    String prefix = 'Current Gradle version'

    /**
    * Method with actual implementation for this task.
    */
    @TaskAction
    def info() {
        println "$prefix: $project.gradle.gradleVersion"
```

```
        }
    }
```

Notice that we must add `import` statements for the classes of the Gradle API. These imports are implicitly added to a build script by Gradle; but if we define the task outside the build script, we must add the `import` statements ourselves.

In our project build file, we have to only create a new `info` task of the `InfoTask` type. Notice that we must use the package name to identify our `InfoTask` class or add an `import sample.InfoTask` statement:

```
// Define new task of type sample.InfoTask.
task info(type: sample.InfoTask) {
    // Set task property/
    prefix = "Running Gradle"
}
```

If we run the build, we can see that Gradle first compiles the `InfoTask.groovy` source file, as follows:

```
$ gradle info
:buildSrc:compileJava UP-TO-DATE
:buildSrc:compileGroovy
:buildSrc:processResources UP-TO-DATE
:buildSrc:classes
:buildSrc:jar
:buildSrc:assemble
:buildSrc:compileTestJava UP-TO-DATE
:buildSrc:compileTestGroovy UP-TO-DATE
:buildSrc:processTestResources UP-TO-DATE
:buildSrc:testClasses UP-TO-DATE
:buildSrc:test UP-TO-DATE
:buildSrc:check UP-TO-DATE
:buildSrc:build
:info
Running Gradle: 2.10
BUILD SUCCESSFUL
Total time: 1.751 secs
```

As a matter of fact, the `build` task of the `buildSrc` directory is executed. We can customize the build of the `buildSrc` directory by adding a `build.gradle` file. In this file, we can configure tasks, add new tasks, and practically do anything we can in a normal project build file. The `buildSrc` directory can even be a multi-project build.

Let's add a new `build.gradle` file in the `buildSrc` directory. We will add a simple action to the `build` task, which prints the `'Done building buildSrc'` value:

```
// File: buildSrc/build.gradle

// Add new action to the build task
// for the buildSrc directory.
build.doLast {
    println 'Done building buildSrc'
}
```

If we run our project build, we can see the following output:

```
$ gradle info
:buildSrc:compileJava UP-TO-DATE
:buildSrc:compileGroovy UP-TO-DATE
:buildSrc:processResources UP-TO-DATE
:buildSrc:classes UP-TO-DATE
:buildSrc:jar UP-TO-DATE
:buildSrc:assemble UP-TO-DATE
:buildSrc:compileTestJava UP-TO-DATE
:buildSrc:compileTestGroovy UP-TO-DATE
:buildSrc:processTestResources UP-TO-DATE
:buildSrc:testClasses UP-TO-DATE
:buildSrc:test UP-TO-DATE
:buildSrc:check UP-TO-DATE
:buildSrc:build
Done building buildSrc
:info
Running Gradle: 2.10
BUILD SUCCESSFUL
Total time: 0.699 secs
```

Writing tests

As the `buildSrc` directory is similar to any other Java/Groovy project, we can also create tests for our task. We have the same directory structure as that of a Java/Groovy project and we can also define extra dependencies in the `build.gradle` file.

If we want to access a `Project` object in our test class, we can use the `org.gradle.testfixtures.ProjectBuilder` class. With this class, we can configure a `Project` object and use it in our test case. We can optionally configure the name, parent, and project directory before using the `build()` method to create a new `Project` object. We can use the `Project` object, for example, to add a new task with the type of our new enhanced task and see if there are any errors. `ProjectBuilder` is meant for low-level testing. The actual tasks are not executed.

In the following JUnit test, we will test whether the property value can be set. We have a second test to check whether the task of the `InfoTask` type is added to the task container of a project:

```
package sample

import org.junit.*
import org.gradle.api.*
import org.gradle.testfixtures.ProjectBuilder

class InfoTaskTest {

    @Test
    void createTaskInProject() {
        final Task newTask = createInfoTask()
        assert newTask instanceof InfoTask
    }

    @Test
    void propertyValueIsSet() {
        final Task newTask = createInfoTask()
        newTask.configure {
            prefix = 'Test'
        }
        assert newTask.prefix == 'Test'
    }

    private Task createInfoTask() {
        // We cannot use new InfoTask() to create a new instance,
        // but we must use the Project.task() method.
        final Project project = ProjectBuilder.builder().build()
        project.task('info', type: InfoTask)
    }
}
```

In our `build.gradle` file in the `buildSrc` directory, we must add a Maven repository and the dependency on the JUnit libraries using the following lines of code:

```
repositories {
    jcenter()
}

dependencies {
    testCompile 'junit:junit:4.12'
}
```

Our test is automatically executed as the `test` task is part of the build process for the `buildSrc` directory.

Creating a task in a standalone project

To make a task reusable for other projects, we must have a way to distribute the task. Also, other projects that want to use the task must be able to find our task. We will see how to publish our task in a repository and how other projects can use the task in their projects.

We have seen how to place the task implementation from the build file in the `buildSrc` directory. The `buildSrc` directory is similar to a normal Gradle build project, so it is easy to create a standalone project for our task. We only have to copy the contents of the `buildSrc` directory to our newly created project directory.

Let's create a new project directory and copy the contents of the `buildSrc` directory. We must edit the `build.gradle` file of our standalone project. Gradle implicitly added the Groovy plugin and dependencies on the Gradle API and Groovy for us when the `build.gradle` file is in the `buildSrc` directory. Now we have a standalone project and we must add these dependencies ourselves.

The following `build.gradle` file has all the definitions necessary to build and deploy our artifact to a local distribution directory. We could also define a corporate intranet repository so that other projects can reuse our `InfoTask` in their projects:

```
apply plugin: 'groovy'
apply plugin: 'maven'

version = '1.0'
group = 'sample.infotask'

// Set the name for the archive file
// with the code. Is used for deploying
```

```
// to Maven repository.
archivesBaseName = 'infotask'

dependencies {
    // Define dependency on Gradle API classes.
    compile gradleApi()

    // Define dependency on the Groovy version
    // that is part of the Gradle distribution.
    compile localGroovy()
}

uploadArchives {
    repositories {
        mavenDeployer {
            // For our example we deploy to a local
            // directory lib.
            repository(url: 'file:../lib')
        }
    }
}
```

When we invoke the `uploadArchives` task to publish our packaged `InfoTask` in the `../lib` directory, we will see the following output:

```
$ gradle uploadArchives
:compileJava UP-TO-DATE
:compileGroovy
:processResources UP-TO-DATE
:classes
:jar
:uploadArchives
BUILD SUCCESSFUL
Total time: 2.223 secs
```

We have published our task, and other projects can use it in their builds. Remember that anything in the `buildSrc` directory of a project is added automatically to the classpath of the build. However, if we have a published artifact with the task, this will not happen automatically. We must configure our build and add the artifact as a dependency of the build script.

We will use the `buildscript{}` script block in our build to configure the classpath of our Gradle project. To include our published `InfoTask` in a new project, we must add the artifact as a `classpath` configuration dependency for our build.

We will create a new directory and add the following `build.gradle` file to the directory:

```
buildscript {
    repositories {
        maven {
            // Set Maven repository to the local
            // directory we also used to publish
            // our custom Gradle task.
            url = 'file:../lib'
        }
    }
    dependencies {
        // Define dependency on the InfoTask implementation
        // for this build script.
        classpath group: 'sample.infotask',
            name: 'infotask',
            version: '1.0'
    }
}

task info(type: sample.InfoTask)
```

Next, we can run the build and see in the output that the `InfoTask` is executed:

```
$ gradle info
:info
Current Gradle version: 2.10
BUILD SUCCESSFUL
Total time: 0.73 secs
```

Creating a custom plugin

One of the great features of Gradle is the support for plugins. A plugin can contain tasks, configurations, properties, methods, concepts, and more to add extra functionality to our projects. For example, if we apply the Java plugin to our project, we can immediately invoke the compile, test, and build tasks. We also have new dependency configurations that we can use and extra properties that we can configure. The Java plugin itself applies the Java base plugin. The Java base plugin doesn't introduce tasks, but it introduces the concept of source sets. This is a good pattern for creating our own plugins, where a base plugin introduces new concepts and another plugin derives from the base plugin and adds explicit build logic-like tasks.

So a plugin is a good way to distribute build logic that we want to share between projects. We can write our own plugin, give it an explicit version, and publish it too; for example, a repository. Other projects can then reuse the functionality by simply applying the plugin to a project. We can create our own plugins and use them in our projects. We will start by defining the plugin in the build file.

Creating a plugin in the build file

We can create a custom plugin right in the project build file. Similar to a custom task, we can add a new class definition with the logic of the plugin. We must implement the `org.gradle.api.Plugin<T>` interface. The interface has an `apply()` method. When we write our own plugin, we must override this method. The method accepts an object as a parameter. The type of the object is the same as the generic `T` type. When we create a plugin for projects, the `Project` type is used. We can also write plugins for other Gradle types, such as tasks. Then we must use the `Task` type.

We are going to create a simple plugin that will print the Gradle version. The plugin adds a new `info` task to the project. The following sample build file defines a new `InfoPlugin` plugin. We will override the `apply()` method and add a new task to the project, named `info`. This task prints the Gradle version. At the top of the build file, we will use the `apply()` method and reference the plugin by the name `InfoPlugin`, which is the class name of the plugin:

```
/**
 * Plugin class that adds a new task to the project.
 */
class InfoPlugin implements Plugin<Project> {

    void apply(Project project) {
        // Add new info task to the project.
        project.tasks.create('info') << {
            println "Running Gradle: $project.gradle.gradleVersion"
        }
    }

}

apply plugin: InfoPlugin
```

From the command line, we can invoke the `info` task when we run Gradle. We can see the Gradle version in the following output:

```
$ gradle info
:info
Running Gradle: 2.10
BUILD SUCCESSFUL
Total time: 0.567 secs
```

The `info` task always prints the same text before the Gradle version. We can rewrite the task and make the text configurable. A Gradle project has an associated `ExtensionContainer` object. This object can hold all settings and properties that we want to pass to a plugin. We can add a JavaBean to `ExtensionContainer` so that we can configure the bean's properties from the build file. The JavaBean is a so-called **extension object**.

In our sample build file, we will first add a new `InfoPluginExtension` class with a `String` property prefix. This is the JavaBean-compliant class that we add to `ExtensionContainer`. In the `apply()` method, we will use the `create()` method of `ExtensionContainer` to add `InfoPluginExtension` with the name `info` to the project. In the build file, we will configure the `prefix` property using the `info` configuration closure. We can also simply reference the `prefix` property through the `info` extension object:

```
/**
 * Simple JavaBean class that acts as the
 * extension point for the InfoPlugin.
 */
class InfoPluginExtension {

    /**
     * Define property that can be set by
     * the user of the InfoPlugin.
     */
    String prefix = 'Running Gradle'

}

/**
 * Plugin class that adds a new task to the project.
 */
class InfoPlugin implements Plugin<Project> {

    void apply(Project project) {
        // Add InfoPluginExtension to the project.
        // The user can add a info{} configuration block in
```

```
        // the build file to configure the plugin.
        project.extensions.create('info', InfoPluginExtension)

        // Add new info task to the project.
        project.tasks.create('info') << {
            // Use prefix set via info extension.
            println "$project.info.prefix: $project.gradle.gradleVersion"
        }
    }

}

apply plugin: InfoPlugin

info {
    prefix = 'Gradle version'
}
```

If we run the `info` task, we will see our configured `prefix` in the output:

```
$ gradle info
:info
Gradle version: 2.10
BUILD SUCCESSFUL
Total time: 0.62 secs
```

Creating a plugin in the project source directory

We have defined the plugin and used it in the same build file. We will see how to extract the plugin code from the build file and put it in a separate source file in the project source directory. Also, we will discuss how to test the plugin.

When we define the plugin in our build file, we cannot reuse it in other projects. We now have the definition and usage of the plugin in the same file. To separate the definition and usage, we can create the plugin class in the `buildSrc` directory of a Gradle project. In a Gradle multi-project, we must use the `buildSrc` directory of the root project. This means that for a multi-project build, we can reuse the plugin in other projects of the multi-project build.

We already discussed when we wrote a custom task that any sources in the `buildSrc` directory are automatically compiled and added to the classpath of the project. First, we will create the `buildSrc/src/main/groovy/sample` directory. In this directory, we will create an `InfoPlugin.groovy` file with the following code:

```groovy
package sample

import org.gradle.api.*

/**
 * Gradle plugin to show Gradle version.
 */
class InfoPlugin implements Plugin<Project> {

    void apply(Project project) {
        // Add InfoPluginExtension to project accessible
        // via info{} configuration block.
        project.extensions.create('info', InfoPluginExtension)

        // Add info task to project.
        project.tasks.create('info') << {
            println "$project.info.prefix: $project.gradle.gradleVersion"
        }
    }

}
```

Next, we will create the `InfoPluginExtension.groovy` file in the directory:

```groovy
package sample

/**
 * Extension class for the InfoPlugin.
 */
class InfoPluginExtension {

    /**
     * Used in InfoPlugin.
     */
    String prefix
}
```

In our build file in the root of the project, we will reference our plugin with the package and class name:

```
// Apply InfoPlugin from buildSrc directory.
apply plugin: sample.InfoPlugin

// Configure InfoPlugin via InfoPluginExtension.
info {
    prefix = 'Gradle version'
}
```

When we run the info task, we will see in the output that first the plugin code is compiled and then the info task is executed:

```
$ gradle info
:buildSrc:clean
:buildSrc:compileJava UP-TO-DATE
:buildSrc:compileGroovy
:buildSrc:processResources UP-TO-DATE
:buildSrc:classes
:buildSrc:jar
:buildSrc:assemble
:buildSrc:compileTestJava UP-TO-DATE
:buildSrc:compileTestGroovy UP-TO-DATE
:buildSrc:processTestResources UP-TO-DATE
:buildSrc:testClasses UP-TO-DATE
:buildSrc:test UP-TO-DATE
:buildSrc:check UP-TO-DATE
:buildSrc:build
:info
Gradle version: 2.10
BUILD SUCCESSFUL
Total time: 1.815 secs
```

Testing a plugin

One of the tasks that are executed for the project in the buildSrc directory is the test task. We can write test cases for testing the plugin code, just like in any other project. We add a build.gradle file in buildSrc and define the dependencies for the JUnit test framework. In the following sample build file, we will add a dependency for JUnit:

```
repositories {
    jcenter()
}

dependencies {
```

```
    testCompile 'junit:junit:4.12'
}
```

Next, we can add an `InfoPluginTest.groovy` test case in
the `buildSrc/src/test/groovy/sample` directory:

```groovy
package sample

import org.gradle.api.*
import org.gradle.testfixtures.ProjectBuilder
import org.junit.*

class InfoPluginTest {

    @Test
    void infoTaskIsAddedToProject() {
        final Project project = ProjectBuilder.builder().build()
        project.apply plugin: sample.InfoPlugin
        assert project.tasks.findByName('info')
    }

    @Test
    void configurePrefix() {
        final Project project = ProjectBuilder.builder().build()
        project.apply plugin: sample.InfoPlugin
        project.info.prefix = 'Sample'
        assert project.info.prefix == 'Sample'
    }

}
```

We use the `ProjectBuilder` class to create a fixture for the `Project` object. We can apply
the plugin to the project and then test to see whether the `info` task is available.
The `Project` object cannot execute tasks in the project; it is only for simple checks like this
one.

When we invoke the `info` task from the command line, our test class is compiled and
executed. If a test fails, the project will abort; but if all tests pass, the project continues.

Creating a plugin in a standalone project

We have defined our plugin in the project source directory, but we cannot reuse it in
another project. We will discuss how to distribute our plugin logic, using a standalone
project. Also, we will see how to use the plugin in other projects.

By placing the plugin code in the `buildSrc` directory, we have separated the definition of the plugin and the usage. The plugin still cannot be used by other projects. To make the plugin reusable, we will create a standalone project and create an artifact with the plugin code and publish the artifact to a repository. Other projects can then get the plugin from the repository and use the build logic from the plugin in the project.

We already have the code for the plugin and the test code in the `buildSrc` directory (from the previous section). We can copy this code to a new directory with the project for the plugin. In this new directory, we must also create a `build.gradle` file. The implicit dependencies and plugin added to a project in the `buildSrc` directory must be made explicit in a standalone project.

Let's create a new Gradle project in the `plugin` directory and also create the `build.gradle` file with the following content:

```
apply plugin: 'groovy'
apply plugin: 'maven'

version = '1.0'
group = 'sample.infoplugin'

// Set name of archive containing the plugin.
archivesBaseName = 'infoplugin'

repositories {
    jcenter()
}

dependencies {
    // Define dependency on the Gradle API.
    compile gradleApi()

    // Define dependency on the Groovy version
    // bundled with Gradle.
    compile localGroovy()

    testCompile 'junit:junit:4.12'
}

uploadArchives {
    repositories {
        mavenDeployer {
            // Define a local directory as the
            // Maven repository where the plugin
            // is deployed to.
            repository(url: 'file:../lib')
```

```
          }
      }
  }
```

Next, we will create the `plugin/src/main/groovy/sample`
and `plugin/src/test/groovy/sample` directories. We copy the `InfoPlugin.groovy`
and `InfoPluginExtension.groovy` files to the `src/main/groovy/sample` directory and
the `InfoPluginTest.groovy` file to the `plugin/src/test/groovy/sample` directory.

So far we have all the ingredients to create an artifact JAR file with the plugin code. The
artifact is deployed to the local `../lib` directory. We can, of course, define any Maven or
Ivy repository to deploy the plugin artifact.

To make sure that Gradle can find the plugin, we must provide a `properties` file in
the `plugin/src/main/resources/META-INF/gradle-plugins` directory with the name
of our plugin. The properties file has a `implementation-class` property key with the full
class name of the `Plugin` class.

We want to name our plugin as `info`, so in the `plugin/src/main/resources/META-INF/gradle-plugins` directory, we will create the `info.properties` file with the
following code:

```
implementation-class = sample.InfoPlugin
```

We are ready to create the artifact with the plugin and upload it to our repository. We will
invoke the `uploadArchives` task and get the following output:

```
$ gradle uploadArchives
:compileJava UP-TO-DATE
:compileGroovy
:processResources
:classes
:jar
:uploadArchives
BUILD SUCCESSFUL
Total time: 4.991 secs
```

The plugin is now in the repository. To use the plugin, we must create a new Gradle project.
We must extend the classpath of this new project and include the plugin as a dependency.
We use the `buildscript{}` script block, where we can configure the repository location
and a `classpath` dependency. For our sample, we will reference the local `../lib`
directory. In the dependencies section, we will set the `classpath` configuration to
the `InfoPlugin` artifact.

The following sample build file contains the definitions:

```
buildscript {
    repositories {
        maven {
            // Define local directory lib
            // as Maven repository. This directory
            // contains the plugin we build ourselves.
            url = 'file:../lib'
        }
    }

    dependencies {
        classpath group: 'sample.infoplugin',
            name: 'infoplugin',
            version: '1.0'
    }
}

// Apply plugin. We can use the value 'info',
// because we packaged our plugin with the file
// info.properties.
apply plugin: 'info'

info {
    // Set prefix property for InfoPlugin.
    prefix = "Gradle version"
}
```

Our project now has the `info` task from the plugin. We can configure the plugin extension through the `info` object or the configuration closure.

If we run the `info` task, we will get the following output:

```
$ gradle info
:info
Gradle version: 2.10
BUILD SUCCESSFUL
Total time: 0.739 secs
```

Summary

In this chapter, we discussed how to create our own enhanced task. We also saw how to add the class definition in our build file and use it directly in the build.

If we put the task definition in the `buildSrc` directory of a Gradle project or multi-project build, we can reuse the task in the context of the Gradle build. Also, we now have a good separation of the definition and configuration of the task.

Then, we discussed how to publish the task as an artifact to a repository. Other projects can include the task in their classpath using the `buildscript{}` script block. Then, we can configure and use the task in the project.

In this chapter, we also discussed how to write our own Gradle plugin. We have seen how to add a plugin class to our Gradle build file. Then you learned using the `buildSrc` directory and place the source code of the plugin there.

Finally, to make the plugin really reusable in other projects, we put the plugin code in a separate project. The plugin code is then packaged into a JAR file and published to a repository. Other projects can then define a dependency in the plugin and use the build logic from the plugin.

In the next chapter, we will see how to use Gradle in continuous integration tools.

11
Gradle in the Enterprise

It is good practice to have a continuous integration tool in a software project. With a continuous integration tool, we can automatically build our software in a controlled environment. In this chapter, we are going to take a look at the support for Gradle in several continuous integration tools.

First, we are going to create a sample Java project and use Git as a version control repository. Then, we are going to see how continuous integration servers, such as **Jenkins**, **JetBrains TeamCity**, and **Atlassian Bamboo**, **support Gradle**.

We will cover the following topics in this chapter:

- Creating a sample Java project
- Using Gradle with Jenkins
- Running Gradle tasks with JetBrains TeamCity
- Learning how to set up Atlassian Bamboo for Gradle

Creating a sample project

Before we can see the support for Gradle in the several continuous integration servers, we need to have a sample project. We are going to create a very simple Java project with a test class and add it to a Git repository in this section.

We have already created a Java project earlier. We are going to reuse the code in this chapter for our sample project. We want a test in our project so that we can see how the continuous integration tools can handle test results. Finally, we want more than one artifact for our project; we also want a JAR file with the compiled classes, source code, and Javadoc-generated documentation.

1. We will first create a `build.gradle` file in a directory with the following contents:

```
// We create a Java project so we need the Java plugin
apply plugin: 'java'

// Set base name for archives.
archivesBaseName = 'gradle-sample'

// Version of the project.
version = '1.1'

// Definine JCenter as repository for downloading
// dependencies.
repositories {
    jcenter()
}

// We have a single dependency on JUnit
// for the testCompile configuration
dependencies {
    testCompile 'junit:junit:4.11'
}

// Extra task to create a JAR file with the sources.
task sourcesJar(type: Jar) {
    classifier = 'sources'
    from sourceSets.main.allSource
}

// Extra task to create a JAR file with Javadoc
// generated documentation.
task docJar(type: Jar, dependsOn: javadoc) {
    classifier = 'docs'
    from javadoc.destinationDir
}

// Add extra JAR file to the list of artifacts
// for this project.
artifacts {
    archives sourcesJar
```

```
    archives docJar
}
```

2. Next, we will create three Java source files in the
   `src/main/java/gradle/sample` directory. We already have an interface with a
   single method to return a welcome message:

```
package gradle.sample;

/**
 * Read welcome message from source and return value.
 */
public interface ReadWelcomeMessage {

    /**
     * @return Welcome message
     */
    String getWelcomeMessage();
}
```

3. We will then create an implementation of this interface and return a `String`
   value:

```
package gradle.sample;

import java.util.ResourceBundle;

/**
 * Simple implementation to return welcome message.
 */
public class ReadWelcomeMessageImpl implements
    ReadWelcomeMessage {

    public ReadWelcomeMessageImpl() {
    }

    /**
     * Return "Welcome to Gradle." String value.
     *
     * @return Welcome to Gradle.
     */
    public String getWelcomeMessage() {
        return "Welcome to Gradle.";
    }
}
```

4. Finally, we have a Java application class that uses the interface and implementation class that we already added:

```java
package gradle.sample;

import java.util.ResourceBundle;

public class SampleApp {

    public SampleApp() {
    }

    public static void main(final String[] arguments) {
        final SampleApp app = new SampleApp();
        app.welcomeMessage();
    }

    public void welcomeMessage() {
        final String welcomeMessage = readMessage();
        showMessage(welcomeMessage);
    }

    private String readMessage() {
        final ReadWelcomeMessage reader =
          new ReadWelcomeMessageImpl();
        final String message = reader.getWelcomeMessage();
        return message;
    }

    private void showMessage(final String message) {
        System.out.println(message);
    }
}
```

5. Let's create a test to verify that our `ReadWelcomeMessageImpl` class returns the expected `String` value. We will add the `ReadWelcomeMessageTest.java` file in the `src/test/java/gradle/sample` directory:

```java
package gradle.sample;

import org.junit.Assert;
import org.junit.Test;

public class ReadWelcomeMessageTest {

    @Test
    public void readWelcomeMessage() {
```

```
final ReadWelcomeMessage reader = new
ReadWelcomeMessageImpl();
final String realMessage =
  reader.getWelcomeMessage();

final String expectedMessage = "Welcome to
Gradle.";

Assert.assertEquals("Get text from
  implementation",expected Message, realMessage);
    }
  }
```

6. To check whether everything is okay, we will run Gradle with the `build` task. We should see the following output:

```
$ gradle build
:compileJava
:processResources UP-TO-DATE
:classes
:javadoc
:docJar
:jar
:sourcesJar
:assemble
:compileTestJava
:processTestResources UP-TO-DATE
:testClasses
:test
:check
:build
BUILD SUCCESSFUL
Total time: 3.337 secs
```

7. We have all the source code, so let's put it in a version control repository. We can use any version control system we want, as long as the continuous integration server supports the version control system. We will create a Git repository for our example as it is easy to set up a local repository and then to use it in the continuous integration tools. In order to use Git, we must first have it installed on our computers. We will create a new Git repository in the current project directory with the `init` command in Git:

```
$ git init
Initialized empty Git repository
in  /Users/mrhaki/Projects/sample-project
```

8. Next, we will add the file to the Git staging area with the `add` command:

```
$ git add .
```

9. We will commit the code to the repository with the `commit` command in Git:

```
$ git commit -m "First commit."
create mode 100644 build.gradle
create mode 100644 build.output.txt
create mode 100644 src/main/java/gradle/sample/
ReadWelcomeMessage.java
create mode 100644 src/main/java/gradle/sample/
ReadWelcomeMessageImpl.java
create mode 100644 src/main/java/gradle/sample/SampleApp.java
create mode 100644 src/test/java/gradle/sample/
ReadWelcomeMessageTest.java
```

Our project is now ready to be used in the continuous integration tools.

Using Jenkins

One of the most popular open source continuous integration tools is Jenkins. The good news is that Jenkins has support for Gradle via the Gradle plugin. Let's see how to use the plugin to add our little Java project to Jenkins.

To install Jenkins on our computer, we must first download the installation files from the Jenkins website. A native installer is available for Mac OS X, Windows, and Linux. We can simply run the installer software to install Jenkins on our computer. We can also download a WAR file and deploy it to a Java web container to install Jenkins. The WAR file is also a Java executable archive. This means that we can simply run the WAR file with the `java -jar` command to execute Jenkins.

Adding the Gradle plugin

1. First, we must install the Gradle plugin in Jenkins.
2. We will launch a web browser and access `http://localhost:8080`. From the Jenkins main page, we will select the **Manage Jenkins** link, which takes us to the appropriate page, as shown in the following image:

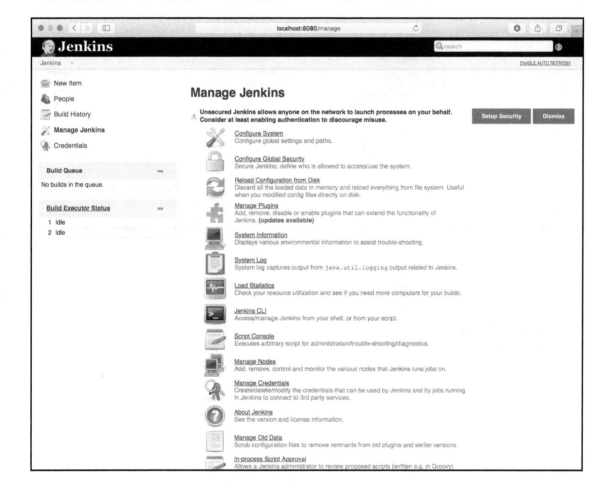

Overview of options to manage Jenkins

3. Here, we will select **Manage Plugins**.

4. On the **Plugin Manager** page, we can use the **Filter** box at the top-right corner to search for **Gradle Plugin**:

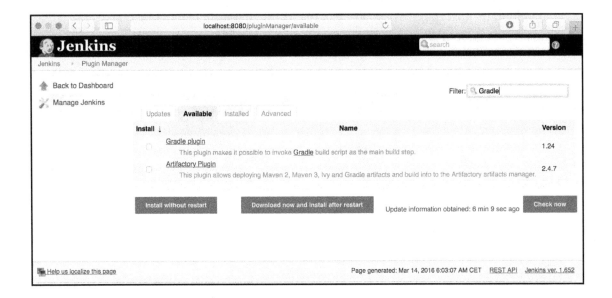

Search results for Gradle plugin

5. We select the plugin and click on the **Install without restart** button. After the installation of the plugin, we see the following screen:

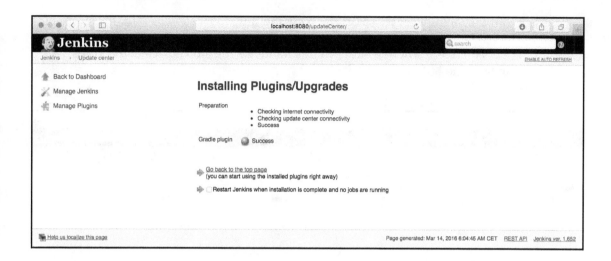

Result after successful installation of the Gradle plugin

6. We need to restart Jenkins to make the plugin active and usable for our Jenkins projects.

Configuring a Jenkins job

Jenkins is now set up with the Gradle plugin and it is time to create a job:

1. From the main page, we select the **New job** link.

2. We get a screen, where we can fill in a name for the job and select the **Freestyle project** radio button:

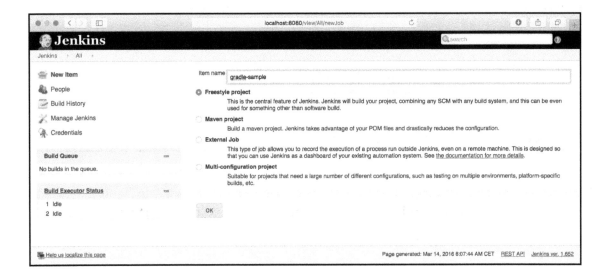

Creating a new job in Jenkins

3. If we have filled in the name and selected the radio button, we can click on the **OK** button. We will go to the **configuration** page of our job. The name of the job is already filled with the value from the previous screen:

Configuring a Jenkins job

4. We must at least define our Git repository in the **Source Code Management** section.

5. Also, we must add a build step in the **Build** section.

6. We select the **Git** radio button to define the location of our Git repository in the URL of the repository field. Note that the Git is not supported by default. We must install the Git client plugin in Jenkins to have Git support.

7. If we select the **Add build step** button in the **Build** section, we can see the **Invoke Gradle script** option. Thanks to the Gradle plugin, we now have this option highlighted in the following screenshot:

Adding a build step to invoke Gradle

8. We will select the **Invoke Gradle script** option, and Jenkins adds new fields to configure our Gradle build:

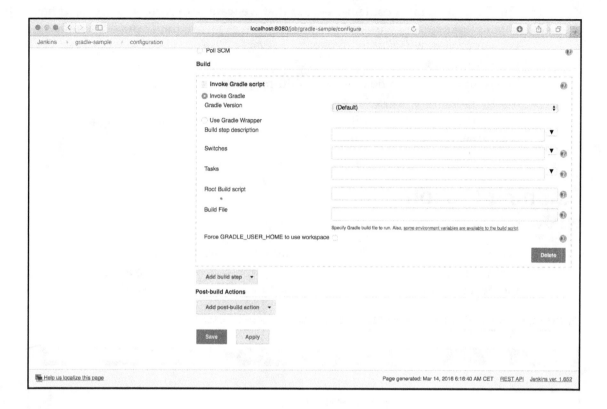

Details for a Gradle build step

9. First, we can choose whether we want to use the Gradle Wrapper for this project. We don't need it for our project, so we leave this unchecked.

10. Next, we can choose **Gradle Version**. We can install multiple Gradle versions for Jenkins, and we can choose the version that we want to use. The default version is the one that is available on the system path. We will discuss how to add more Gradle versions to Jenkins later.

11. We can give our build step a short description in the **Build step description** field.

12. The **Switches** field can contain the Gradle command-line options that we want to use. For example, to exclude a task, we can set the value for the **Switches** field to `-x <taskName>`.

13. The **Tasks** field must contain the tasks that we want to execute. If our project has default tasks set and we want to run those, we can leave the **Tasks** field empty. For our project, we want to invoke the `clean` and `build` tasks, so we will set the value to `clean build`.

14. The **Root Build script** field is for a multi-project build, where the root script is not in a default location. We can define the custom location here.

15. If a Gradle project has a build file name other than the default `build.gradle`, we can set the value in the **Build File** field.

Running the job

We have the basic setup for running our Gradle project:

1. We will click on the **Save** button and close the configuration.

2. We will return to the job page. On the left-hand side, we can see a menu with the **Build Now** link. We will click on the link and Jenkins will start the job:

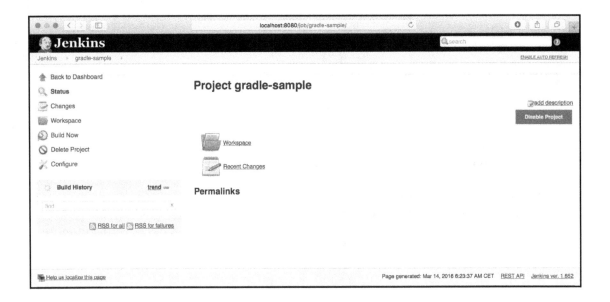

Overview of the Gradle job we have configured

Our code will be checked from the Git repository, and the `clean` and `build` Gradle tasks are run.

3. If the job is done, we can see the build result. From the build result page, we can see the console output when we click on the **Console Output** link:

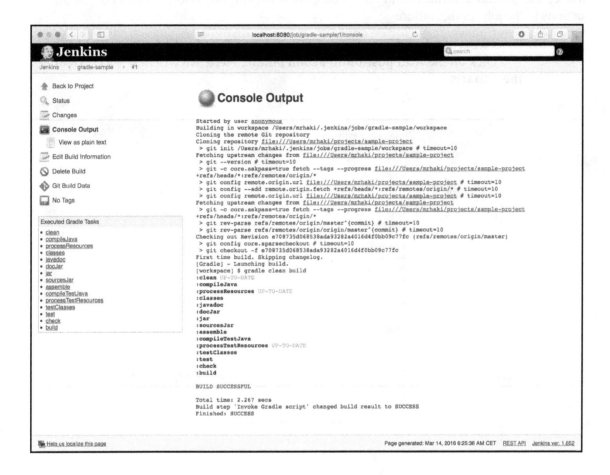

Console output for running Gradle job in Jenkins

On the left-hand side, we can also see all the Gradle tasks that have been executed. We can click on the links and jump directly to any output of the task.

Configuring artifacts and test results

To see the generated artifacts and test results, we must add the following two post-build actions to the job configuration:

1. First, we will select the configure job link. In the **Post-build Actions** section, we will click on the **Add post-build action** button. Here, we will first select **Archive the artifacts**:

Adding build step for archiving artifacts

2. Next, we will select **Publish JUnit test result report**:

Adding build step to publish test results

3. The artifacts are saved in the `build/libs` directory of our project. So, in the **Files to archive** field, we will enter `build/libs/.jar`. We will also set the value for the **Test report XMLs** field to `build/test-results/.xml`:

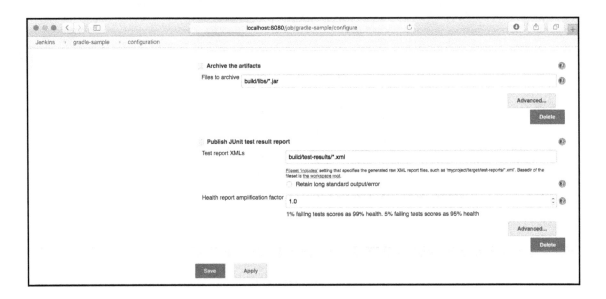

Configuration for the build steps

4. The configuration is done, so we click on the **Save** button. We can run the job again, and this time, we will see the artifacts of our projects as downloadable links on the job page. The test results are also shown, and we can even see more details if we click on the **Test Result** link:

Job overview page with published test results and archived artifacts

Adding Gradle versions

We can add extra Gradle versions to Jenkins. If, for example, some projects rely on Gradle 2.10 and others on Gradle 2.11, we can add other Gradle versions to Jenkins. Let's see how we can add another Gradle version to Jenkins:

1. From the **Manage Jenkins** page, we will select **Configure System**. The page has a **Gradle** section, where we can add new Gradle installations:

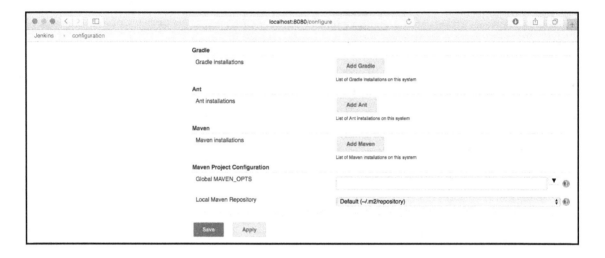

Option to add a new Gradle version in Jenkins

2. If we click on the **Add Gradle** button, we can define a name for our Gradle installation in the **Gradle name** field.

3. We will also see an **Install automatically** checkbox. If this is checked, Jenkins will download a Gradle version for us from the Internet. We can select the version from the **Version** drop-down box:

Configuration to automatically install Gradle version

4. If we want to use a locally-installed instance of Gradle, we must uncheck the **Install automatically** checkbox. Now, we can set the Gradle location in the **GRADLE_HOME** field:

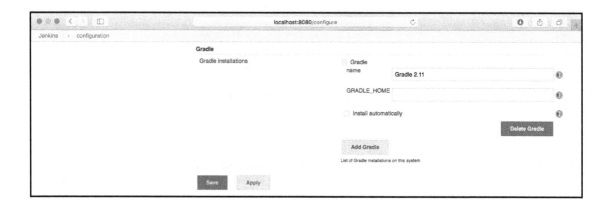

Configuration for existing Gradle installation

5. We must click on the **Save** button to save the changes. Now, we can choose the correct Gradle version in the jobs.

Using JetBrains TeamCity

JetBrains TeamCity is a commercial continuous integration server. TeamCity has a Professional Server license. This means that we can create 20 build configurations and one build agent. If we need more configurations or build agents, we can purchase other licenses. In this section, we will see how to create a build plan with Gradle.

We can download installer software for Mac OS X, Windows, and Linux from the JetBrains TeamCity website. We run the installer software to install TeamCity on our computer. TeamCity is also available as an archive for all platforms. To install the archive, we only have to unpack the contents to a directory on our computer. TeamCity is also available as a WAR file, which can be deployed to a Java web container.

Creating a project

In TeamCity we must create a project with the build configuration we want to be executed. Let's see how we can add a project:

1. After we install TeamCity, we will open a web browser and go to `http://localhost:8111/`. We can create a new project from the **Administration** page. We can also define the name of our project and provide a short description:

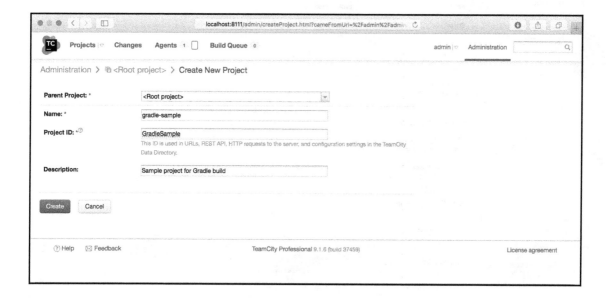

Creating a new project in TeamCity

2. We will then click on the **Create** button to create the project and go to an overview page of our project:

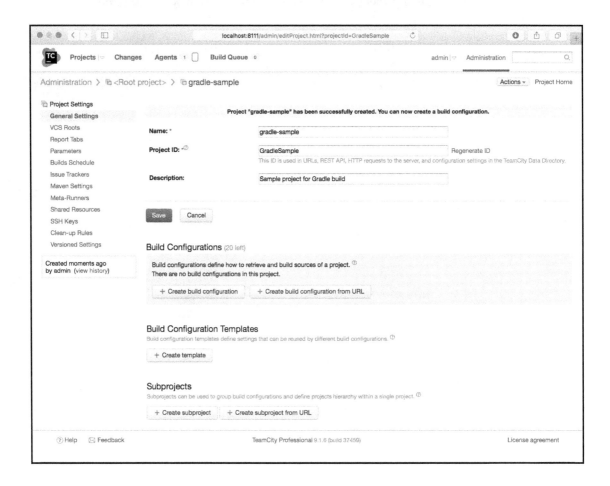

Project overview page

3. It is time to add a new build configuration. We will click on the **Create build configuration** button in the **Build Configurations** section to add a build configuration:

Creating a new build configuration

4. We will click on the **Create** button to create the project and go to the version control settings page of our project. Here, we fill in the properties of our local Git repository:

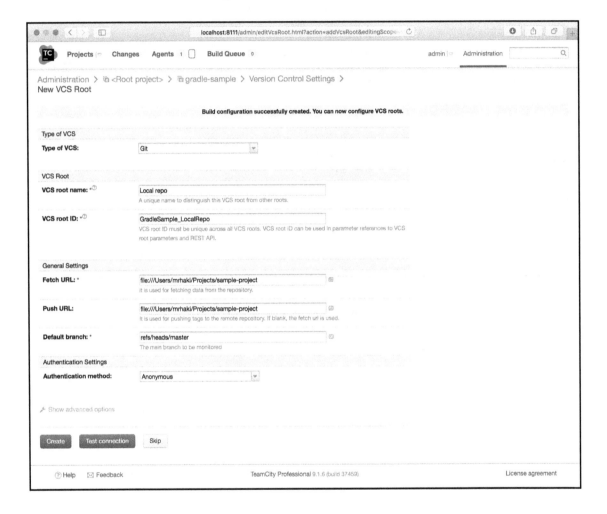

Configuration for version control management

5. We will click on the **Create** button to create the project and go to an overview page of our project:

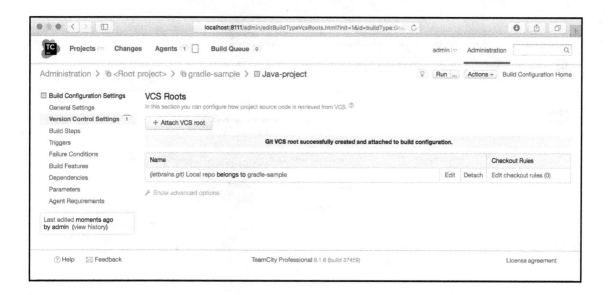

Overview of configuration for version control

6. We will define the artifacts of our project on the **General Settings** page. We can define the path of the artifacts in our project in the **Artifact paths** field. Here, We defined the value `build/libs/*.jar` in the **Artifact paths** field.:

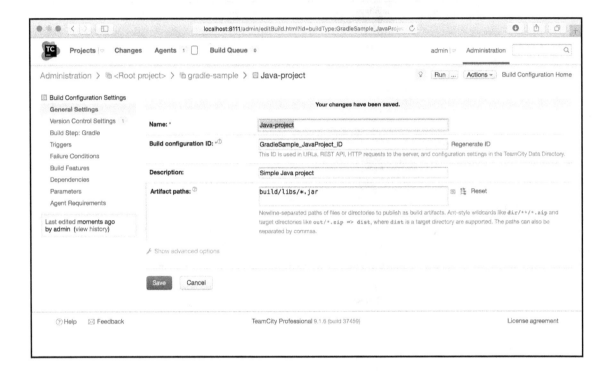

Configuration of the artifacts of the project

7. On the project overview screen, we will click on the **Add Build Step** button. We are taken to a new screen, where we can select the **Runner type** of the build. Here, we will select the **Gradle** runner and click on the **Save** button:

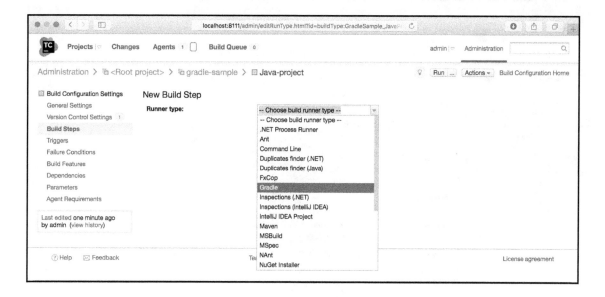

Defining a new build step with Gradle

8. We are on the configuration page for the build step now, as shown in the following screenshot:

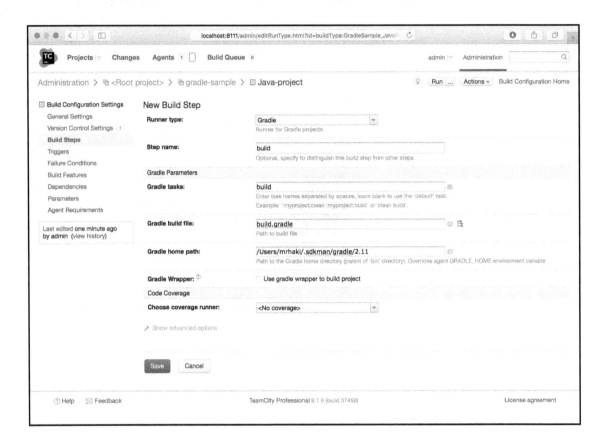

Configuration for Gradle build step

9. We can fill a descriptive name for this build step in the **Step name** field. In the **Gradle Parameters** section, we can set the tasks in the **Gradle tasks** field. For our project, we want to invoke the `build` task, so we will fill `build`. Note that we can enable **Incremental building** for multi-project builds. TeamCity will use the `buildDependents` task.

10. To set the Gradle version, we will fill the **Gradle home path** field. Extra command-line parameters can be filled in the **Additional Gradle command line parameters** field.

11. If our project has a Gradle Wrapper, we can check the **Gradle Wrapper** checkbox. TeamCity will then use the `gradlew` or `gradlew.bat` scripts, instead of the Gradle home path location, to run Gradle.

Running the project

We can save the build configuration, and we are now ready to run it as follows:

1. At the top-right side, we can see the **Run** button with an ellipsis. When we click on the ellipsis, we will get a dialog window with options that we can set before we run the build, as shown in the following screenshot:

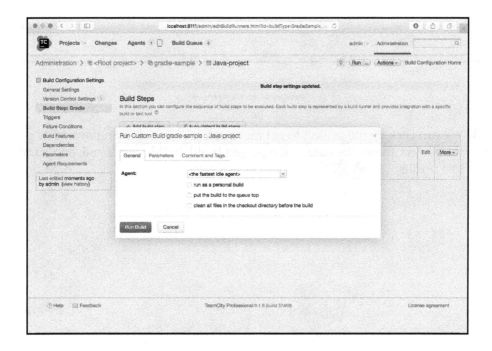

Running the project with the Gradle build step

We will leave all the options unchanged and click on the **Run Build** button.

2. TeamCity instructs the build agent to run our build configuration. The code is checked from the repository, and the `build` Gradle task is invoked. On the **Projects** page, we will see a summary of the build:

Results after running the project

3. We can click on the project to get more details. The following overview page of the project shows the date of the project build, build agent used, and summary of test results:

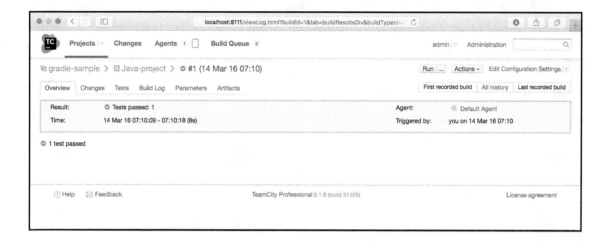

More details for a project that has run

4. If we click on the **Tests** tab, we will see the tests that have run and the time it took to execute them:

Overview of test results

5. The **Build Log** tab page shows the output of the build process. We will see detailed information here:

TeamCity logging for running the project

6. Finally, on the **Artifacts** page, we will see the generated JAR files. We can click on the filename and see the contents of the files:

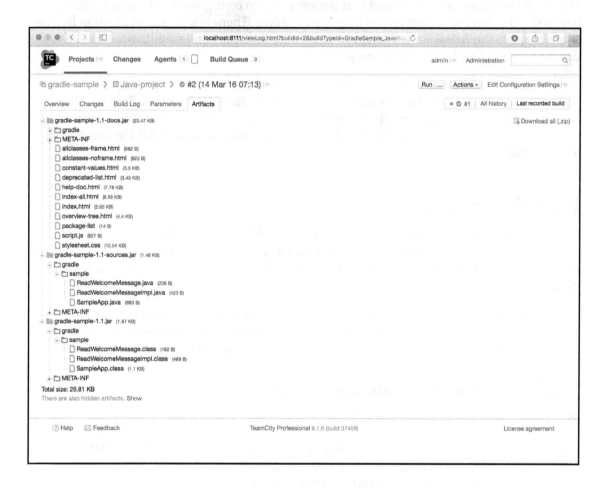

Overview of artifacts for the project

Using Atlassian Bamboo

The last continuous integration tool that we are going to configure is Atlassian Bamboo. Bamboo is a commercial continuous integration server. There is a 30-day evaluation license available from the Atlassian website. We will discuss how to configure Bamboo to use Gradle as a build tool for our Java project.

We can install Bamboo on our local computer. We will first need to download the installation package from the Bamboo website. We can choose native installers for Mac OS X, Windows, and Linux. Alternatively, we can simply download a packaged version and unzip it in a directory on our computer. Finally, we can download a WAR file and deploy it to a web container.

Defining a plan

Bamboo has no Gradle runner or plugin, but we can define a build plan and add the so-called script task. A script task can run any script as part of the build plan. To make sure that Bamboo can build our Java project, we must add the Gradle Wrapper scripts to the project.

We will run the `wrapper` task in our local Java project directory. We now have the `gradlew` and `gradlew.bat` script files. Also, the `gradle` directory is created with the configuration for the Gradle Wrapper. We add the directory and files to our Git repository, as follows:

```
$ git add .
$ git commit -m "Add Gradle wrapper output."
```

We are now ready to create a new build plan in Bamboo:

1. We will start a web browser and open `http://localhost:8085/`. After we have logged in to Bamboo, we will select the **Create Plan** link. We will go to a new page, where we can set the properties of the build plan:

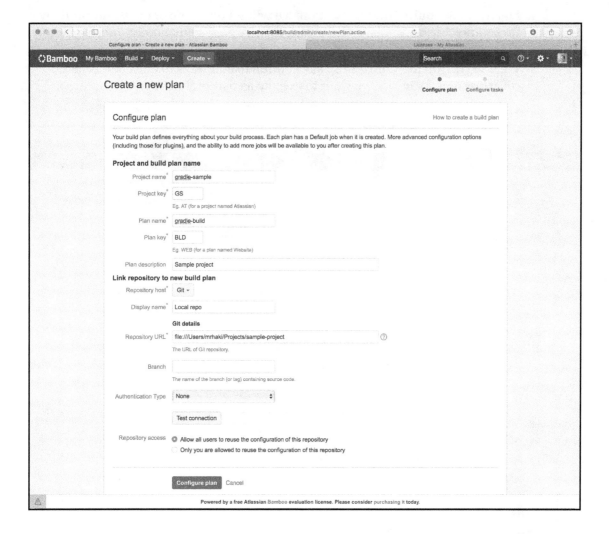

Creating a new plan in Bamboo

2. We must define a project name in the **Project name** field. Bamboo also expects a short identifier in uppercase characters as the project key in the **Project Key** field. The plan that is part of the project also has a name and key; we fill the **Plan name** and **Plan key** fields. We can set a short description in the **Plan description** field.

3. In the **Source Repositories** section, we can define the Git repository location for our project.

4. Finally, in the **Build Strategy** section, we will set the value of the **Build Strategy** drop-down box to Manual. This means that we have to manually start the build via the run action in the Bamboo user interface.

5. We will click on the **Configure Tasks** button to add tasks to our plan. A task contains some logic that we want to execute as part of the plan:

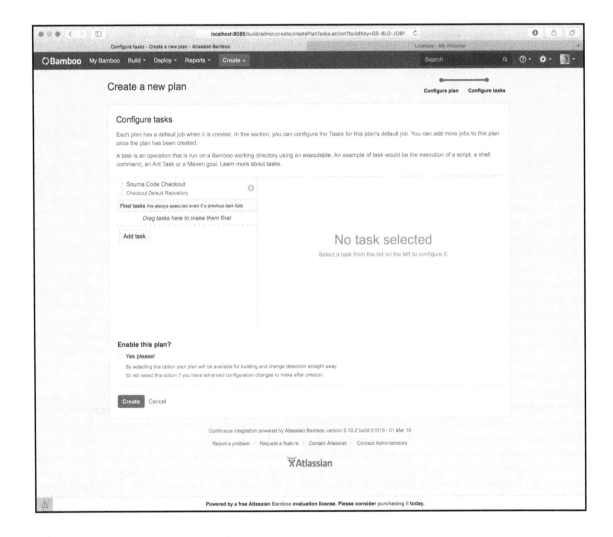

Adding a new task to the plan

6. The first task is automatically added and it is responsible to check the source code of the Git repository. We will click on the **Add task** button to create a new task:

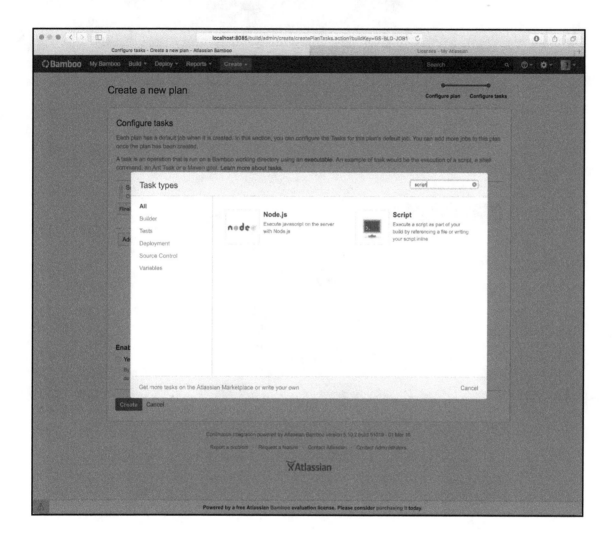

Searching for script task

7. A dialog window will appear, where we will select the **Script** task from the **Builder** section. With this task, we can configure the Gradle Wrapper scripts to be executed.

8. We will return to the tasks window and we fill in the fields under the **Script** configuration:

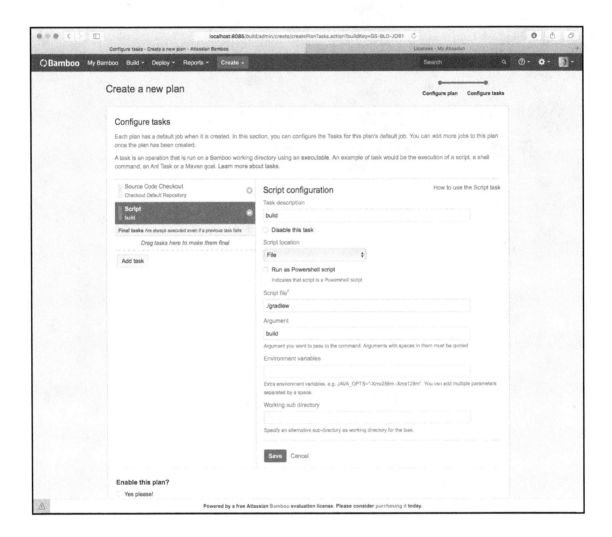

Configuring the script task

9. We fill a description in the **Task description** field. Script location must be set to **File** instead of **Inline**. The **Script** file field has the location of the gradlew or gradlew.bat script that we want invoked.

10. In the **Argument** field, we will pass the arguments to the `gradlew` script. We want to invoke the `build` task, so we set the value to `build`.

11. We are ready to click on the **Save** button to save our script task configuration. The task is added to the list of tasks, as shown in the following screenshot:

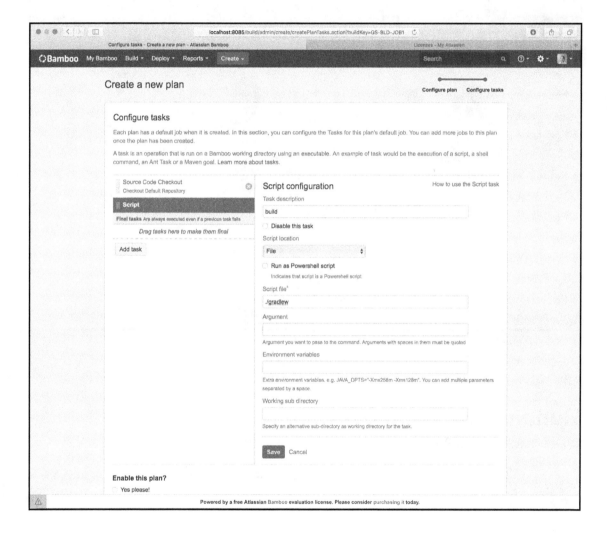

Configuration for the script task to run Gradle

12. We can enable the plan in the **Enable this Plan?** section by checking the **Yes please!** checkbox. Next, we will click on the **Create** button to finish the configuration and save the plan in Bamboo.

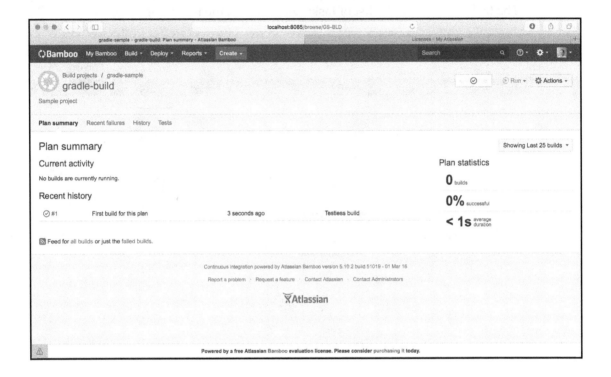

Overview of plan

Running the build plan

We are now ready to run the build:

1. Click on the **Run** button at the top-right side of the page. While the build is running, we can see some of the log output. After the build is finished, we can see the results.

2. We also want to add the project artifacts to our plan, and the test results as well. Therefore, we will select the **Configure plan** option from the **Actions** menu:

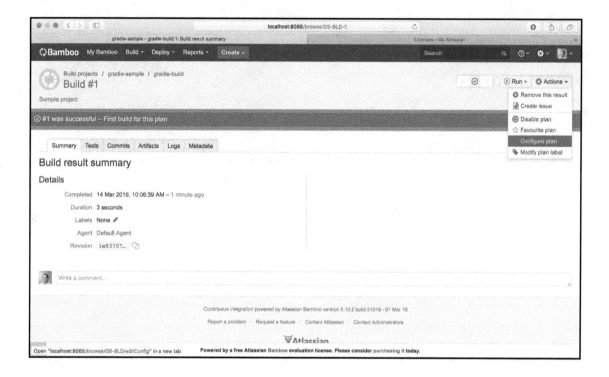

Build results after running the plan

3. We will then go to the **Artifacts** tab page and click on the **Create definition** button to add a new artifact definition:

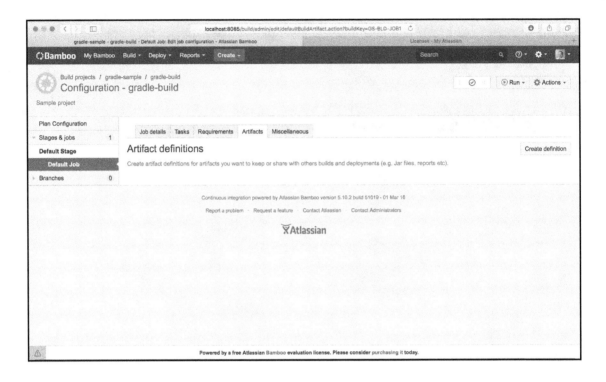

Defining artifacts for the plan

4. We will see a dialog window and we can define **Name**, **Location**, and **Copy Pattern** of the artifacts here:

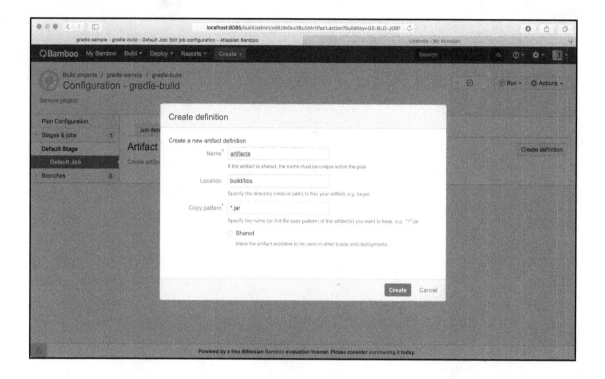

Configuration for artifacts

5. We fill `artifacts` in the **Name** field and `build/libs` in the **Location** field. The **Copy pattern** field is filled with the `*.jar` value to include all JAR files. We then click on the **Create** button to finish the configuration of the artifacts.

6. Next, we will select the **Tasks** tab page and click on the **Add task** button to create a new task.

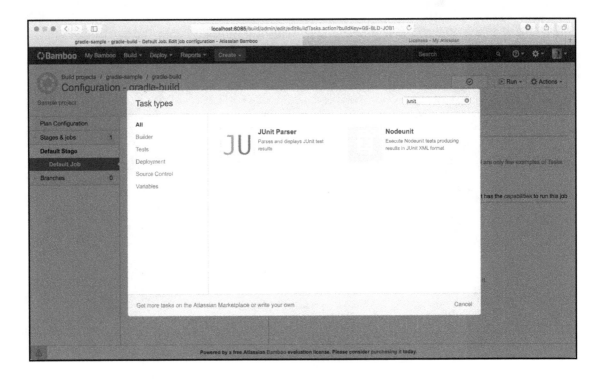

Searching for task to publish test results

7. In the dialog window with **Tasks** types, we will select **JUnit Parser** from the **Tests** section. Bamboo shows the configuration fields for this task:

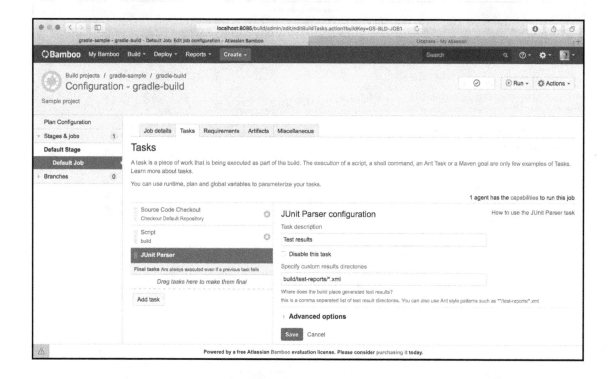

Configuration for test results task

8. We will then set **Task description** with the Test results value. In the **Specify custom results directories** field, we will set the build/test-results/*.xml pattern.

9. We are now ready to run our plan again; but this time, we have the test results:

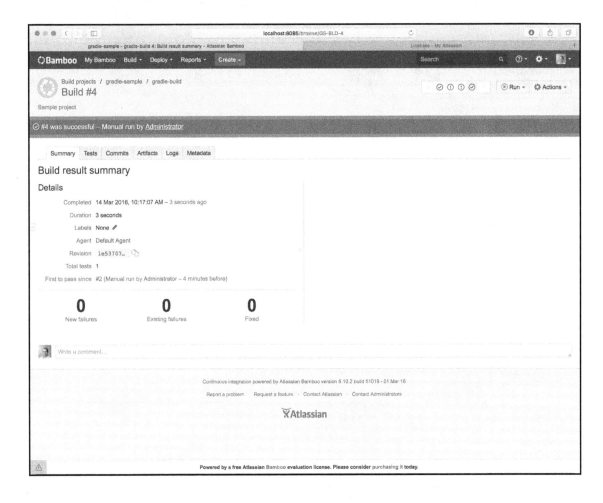

Summary of build results

10. We will click on the **Artifacts** tab and see that the plan has produced artifacts:

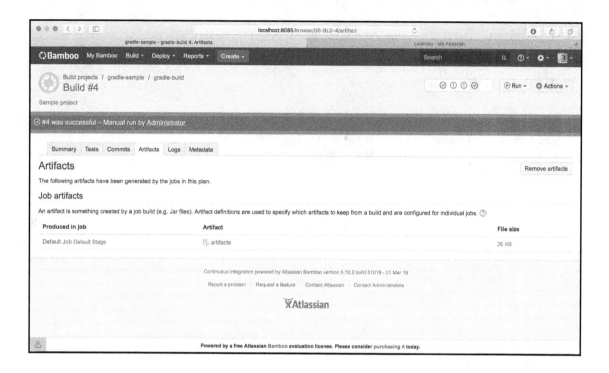

Overview of artifacts for the plan

11. If we click on the **artifacts** link, we are taken to a page where we can download each artifact JAR file, as shown in the following screenshot:

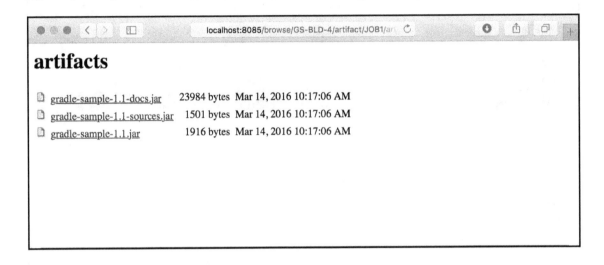

Links for downloading artifacts

Summary

In this chapter, we have discussed how we should configure continuous integration tools, such as Jenkins, JetBrains TeamCity, and Atlassian Bamboo, to build our Java project with Gradle.

Jenkins and TeamCity have good support for Gradle builds. We can choose to use either a locally-installed Gradle version or the Gradle task wrapper scripts. Defining which tasks to run is easy.

Bamboo has no real support for Gradle builds. We can use the script build option and Gradle task wrapper support to work around this. This way, we can still run Gradle builds with Bamboo.

In the next chapter, we will discuss how to integrate Gradle with **Integrated Development Environments (IDEs)** such as Eclipse and JetBrains IntelliJ IDEA.

12
IDE Support

When we develop applications, we usually use an **integrated development environment** (**IDE**). An IDE provides support for writing code for our applications. We can write our code in Java, Groovy, or Scala. We have seen how to use Gradle to define, for example, library dependencies to compile the code. We want to use the same information that we have defined in a Gradle build file in a project in our favorite IDE.

In this chapter, we will discuss how to use Gradle plugins to generate the project files with classpath dependencies for Eclipse and JetBrains IntelliJ IDEA. We will also discuss how to customize the file generation to add extra configuration data.

Next, we will see the Eclipse and IntelliJ IDEA support for running Gradle tasks from within the IDE.

In this chapter, we will cover the following subjects:

- Using the Eclipse plugin
- Using the IDEA plugin
- Integrating Gradle with Eclipse
- Running Gradle scripts from IDEA IntelliJ

Using the Eclipse plugin

The Eclipse plugin can generate the project files necessary to import the project in Eclipse. In this section, we will see the tasks that are added by the plugin and how to customize the generated output.

If we have a Java project and we want to import the project into Eclipse, we must use the Eclipse plugin to generate the Eclipse project files. Each Eclipse project has a `.project` and `.classpath` file as minimum. The `.project` file contains the metadata about the project, such as the project name. The `.classpath` file contains classpath entries for the project. Eclipse needs this in order to be able to compile the source files in the project. The Eclipse plugin will try to download the artifact with source files belonging to a dependency as well. So, if we import the project into Eclipse and the source files are available, we can directly see the source of dependent class files.

For a Java project, an additional **Java Development Tools** (**JDT**) configuration file is created in the `.settings` folder. The name of the file is `org.eclipse.jdt. core.prefs`.

Let's create a simple Gradle build file for a Java project. The code for the build file is shown in the following code snippet:

```
apply plugin: 'java'

// Apply the Eclipse plugin.
apply plugin: 'eclipse'

version = 1.0

sourceCompatibility = 1.8
targetCompatibility = 1.8

description = 'Sample project'

ext {
    slf4jVersion = '1.7.18'
    slf4jGroup = 'org.slf4j'
}

configurations {
    // Extra configuration.
    extraLib
}

repositories {
    jcenter()
}

dependencies {
    testCompile 'junit:junit:4.11'

    extraLib "$slf4jGroup:slf4j-api:$slf4jVersion",
      "$slf4jGroup:slf4j-simple:$slf4jVersion"
```

```
}
```

We will apply the Java and Eclipse plugins for our project. We will set some project properties, such as version, description, source, and target compatibility. We will define a dependency on JUnit for the testCompile configuration. Also, we will add an extra custom configuration with a dependency on the SLF4J logging library.

First, let's see the tasks that are added to our project by the Eclipse plugin. We will invoke the tasks task and look at all the tasks in our plugin, as shown in the following command output:

```
$ gradle tasks --all
:tasks
. . .
IDE tasks
---------
cleanEclipse - Cleans all Eclipse files.
cleanEclipseClasspath
cleanEclipseJdt
cleanEclipseProject
eclipse - Generates all Eclipse files.
eclipseClasspath - Generates the Eclipse classpath file.
eclipseJdt - Generates the Eclipse JDT settings file.
eclipseProject - Generates the Eclipse project file.
. . .
```

The eclipse task is dependent on the following three tasks: eclipseClasspath, eclipseJdt, and eclipseProject. Each task generates a single file. The eclipseClasspath task generates the .classpath file, eclipseProject generates the .project file, and eclipseJdt generates org.eclipse.jdt.core.prefs.

When we execute the eclipse task from the command line, we get the following output:

```
$ gradle eclipse
:eclipseClasspath
:eclipseJdt
:eclipseProject
:eclipse
BUILD SUCCESSFUL
Total time: 1.223 secs
```

Note that the sources of the JUnit library are downloaded. We now have the .classpath and .project files in our project folder. In the .settings folder, we have the org.eclipse.jdt.core.prefs file.

The `.project` file has the following contents:

```
<?xml version="1.0" encoding="UTF-8"?>
<projectDescription>
    <name>eclipse</name>
    <comment>Sample project</comment>
    <projects/>
    <natures>
      <nature>org.eclipse.jdt.core.javanature</nature>
    </natures>
    <buildSpec>
      <buildCommand>
          <name>org.eclipse.jdt.core.javabuilder</name>
          <arguments/>
      </buildCommand>
    </buildSpec>
    <linkedResources/>
</projectDescription>
```

The `name` element is filled with the project's folder name. We will discuss how to change this later in the chapter. The `comment` element contains our project description. We have applied the Java plugin to our project, and hence, the Java `nature` and `buildCommand` are added to the project configuration.

If we look at the `.classpath` file, we can see a `classpathentry` element with the JUnit dependency, as shown in the following code snippet:

```
<?xml version="1.0" encoding="UTF-8"?>
<classpath>
    <classpathentry kind="output" path="bin"/>
    <classpathentry kind="con"
        path="org.eclipse.jdt.launching.JRE_CONTAINER/
        org.eclipse.jdt.internal.debug.ui.launcher.StandardVMType/
        JavaSE-1.8/"/>
    <classpathentrysourcepath="/Users/mrhaki/.gradle/caches/
        modules-2/files-2.1/junit/junit/4.11/
        28e0ad201304e4a4abf999ca0570b7cffc352c3c/
        junit-4.11-sources.jar" kind="lib"
        path="/Users/mrhaki/.gradle/caches/modules-2/files-
        2.1/junit/junit/4.11/
        4e031bb61df09069aeb2bffb4019e7a5034a4ee0/junit-4.11.jar"/>
    <classpathentry sourcepath="/Users/mrhaki/.gradle/caches/
        modules-2/files-2.1/org.hamcrest/hamcrest-core/1.3/
        1dc37250fbc78e23a65a67fbbaf71d2e9cbc3c0b/hamcrest-core-1.3-
        sources.jar" kind="lib" path="/Users/mrhaki/.gradle/caches/
        modules-2/files-2.1/org.hamcrest/hamcrest-core/1.3/
        42a25dc3219429f0e5d060061f71acb49bf010a0/
```

```
        hamcrest-core-1.3.jar"/>
</classpath>
```

The `classpathentry` element has a reference to the location in the Gradle cache of the downloaded JUnit library. Note that the `sourcepath` attribute references the source files.

The last generated `org.eclipse.jdt.core.prefs` file has the following contents:

```
#
#Mon Mar 14 21:28:13 CET 2016
org.eclipse.jdt.core.compiler.debug.localVariable=generate
org.eclipse.jdt.core.compiler.compliance=1.8
org.eclipse.jdt.core.compiler.codegen.unusedLocal=preserve
org.eclipse.jdt.core.compiler.debug.sourceFile=generate
org.eclipse.jdt.core.compiler.codegen.targetPlatform=1.8
org.eclipse.jdt.core.compiler.problem.enumIdentifier=error
org.eclipse.jdt.core.compiler.debug.lineNumber=generate
eclipse.preferences.version=1
org.eclipse.jdt.core.compiler.codegen.inlineJsrBytecode=enabled
org.eclipse.jdt.core.compiler.source=1.8
org.eclipse.jdt.core.compiler.problem.assertIdentifier=error
```

We can see that the source and target compatibility that we defined in the Gradle build file are used for the `org.eclipse.jdt.core.compiler.source`, `org.eclipse.jdt.core.compiler.codegen.targetPlatform`, and `org.eclipse.jdt.core.compiler.compliance` properties.

Customizing generated files

We have several options to customize the configuration in the generated files. The Eclipse plugin adds a DSL to configure model objects that represent Eclipse configuration objects. If we use the DSL to configure the objects, these newly configured objects are merged with the existing configuration before the file is generated. We can also hook into the generation process and work directly on the model objects, before and after the configuration is merged and the file is generated. Finally, we can even use a hook to work directly on the XML structure before the configuration file is generated.

The following steps describe the complete configuration file generation life cycle:

1. First, the file is read from the disk or a default file is used if the file is not available.
2. Next, the `beforeMerge` hook is invoked. The hook accepts the model object for the configuration file as an argument.

3. The implicit configuration information from the Gradle build file and the configuration that is defined using the DSL are merged.
4. Then, the `whenMerged` hook is executed. The hook accepts the model object for the configuration file as an argument.
5. The `withXml` hook is invoked. XML manipulation can happen here before the file is written to the disk.
6. Finally, the configuration file is written to the disk.

Customizing using DSL

When the Eclipse plugin generates the files, it will look in the Gradle build file for necessary information. For example, if we set the `description` property of the `Project` object, the comment section in the `.project` file will be filled with the value of this property.

The Eclipse plugin also adds a configuration script block with the name eclipse. The configuration can be described using a simple DSL. At the top level, we can add the path variables that will be used to replace absolute paths in `classpath` entries. The `org.gradle.plugins.ide.eclipse.model.EclipseModel` object is used, and the `pathVariables()` method of this class must be used to define a path variable.

Next, we can define the configuration information for the `.project` file in the project section. The `org.gradle.plugins.ide.eclipse.model.EclipseProject` model object is used to model the Eclipse project configuration. We can, for example, use the `name` property to change the name of the project in the generated `.project` file. It is good to know that Gradle can generate unique project names for a multi-project build. A unique name is necessary to import the projects in Eclipse. During the `.project` file generation, all projects that are part of the multi-project must be known. So, it is best to run the `eclipse` or `eclipseProject` task from the root of the project. Also, methods for adding project natures and new build commands are available.

To customize the `.classpath` file generation, we can use the `classpath` section of the Eclipse configuration closure. Here, the `org.gradle.plugins.ide.eclipse.model.EclipseClasspath` object is used to model the classpath entries of the Eclipse project. We can use the `plusConfigurations` and `minusConfigurations` properties to add or remove dependency configurations from the generated `.classpath` file. By default, the associated source files for a dependency are downloaded, but we can also set the `downloadJavadoc` property to `true` to download the Javadoc associated with the dependency.

The `jdt` section of the Eclipse configuration closure can be used to change the source and target compatibility versions. By default, Gradle Java plugin settings are used, but we can override it here. The `org.gradle.plugins.ide.eclipse.model.EclipseJdt` object is used to model the Eclipse configuration.

In the following build file, we will discuss an example of all the possible methods and properties that we can use with the DSL to customize the generated `.project`, `.classpath` and `org.eclipse.jdt.core.prefs` files:

```
apply plugin: 'java'
apply plugin: 'eclipse'

version = 1.0

description = 'Sample project'

ext {
    slf4jVersion = '1.7.18'
    slf4jGroup = 'org.slf4j'
}

configurations {
    extraLib
}

repositories {
    jcenter()
}

dependencies {
    testCompile 'junit:junit:4.11'

    extraLib "$slf4jGroup:slf4j-api:$slf4jVersion",
      "$slf4jGroup:slf4j-simple:$slf4jVersion"
}

eclipse {
    pathVariables 'APPSERVER_HOME': file('/apps/appserver/1.0')

    // Customize .project file.
    project {
        // Override default project name from project
        // and set explicitly.
        name = 'sample-eclipse'

        // Set comment section in .project file.
        comment = 'Eclipse project file build by Gradle'
```

```
    // Add new natures like Spring nature.
    natures 'org.springframework.ide.eclipse.core.springnature'

    // Add build command for Spring.
    buildCommand
      'org.springframework.ide.eclipse.core.springbuilder'

      // If using location attribute
      // then type 1 is file, 2 is folder
      linkedResource name: 'config', type: '2',
        location: file('/opt/local/config')

      // If using locationUri attribute
      // then type 1 for file/folder, 2 is virtual folder
      linkedResource name: 'config2', type: '1',
        locationUri: 'file:../config'

      // Define reference to other project. This is not
      // a build path reference.
      referencedProjects 'other-project'
  }

  // Customize .classpath file.
  classpath {
      // Add extra dependency configurations.
      plusConfigurations += configurations.extraLib

      // Remove dependency configurations.
      minusConfigurations += configurations.testCompile

      // Included configurations are not exported.
      noExportConfigurations += configurations.testCompile

      // Download associated source files.
      downloadSources = true

      // Download Javadoc for dependencies.
      downloadJavadoc = true

      // Add extra containers.
      containers 'ApacheCommons'

      // Change default output dir (${projectDir}/bin)
      defaultOutputDir file("$buildDir/eclipse-classes")
  }

  // Customize org.eclipse.jdt.core.prefs file.
  jdt {
```

```
        sourceCompatibility = 1.8
        targetCompatibility = 1.8
    }
}
```

Customizing with merge hooks

Using the DSL to customize file generation is very elegant. Remember from the configuration file generation steps that this information is used right after the `beforeMerged` hook and before the `whenMerged` hook. These hooks take a model object as an argument that we can use to customize. We can use the merge hooks if we want to do something that is not possible using the project configuration or DSL.

The merge hooks can be defined in the Eclipse configuration closure. For each file, we can define a configuration closure for the `beforeMerged` and `whenMerged` hooks. These methods are part of the `org.gradle.plugins.ide.api.XmlFileContentMerger` class. Gradle will delegate the configuration closures to the methods of this class. The `beforeMerged` hook is useful to overwrite or change existing sections in the configuration file. The `cleanEclipse` task cleans all the sections in a configuration file; and by using the `beforeMerged` hook, we can define the parts that need to be cleaned or overwritten ourselves.

The `whenMerged` hook is the preferred way of changing the model object. When this hook is invoked, the model object is already configured with all the settings from the project configuration and DSL.

Each file is represented by the file property of the Eclipse configuration closures. For example, to add a merge hook to the `.project` file generation, we will define it using the `eclipse.project.file` property.

The following table shows the class that is passed as an argument for the merge hooks closures:

Model	Merge hook argument	Description
Project	`org.gradle.plugins.ide.eclipse.model.Project`	This is the model object with properties for the `.project` file generation
Classpath	`org.gradle.plugins.ide.eclipse.model.Classpath`	This is the model object with properties for the `.classpath` file generation

Jdt	`org.gradle.plugins.ide.eclipse.model.Jdt`	This is the model object with properties for the `org.eclipse.jdt.core.prefs` file generation

For the `Jdt` model, we have an additional `withProperties()` method to change the contents of the file. This method has a closure with an argument of the `java.util.Properties` type.

In the following example build file, we will use the merged hooks to change the configuration in the `.project`, `.classpath`, and `org.eclipse.jdt.core.prefs` files:

```
apply plugin: 'java'
apply plugin: 'eclipse'

version = 1.0

description = 'Sample project'

ext {
    slf4jVersion = '1.7.18'
    slf4jGroup = 'org.slf4j'
}

configurations {
    extraLib
}

repositories {
    jcenter()
}

dependencies {
    testCompile 'junit:junit:4.11'

    extraLib "$slf4jGroup:slf4j-api:$slf4jVersion",
             "$slf4jGroup:slf4j-simple:$slf4jVersion"
}

eclipse {
    // Customize .project file.
    project {
        file {
            beforeMerged { project ->
                // We can access the internal object structure
                // using merge hooks.
```

```
            project.natures.clear()
        }

        // Instead of using the DSL we use the afterMerged
        // hook to customize the .project and .classpath files.
        afterMerged { project ->
            // Set name.
            project.name = 'sample-eclipse'

            // Set comment for .project file.
            project.comment = 'Eclipse project file build by Gradle'
        }

    }
}

// Customize .classpath file.
classpath {
    file {
        beforeMerged { classpath ->
            // Remove lib classpath entries.
            classpath.entries.removeAll {
                it.kind == 'lib'
            }
        }




    }
}

// Customize org.eclipse.jdt.core.prefs file.
jdt {
    file {

        whenProperties { properties ->
            properties.extraProperty = 'value'
        }
    }
}
}
```

Customizing with an XML manipulation

We have seen how to customize the configuration file generation with project configuration, DSL, and merge hooks. At the lowest level, there is a hook to change the XML structure before it is written to disk. Therefore, we must implement the `withXml` hook. We will define a closure, and the first argument of the closure is of the `org.gradle.api.XmlProvider` type. The class has the `asNode()` method, which returns the root of the XML as a Groovy node. This is the easiest object to alter the XML contents. The `asString()` method returns a `StringBuilder` instance with the XML contents. Finally, the `asElement()` method returns an `org.w3c.dom.Element` object.

The `asNode()` method returns the Groovy `groovy.util.Node` class. With this node class, we can easily add, replace, or remove nodes and attributes.

In the following example build file, we can see different ways to manipulate the XML structure:

```
apply plugin: 'java'
apply plugin: 'eclipse'

version = 1.0

description = 'Sample project'

repositories {
    jcenter()
}

dependencies {
    testCompile 'junit:junit:4.11'
}

eclipse {
    // Change .project file.
    project {
        file {
            withXml { xml ->
                def projectXml = xml.asNode()
                projectXml.name = 'sample-eclipse'

                def natures = projectXml.natures
                natures.plus {
                    nature {
                        'org.springframework.ide.eclipse.core.springnature'
                    }
                }
```

```
            }
        }
    }

    // Change .classpath file.
    classpath {
        file {
            withXml { xml ->
                def classpathXml = xml.asNode()
                classpathXml.classpathentry
                    .findAll { it.@kind == 'con' }*.@exported = 'true'
            }
        }
    }

}
```

We have seen all the different options to change the configuration files. Configuration changes, which we would normally make in Eclipse, can now be done programmatically in a Gradle build file.

Merging configuration

If a file already exists, Gradle will try to merge extra information with existing information. Depending on the section, the information will be amended to the existing configuration data or will replace the existing configuration data. This means that if we make changes to our project settings in Eclipse, they will not be overwritten even if we invoke one of the eclipse tasks.

To completely rebuild the project files, we must use the cleanEclipse tasks. For each project file, there is a corresponding cleanEclipse task. For example, to rebuild the .project file, we will invoke the cleanEclipseProject task before eclipseProject. Any changes that we have made manually are removed and a new .project file is generated by Gradle, with the settings from our Gradle build file.

Configuring WTP

We can add **Web Tools Platform** (**WTP**) to Eclipse in order to add support for Java enterprise applications. We will get support for web applications (WAR) and enterprise applications (EAR). To generate the correct configuration files, we must add another plugin to our Gradle build file. We will add the Eclipse WTP plugin to the project and also the War or Ear plugin.

Let's create a build file and add the War and Eclipse WTP plugins, as follows:

```
apply plugin: 'java'
apply plugin: 'war'

// Include the eclipse-wtp plugin.
apply plugin: 'eclipse-wtp'

version = 1.0

description = 'Sample project'

repositories {
    jcenter()
}

dependencies {
    testCompile 'junit:junit:4.11'
}
```

The Eclipse WTP plugin adds several new tasks to our Gradle build. In the following snippet, we will invoke the `tasks` task to see which tasks are added:

```
$ gradle tasks --all
:tasks
...
IDE tasks
---------
cleanEclipse - Cleans all Eclipse files. [cleanEclipseWtp]
cleanEclipseClasspath
cleanEclipseJdt
cleanEclipseProject
cleanEclipseWtp - Cleans Eclipse wtp configuration files.
cleanEclipseWtpComponent
cleanEclipseWtpFacet
eclipse - Generates all Eclipse files. [eclipseWtp]
eclipseClasspath - Generates the Eclipse classpath file.
eclipseJdt - Generates the Eclipse JDT settings file.
eclipseProject - Generates the Eclipse project file.
eclipseWtp - Generates Eclipse wtp configuration files.
eclipseWtpComponent - Generates the Eclipse WTP component settings file.
eclipseWtpFacet - Generates the Eclipse WTP facet settings file.
...
```

The Eclipse WTP plugin includes the Eclipse plugin as well. We get all the tasks that we have seen earlier, but new tasks are also added for WTP configuration files. The `eclipseWtp` task depends on `eclipseWtpComponent` and `eclipseWtpFacet` to generate the corresponding configuration files. Note that now the Eclipse task itself also depends on `eclipseWtp`.

For each of these tasks, there is a corresponding `clean` task. These clean tasks will delete the configuration files.

If we execute the eclipse task, we will get the following configuration files: `.project`, `.classpath`, and `org.eclipse.jdt.core.prefs`. We also get additional configuration files in the `.settings` folder, with the names `org.eclipse.wst.common.component` and `org.eclipse.wst.common.project.facet.core.xml`:

```
$ gradle eclipse
:eclipseClasspath
:eclipseJdt
:eclipseProject
:eclipseWtpComponent
:eclipseWtpFacet
:eclipseWtp
:eclipse
BUILD SUCCESSFUL
Total time: 0.926 secs
```

The contents of the `.project` file show that the Eclipse WTP plugin added additional natures and build commands, which are shown as follows:

```
<?xml version="1.0" encoding="UTF-8"?>
<projectDescription>
    <name>eclipse</name>
    <comment>Sample project</comment>
    <projects/>

    <natures>
      <nature>org.eclipse.jdt.core.javanature</nature>
      <nature>org.eclipse.wst.common.project.facet.core.nature
    </nature>
      <nature>org.eclipse.wst.common.modulecore.ModuleCoreNature
    </nature>
      <nature>org.eclipse.jem.workbench.JavaEMFNature</nature>
    </natures>
    <buildSpec>
      <buildCommand>
        <name>org.eclipse.jdt.core.javabuilder</name>
```

```
                <arguments/>
          </buildCommand>
          <buildCommand>
            <name>org.eclipse.wst.common.project.facet.core.builder
               </name>
                <arguments/>
          </buildCommand>
          <buildCommand>
            <name>org.eclipse.wst.validation.validationbuilder</name>
                <arguments/>
          </buildCommand>
        </buildSpec>
        <linkedResources/>
    </projectDescription>
```

In the `.classpath` configuration file, an
additional `org.eclipse.jst.j2ee.internal.web.container` container is added, as
shown in the following code snippet:

```
<?xml version="1.0" encoding="UTF-8"?>
<classpath>
    <classpathentry kind="output" path="bin"/>
    <classpathentry kind="con"
       path="org.eclipse.jdt.launching.JRE_CONTAINER/
       org.eclipse.jdt.internal.debug.ui.launcher.StandardVMType/
       JavaSE-1.8/"/>
    <classpathentry kind="con"
       path="org.eclipse.jst.j2ee.internal.web.container"/>
    <classpathentry sourcepath="/Users/mrhaki/.gradle/caches/
       modules-2/files-2.1/junit/junit/
       4.11/28e0ad201304e4a4abf999ca0570b7cffc352c3c/
       junit-4.11-sources.jar" kind="lib" path=
       "/Users/mrhaki/.gradle/caches/modules-2/files-
       2.1/junit/junit/4.11/
       4e031bb61df09069aeb2bffb4019e7a5034a4ee0/
       junit-4.11.jar">
      <attributes>
        <attribute name="org.eclipse.jst.component.nondependency"
           value=""/>
      </attributes>
    </classpathentry>
    <classpathentry sourcepath="/Users/mrhaki/.gradle/caches/
       modules-2/files-2.1/org.hamcrest/hamcrest-
       core/1.3/1dc37250fbc78e23a65a67fbbaf71d2e9cbc3c0b/
       hamcrest-core-1.3-sources.jar" kind="lib"
       path="/Users/mrhaki/.gradle/caches/modules-2/files-
       2.1/org.hamcrest/hamcrest-
       core/1.3/42a25dc3219429f0e5d060061f71acb49bf010a0/
```

```
          hamcrest-core-1.3.jar">
            <attributes>
              <attribute
                name="org.eclipse.jst.component.nondependency"
                value=""/>
            </attributes>
        </classpathentry>
    </classpath>
```

The contents of the `org.eclipse.jdt.core.prefs` file in the `.settings` folder are not different from the standard Eclipse plugin. The `org.eclipse.wst.common.component` file has the following contents:

```
<?xml version="1.0" encoding="UTF-8"?>
<project-modules id="moduleCoreId" project-version="2.0">
    <wb-module deploy-name="eclipse">
        <property name="context-root" value="eclipse"/>
    </wb-module>
</project-modules>
```

Here, we find information for the web part of our project.

The last generated file in the `.settings` folder is
the `org.eclipse.wst.common.project.facet.core.xml` file; here, we see the servlet and Java versions. The file has the following contents:

```
<?xml version="1.0" encoding="UTF-8"?>
<faceted-project>
    <fixed facet="jst.java"/>
    <fixed facet="jst.web"/>
    <installed facet="jst.web" version="2.4"/>
    <installed facet="jst.java" version="1.8"/>
</faceted-project>
```

Using the IntelliJ IDEA plugin

IntelliJ IDEA from JetBrains is another IDE that we can use to develop applications. Gradle has the IDEA plugin to generate the project files for IntelliJ IDEA. This means that we can simply open the project in IntelliJ IDEA. The dependencies are set correctly to compile the project in the IDE. In this section, we will see how to generate these files and customize file generation.

IntelliJ IDEA supports a folder-based and file-based format for the project files. The IDEA plugin generates files for the file-based format. The file format for the project files is XML. The workspace project file has the .iws extension and contains personal settings. The project information is stored in a file with the .ipr extension. The project file can be saved in a version control system as it doesn't have a reference to local paths. The workspace project file has a lot of personal settings and this shouldn't be put in a version control system.

For a Java project, we have a third project file with the .iml extension. This file contains dependency references with local path locations. We shouldn't put this file in a version control system. The IDEA plugin can just, like the Eclipse plugin, download associated source files for a dependency. We can also configure and download the associated Javadoc files. The IDEA plugin works together with the Java plugin. If we have a Gradle build file and we apply both Java and IDEA plugins, a specific Java configuration is added to the project files.

Let's create an example build file and apply the IDEA plugin, as shown in the following code snippet:

```
apply plugin: 'java'
apply plugin: 'idea'

version = 1.0

sourceCompatibility = 1.8
targetCompatibility = 1.8

description = 'Sample project'

ext {
    slf4jVersion = '1.7.18'
    slf4jGroup = 'org.slf4j'
}

configurations {
    extraLib
}

repositories {
    jcenter()
}

dependencies {
    testCompile 'junit:junit:4.11'
```

```
        extraLib "$slf4jGroup:slf4j-api:$slf4jVersion",
                "$slf4jGroup:slf4j-simple:$slf4jVersion"
}
```

First, we will execute the `tasks` task and see which tasks are added by the plugin, as follows:

```
$ gradle tasks --all
:tasks
...
IDE tasks
---------
cleanIdea - Cleans IDEA project files (IML, IPR)
cleanIdeaModule
cleanIdeaProject
idea - Generates IDEA project files (IML, IPR, IWS)
ideaModule - Generates IDEA module files (IML)
ideaProject - Generates IDEA project file (IPR)
ideaWorkspace - Generates an IDEA workspace file (IWS)
...
```

We have an idea task that is dependent on the following three other tasks: `ideaWorkspace`, `ideaModule`, and `ideaProject`. Each of these tasks can generate a project file. To remove the module and project files, we can execute either the `cleanIdeaModule` and `cleanIdeaProject` tasks or simply the `cleanIdea` task. There is no `cleanIdeaWorkspace` task as the workspace file contains personal settings. These settings are probably set via the user interface of IntelliJ IDEA and shouldn't be removed by a Gradle task.

When we run the `idea` task from the command line and look at the output, which is as follows; we will see that all the tasks are executed and we now have three project files:

```
$ gradle idea
:ideaModule
:ideaProject
:ideaWorkspace
:idea
BUILD SUCCESSFUL
Total time: 1.057 secs
```

Customizing file generation

The IDEA plugin has several ways to customize the configuration in generated files, just like the Eclipse plugin. The plugin will look in the project settings and use the information in the generated files. For example, we can set the source and target compatibility versions in our Gradle project and the plugin will use them to set a correct value in the generated project file.

We can use a DSL to change the configuration information before the file is generated. Gradle also offers hooks where we can manipulate model objects before and after the project information and DSL configuration is applied. To change the generated XML structure, we can implement the withXml hook. We can alter the XML just before it is written to the disk. To change the contents of the workspace file, we should use the withXml hook. The workspace file has an empty model object and has no DSL as the contents are very specific and contain a lot of personal settings.

Running Gradle in Eclipse

We can generate the Eclipse project files using the Eclipse plugin. We can also import a Gradle build file in Eclipse and then execute Gradle tasks from within Eclipse. In this section, we will see how to install the Gradle plugin in Eclipse and also how to use it to import a Gradle build file and execute tasks.

Gradle developed an Eclipse plugin, named **Buildship**. The plugin adds Gradle integration to the Eclipse IDE. The plugin has an import wizard to import existing Gradle builds. Multi-project builds are also supported by it.

The plugin keeps track of dependencies defined in the Gradle build file as project dependencies. This means that if we change a dependency in the build file, the Eclipse classpath will be updated with the change so that the compiler can use it.

To execute the tasks, the plugin adds an additional view to Eclipse. From the view, we can execute the tasks. The Eclipse launching framework is used to execute the tasks.

Installing the buildship plugin

The following steps can be used to install the buildship plugin:

1. To install the plugin, we will use the Eclipse marketplace. From the **Help** menu, we will select **Eclipse Marketplace…**. We will see then a new dialog window. In the **Search** field, we will type `buildship` and wait for the search result, as shown in the following screenshot:

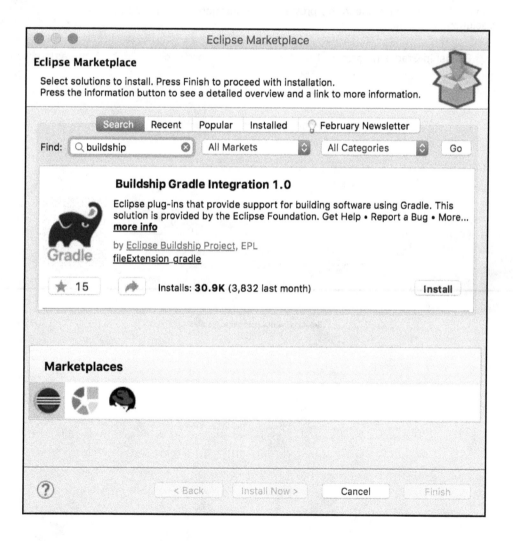

Searching Buildship plugin in the Eclipse Marketplace

2. We then click on the **Install** button to install the plugin in our Eclipse IDE. In the install dialog window, we will select the plugin features and click on the **Confirm** button:

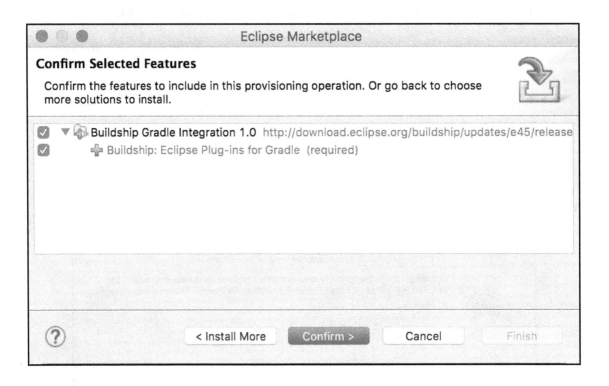

Selecting the Buildship plugin features

3. We have to accept the licenses, and Eclipse downloads the plugin components. Restart Eclipse after all the plugin components have been downloaded:

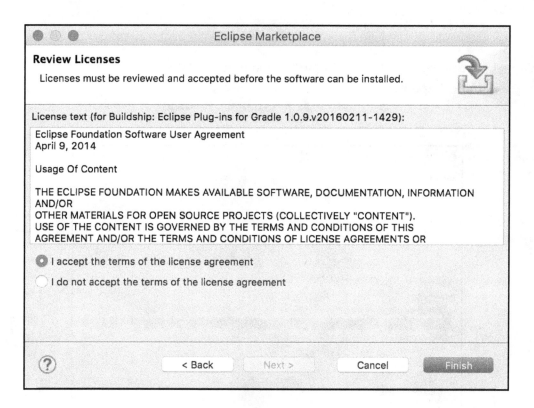

License for the Buildship plugin

Importing a Gradle project

After we have installed the plugin, we can use the import wizard to import a Gradle project. We will use a very simple Java project with the following build file:

```
apply plugin: 'java'

version = '1.0'
group = 'sample.gradle'

description = 'Sample Java project'

repositories {
```

```
        jcenter()
}

dependencies {
        testCompile 'junit:junit:4.11'
}
```

1. In Eclipse, we select the **Import** option from the **File** menu.
2. In the Import dialog window, we will select the `Gradle Project` option before we click on the **Next** button, as shown in the following screenshot:

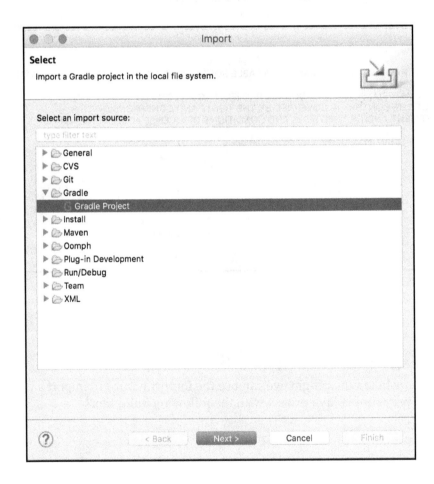

Importing a Gradle project

3. In the next step of the import wizard, we must specify the root folder for our Gradle project. For a multi-project build, we should select the root folder. If we only have a single project, we can select the project folder then.

4. We will click on the **Next** button to look at other options. However, we can also click on the **Finish** button to import the project into Eclipse:

Import Gradle Project overview

5. In the **Import Gradle Project** dialog window, we can specify some extra options:

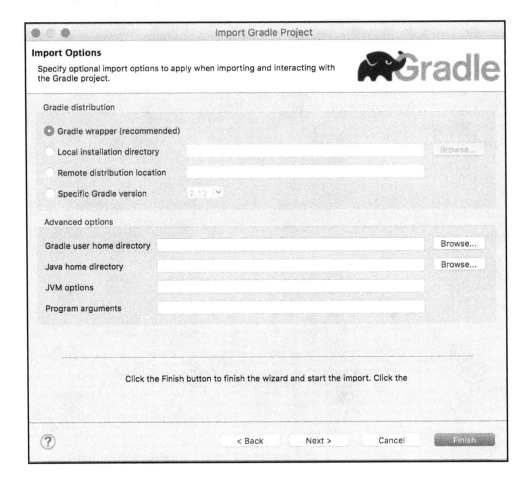

Configuration for importing Gradle project

6. In the **Gradle distribution** section, we can specify the Gradle location and distribution that we want to use to build our project. We use the default **Gradle wrapper (recommended)** option to use the wrapper find in the project. We can also choose a **Local installation directory** to reference a Gradle installation on our computer. With the **Remote distribution location** option, we can set a download location for a Gradle distribution. This could, for example, also be corporate intranet site with a distribution.

7. Finally, we can use **Specific Gradle version** to select a version. The version is downloaded to our computer if we don't have it already.

8. In the **Advanced options** section, we can specify some more option for running Gradle. For example, to change the GRADLE_USER_HOME directory or extra command-line options.

9. We will click on the **Next** button and get an overview of all settings before the project is imported:

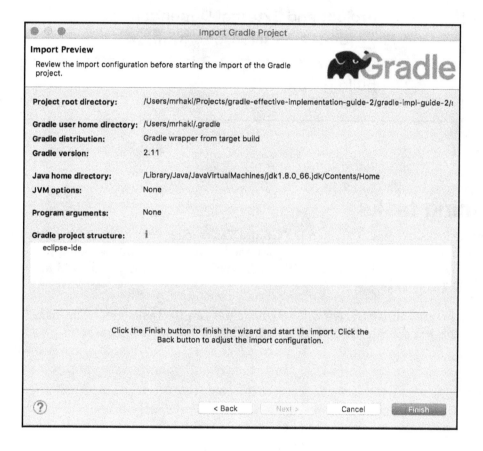

Preview of options for importing a Gradle project

10. Next, we will click on the **Finish** button to import the project into Eclipse:

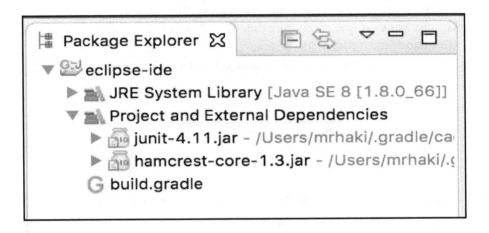

Imported Gradle project in Eclipse

Running tasks

To execute tasks, we will first open the **Gradle Tasks** view. Normally, it is already visible at the bottom of our workspace. If not, we can open it from the **Window** menu, we will select **Show View** and then **Other...**. We will type gradle in the search field to search for the **Gradle Tasks** view.

1. In our workspace, we will now have the **Gradle Tasks** view. The tasks for this project are then displayed as shown in the following screenshot:

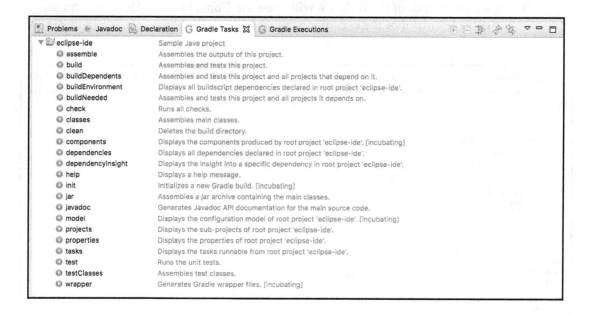

Overview of Gradle task in the Gradle Tasks view

2. To execute a task, we will simply have to double-click on the task name. In the **Gradle Executions** view, we can see the tasks that are executed and the time each task took:

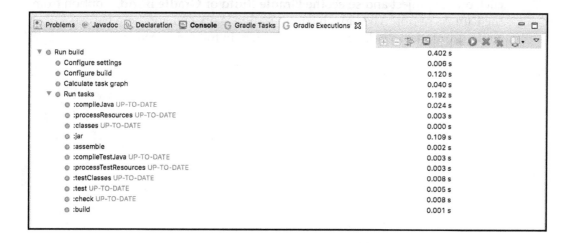

Results after running a Gradle task

3. To see the output of the task, we will open the **Console** view. Here, we can see the console output of the executed task:

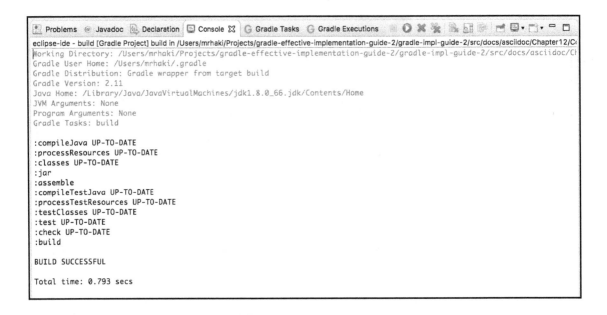

```
 Problems  @ Javadoc  Declaration  Console ⊠  G Gradle Tasks  G Gradle Executions

eclipse-ide - build [Gradle Project] build in /Users/mrhaki/Projects/gradle-effective-implementation-guide-2/gradle-impl-guide-2/src/docs/asciidoc/Chapter12/C
Working Directory: /Users/mrhaki/Projects/gradle-effective-implementation-guide-2/gradle-impl-guide-2/src/docs/asciidoc/Ch
Gradle User Home: /Users/mrhaki/.gradle
Gradle Distribution: Gradle wrapper from target build
Gradle Version: 2.11
Java Home: /Library/Java/JavaVirtualMachines/jdk1.8.0_66.jdk/Contents/Home
JVM Arguments: None
Program Arguments: None
Gradle Tasks: build

:compileJava UP-TO-DATE
:processResources UP-TO-DATE
:classes UP-TO-DATE
:jar
:assemble
:compileTestJava UP-TO-DATE
:processTestResources UP-TO-DATE
:testClasses UP-TO-DATE
:test UP-TO-DATE
:check UP-TO-DATE
:build

BUILD SUCCESSFUL

Total time: 0.793 secs
```

Console output after running a Gradle task

4. We can also use the launch framework of Eclipse to run tasks. We must right-click on the project and select the **Gradle Build** or **Gradle Build...** option from the **Run As** option. The launch configuration is opened and here we can configure the tasks to be executed, as shown in following screenshot:

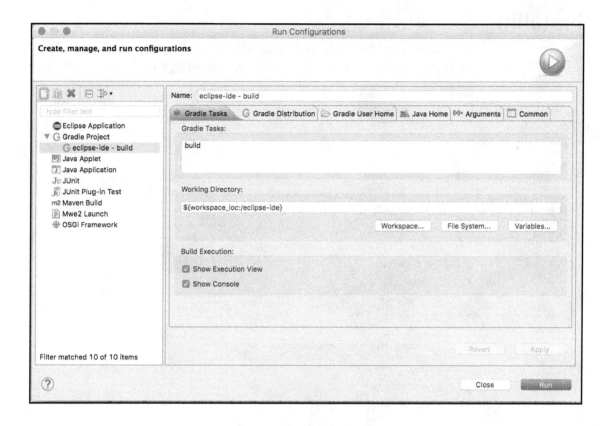

Configuring a Gradle task as run configuration

5. Here we can type the name of the Gradle task that we want to execute.

Running Gradle in IntelliJ IDEA

We can generate IDEA project files with the IDEA plugin in our build file. IntelliJ IDEA has a Gradle plugin to import a Gradle project without first creating the project files. In this section, we will discuss how to use the Gradle plugin with IntelliJ IDEA 15 Community Edition or Ultimate.

We use the same project that was used with the Eclipse Gradle plugin to import the project into IntelliJ IDEA.

Installing the plugin

The Gradle plugin can be installed through the IntelliJ IDEA plugin manager. We need to go to IDE Settings in the Settings window, as shown in the following screenshot:

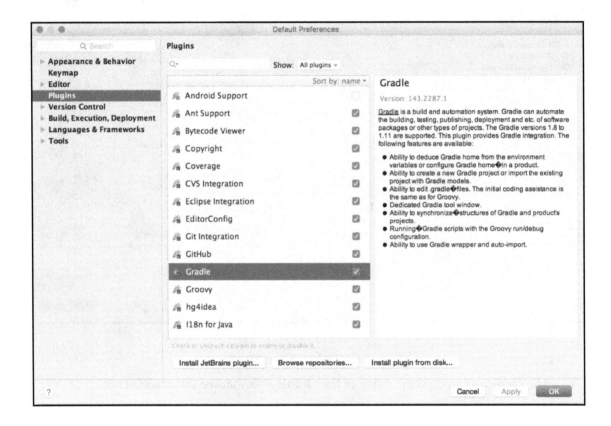

Selecting the Gradle plugin from the list of available plugins

We will select the **Gradle** plugin to install it in the IDE. Once we have installed the plugin, we can then import a project. By default, it is already installed.

Importing a project

To import an existing Gradle project, perform the following steps:

1. We will start the **Import Project** wizard from the startup screen. Alternatively, we will select the **Project from existing sources...** option from the **File** menu. IntelliJ IDEA shows a dialog window in which we can choose the source of the new project, as shown in the following screenshot:

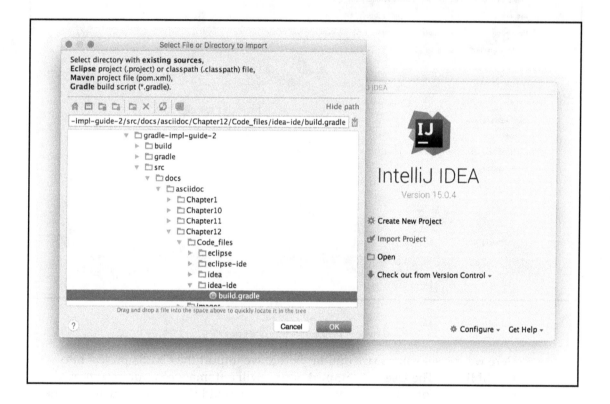

Selecting Gradle build file to import into IDEA

2. We will click on the **OK** button. IntelliJ IDEA shows a new dialog window where we can fill in some extra details:

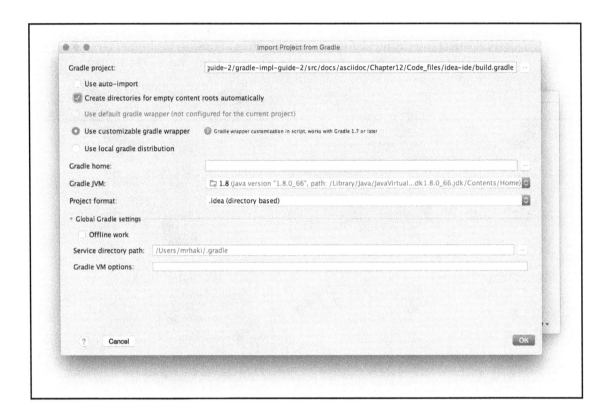

Overview of options for importing a Gradle project

3. Here we can set some extra options before we import the Gradle project into IntelliJ IDEA. The **Use auto-import** option will automatically add new modules to our project for a multi-module project or the build file is executed again when we make a change and the IDEA project is updated automatically.

4. With the **Create directories for empty content roots automatically** option, IntelliJ IDEA will create directories based on source sets in our Gradle build. For example, when we apply the java plugin, the `src/main/java`, `src/main/resources`, `src/test/java`, and `src/test/resources` directories are created.

5. We can also specify the Gradle version that need to be used. We can choose a wrapper configured for the project, if it is available with the **Use default gradle wrapper** option. However, if the wrapper is not in our project, we can create one with the **Use customizable gradle wrapper** option.

6. Finally, we can select a Gradle distribution that is already installed on our computer with **Use local gradle distribution**.

7. If we need another Gradle home directory, we can set a value in the **Gradle home** field. We can also set the JDK used by Gradle with the **Gradle JVM** option.

8. We can use two formats for an IntelliJ IDEA project: directory-based or file-based. We select the option we want with the **Project format**.

9. We can access extra options if we click on the arrow next to **Global Gradle settings**. We can also specify to work offline with the **Offline work** checkbox.

10. To change the Gradle user home directory, we can set the value for the **Service directory path**. Any Gradle VM options that we want to be applied for all build task will be set in the **Gradle VM options** field.

11. To create our project, we will click on the **OK** button.

12. We can see the project and its dependencies, as shown in the following screenshot:

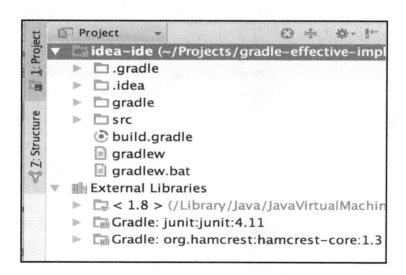

Gradle project is created in IntelliJ IDEA

Running tasks

To see the Gradle project dependency structure, we can also open the Gradle window:

1. Here we can see all tasks and dependencies defined in the build file. We must click on the **Refresh** button to use the latest changes in the `build.gradle` file. For example, if we add a new `org.slf4j:slf4j-api:1.7.18` compile dependency, we must click on the refresh button to see the changes.

2. From the Gradle window, we can double-click on a task name to start it. The tasks are grouped by the task groups from the Gradle build file:

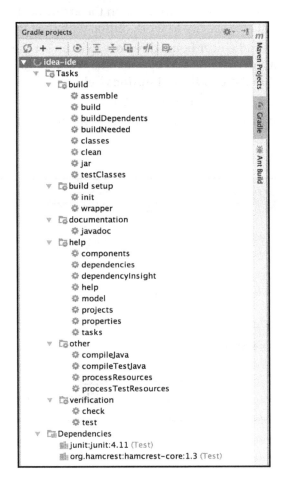

Overview of tasks

3. For example, we can double-click on `build` to start the `build` task. We can also click on the **Run** button. We get a new dialog window, where we can choose the task and project to run:

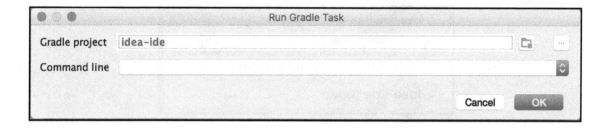

Options for running a Gradle task

4. The output is the task, as shown in the **Run** window. Here we can see the execution of the task and the corresponding status and output:

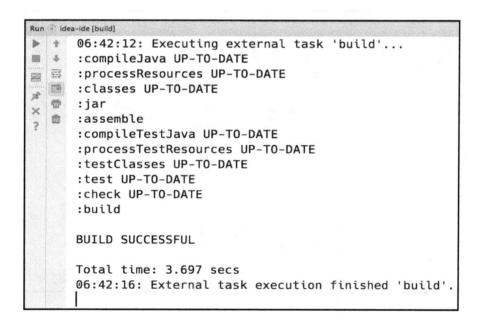

Console output after running a Gradle task

5. Another way to start a task is via **Run Configurations** of IntelliJ IDEA. First, we must create a new configuration. In the toolbar, we click on the configuration list box and select **Edit configurations...**, as shown in the following screenshot:

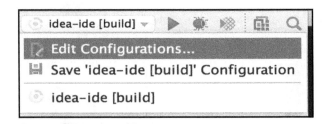

Selecting Edit Configurations options

6. In the dialog window, we can specify the options needed to run the build. We can type the task name in the **Tasks** field. If we click the **OK** button, we have a new configuration that we can run to execute the task:

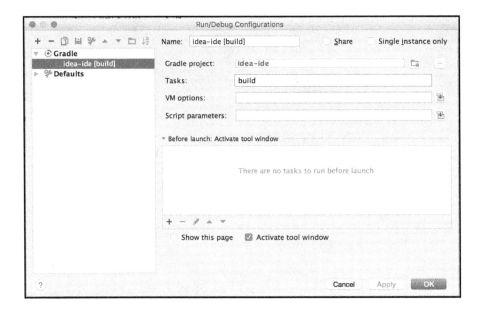

Run configuration for a Gradle task

Summary

When we develop applications, we usually develop the code with an IDE. In this chapter, we saw how to use the Gradle plugins in Eclipse, Eclipse WTP, and IDEA to generate project files for Eclipse and IntelliJ IDEA.

The plugins have a DSL to change the configuration before the files are generated. We can also use hooks to change the model objects before and after the DSL is applied. At the lowest level, we can use the `withXml` hook to alter the XML content before the file is written to the disk.

Both Eclipse and IntelliJ IDEA have plugins to import an existing Gradle project. We can then work with the project from within the IDE. Extra dependencies or changes are reflected in the classpath project files so that the code can be compiled with the IDE's compiler. We can also run Gradle tasks from within the IDE, so we don't have to leave our favorite IDE if we want to use Gradle.

In this book, we have seen the power of Gradle as a build tool. The Gradle syntax is very consistent and compact. If we know the basics, we can accomplish many things. We discussed how to add functionality to a build file with tasks. We have seen how to use Gradle in Java, Groovy, and Scala projects. We saw Gradle's features to work with multi-projects. We also discussed how to create custom tasks and plugins to enable reusing build logic across projects. After reading this book, you will be able to use Gradle in your software development. Using Gradle, we can have great flexibility in our projects and still rely on sold convention-over-configuration defaults. We can start simple and gradually expand the build script with more functionality. With this book, you will get started quickly and have successful Gradle implementation in your projects.

Index

Java plugin, properties
  archivesBaseName 108
  manifest 108
  metaInf 108
  sourceCompatibility 108
  sourceSets 108
  targetCompatibility 108
Java plugin
  using 96, 97, 98, 99
Java project
  creating 257, 258, 260
Java Virtual Machine (JVM) 8
Javadoc documentation
  archives, assembling 111, 112
  creating 110
JDepend plugin
  using 228
Jenkins
  artifacts, configuring 272, 273, 274, 275
  Gradle plugin, adding 263, 264, 265
  Gradle versions, adding 276, 277, 278
  job, configuring 266, 267, 268, 269, 270
  job, running 270, 271
  test results, configuring 272, 273, 274, 275
  using 262
JetBrains TeamCity
  about 278
  project, creating 279, 280, 281, 282, 283,
    284, 285, 286, 287
  project, running 287, 288, 290, 291
  using 278
Jetty plugin
  jettyRun task 197
  jettyRunWar task 197
  jettyStop task 197
  URL 197
  using 197, 198, 199
JUnit 141

L

lib dependencies 192
local directory repository
  adding 125
Local Groovy dependency 126
logging options 20, 21

logging
  output, controlling 88, 89
  using 82, 84, 86, 87

M

Maven 115
Maven central repository
  about 119, 170
  URL 120
Maven local repository 119
Maven Project Object Model (POM) 167
Maven repository
  about 119
  adding 120, 122
  artifacts, uploading 167, 168
merge hooks
  used, for customizing generated file 315
multi-project builds
  configuration dependencies, defining 188, 189
  flat layout, using 180
  projects, defining 181, 182, 184
  projects, filtering 184
  task dependencies, defining 187
  tasks, executing by project path 179, 180
  tasks, invoking 178
  working with 177
multiple tasks
  executing 17

P

plugins
  need for 93
PMD plugin
  using 221, 222, 223, 224
Pretty Good Privacy (PGP) 170
project dependency
  about 126
  using 132
project properties
  adding, via environment variables 81
  custom properties, defining 78
  defining 76, 77, 78
  defining, external file used 79
  defining, via system properties 80
  passing, via command line 80

project source directory
  custom plugin, creating 248, 249, 250
  custom task, creating 239, 240, 241
properties
  directory properties 107
  working with 106, 107, 108, 109

R

repositories
  about 119
  Bintray JCenter repository 119
  Flat directory repository 119
  Ivy repository 119
  local directory repository, adding 125
  Maven central repository 119
  Maven local repository 119
  Maven repository 119

S

Scala plugin, properties
  allScala 210
  scala 210
  scala.srcDirs 210
Scala plugin
  documentation, creating 211, 212
  using 207, 208, 209, 210, 211
Simple Logging Facade for Java (SLF4J) Logger
    interface 82
Software Development Kit Manager (SDKMAN!)
  about 11
  installing 11, 12
source sets, property
  allJava 100
  allSource 100
  java 100
  java.srcDirs 100
  name 101
  output 100
  output.classesDir 100
  output.resourcesDir 101
  resources 100
  resources.srcDirs 100
source sets
  about 99
  creating 102, 104

custom configuration 105
Stack Trace Output section
  Exceptions Only option 30
  Full Stack Trace (-S) 30
  Standard Stack Trace (-s) option 30
system properties
  properties, defining 80

T

task dependencies
  defining 39, 40
  defining, via closures 41
  defining, via tasks 41
task groups 45
task name abbreviation 17
task rules
  using 49
tasks, skipping
  about 53
  from command line 56
  onlyIf predicates, using 53
  StopExecutionException exception, throwing 54,
    55
  tasks, disabling 55, 56
  tasks, enabling 55, 56
  updated task, skipping 57, 58, 59
tasks
  accessing, as project properties 50
  actions, defining with Action interface 37
  adding 47, 48
  additional properties, adding 51, 52
  common pitfalls, avoiding 52
  defining 35, 36
  description, adding 45
  grouping 45
  information, obtaining 46
  organizing 43
TestNG 141
tests
  determining 154
  executing 141, 145
  test output, logging 155
  test process, configuring 152
  test report directory, modifying 157
  TestNG, using 148, 149, 151

www.ingramcontent.com/pod-product-compliance
Lightning Source LLC
Chambersburg PA
CBHW062051050326

40690CB00016B/3053